OUTSIDE THE BOX

Outside the Box

HOW GLOBALIZATION CHANGED
FROM MOVING STUFF TO
SPREADING IDEAS

MARC LEVINSON

PRINCETON UNIVERSITY PRESS

PRINCETON & OXFORD

Copyright © 2020 by Marc Levinson

Requests for permission to reproduce material from this work
should be sent to permissions@press.princeton.edu

Published by Princeton University Press
41 William Street, Princeton, New Jersey 08540
6 Oxford Street, Woodstock, Oxfordshire OX20 1TR

press.princeton.edu

ISBN 978-0-691-19176-8
ISBN (e-book) 978-0-691-20583-0

British Library Cataloging-in-Publication Data is available

Editorial: Joe Jackson and Jacqueline Delaney
Production Editorial: Jenny Wolkowicki
Jacket design: Karl Spurzem
Production: Erin Suydam
Publicity: Kate Farquhar-Thomson and James Schneider
Copyeditor: Maia Vaswani

Jacket image: Shutterstock

This book has been composed in Arno Pro

Printed on acid-free paper. ∞

Printed in the United States of America

10 9 8 7 6 5 4 3 2 1

CONTENTS

Introduction

ON AUGUST 16, 2006, at five thirty in the afternoon, five tugboats dragged *Emma Maersk* from the Odense Steel Shipyard and towed her backward to the sea. Whether new or old, ships generally sail forward, not backward, but there was nothing typical about *Emma Maersk*. The length of four soccer fields, her keel nearly a hundred feet below her deck, the light blue vessel was so enormous she could barely escape the confines of the shallow Odense Fjord. As she passed through the Gabet, the narrow gap between the fjord and the deeper waters beyond, the thousands of Danes lining the beaches were treated to an extraordinary sight. On her launch day, because *Emma* carried neither cargo nor fuel, she rode high in the water, partially exposing her white underside and showing off the massive bronze propeller that would normally turn silently beneath the waves. It was, as everyone knew from news reports, by far the largest propeller ever cast.

Emma Maersk was a bet on globalization. Owned by Maersk Line, part of a venerable Danish conglomerate, she dwarfed every vessel that had preceded her in the fifty-year history of container shipping. Save for a handful of oil supertankers, there had never been a ship so large. *Emma* and the seven similar ships that were to follow cost $154 million apiece, much more than any containership had cost before, and the price seemed a bargain. If the new vessels were loaded to capacity, they would be able to transport the world's trade more cheaply than any other ships afloat. As the world economy expanded and long-distance trade increased with it, Maersk Line's leaders expected, that cost advantage would enable their company to capture a growing share.

Containerships are the workhorses of globalization, carrying steel boxes stuffed with everything from washing machines to waste paper vast distances on regular schedules, meshing with trucks, trains, and barges to serve cities miles inland. International cargo that is time sensitive or highly valuable—diamonds, disc drives—usually flies across the oceans, but almost everything else churned out by factories and much that comes from farms is packed into standard containers forty feet long and eight feet across. In the final decades of the twentieth century, containers all but erased transportation costs as a factor in decisions about where to make things, where to grow things, and how to move goods to customers. They helped reshape world trade, making it feasible to combine parts from a dozen countries into a finished car and delivering wine from Australia to California, a distance of seven thousand miles, for perhaps fifteen US cents a bottle. They lay behind the startling transformation of China into the world's largest manufacturing nation—and behind the desolation of long-standing manufacturing centers, from Detroit to Dortmund, as distinct national markets, protected by high transportation costs, merged into a nearly seamless global one.

Since the first containership steamed from Newark to Houston in 1956, each generation of vessels had been larger and more cost-effective than its predecessors. *Emma* and her sister ships were commissioned in the expectation that this trend would continue, making it even easier for families to enjoy fresh strawberries in wintertime and enabling manufacturers to weld longer, more complex supply chains linking factories and distribution centers thousands of miles apart. Dozens of even larger ships would soon follow in *Emma*'s wake, some able to carry more cargo than eleven thousand over-the-road trucks. But just as a race to build monumental skyscrapers often heralds an economy poised for a correction—the Empire State Building in New York, planned in the late 1920s to be the world's tallest building, sat largely empty through the Great Depression of the 1930s—so the construction of ships too big to call at most of the world's ports was an early indicator of excessive exuberance. Unremarked at the time of *Emma Maersk*'s launch, the era of ceaseless growth in goods trade was about to draw to a close. Those who assumed that globalization would stay on the course it had followed since the aftermath of World War Two would pay a steep price.

———

"Globalization" is not a recent concept. The word seems to have made its first appearance in Belgium in 1929: physician and educator J. O. Decroly used "globalization" to refer to a young child's developing attention to the broader world rather than itself alone. Over time, the term has had many other meanings: the idea that giant companies can sell the same product everywhere rather than different models in each country; the transmission of ideas from one country to another; the flag-waving enthusiasm of Americans and Kenyans and Chinese for English soccer teams led by non-British stars.[1] The worldwide diffusion of religions is a form of globalization, as are the spread of disease and the large-scale migration of people in search of personal safety, political or social freedom, or greater economic opportunity. So, of course, is the increasing intensity of economic exchange across international frontiers.

The world was in some ways highly globalized long ago; as the historians Jürgen Osterhammel and Niels P. Petersson put it, "In a certain sense, the 'Americanization' of Germany did not begin in 1945 but rather in the eighteenth century, with the introduction of the potato." But globalization, as that term is used today, erupted with the birth of industrial capitalism in the nineteenth century, as Europe's colonial powers spun commercial webs across Africa and Asia, protecting their interests with armies, navies, and professional corps of colonial civil servants. Erstwhile manufacturing centers, notably India, were unable to match the higher productivity of European factories, and as their textiles became uncompetitive with foreign products, they sank into the role of commodity exporters. During this First Globalization, international lending was routine, and in many countries exports and imports accounted for large shares of economic activity. Migrants crossed borders by the tens of millions, and motifs from China and Tahiti found their way into European art. The world seemed to have become so interconnected that war was impossible—until the eruption of World War One in August 1914 brought the First Globalization to an abrupt end.[2]

The process of globalization paused from 1914 until roughly 1947, through two world wars, numerous regional wars, and a great depression. While multinational corporations expanded during those years, many of the financial, commercial, and human links across borders eroded. In some quarters, this retreat was welcomed; in 1943, the US congresswoman Clare Boothe Luce criticized Vice President Henry Wallace, who prided himself on his global perspective, for spouting "globaloney." After much criticism, Luce abandoned the term in favor of "global nonsense." But in the wake of her coinage, words such as "globalistic," "globalitis," and "globalism" made their way into the American vocabulary, being employed to disparage immigration, foreign trade, and even proposals for international cooperation.[3]

Globalization began anew in the late 1940s, after the Allied victory in World War Two. This development was supported by a less rigid system of exchange rates and a concerted effort to lower barriers to trade in raw materials and manufactured goods. The result was a quarter-century of robust economic growth in all the world's rich economies and many of the poor ones. Despite the economic crises of the 1970s, trade in manufactured goods, measured by the volume of goods traded, was roughly fifteen times as high in 1986 as it had been in 1950. With prices soaring, the oil market became thoroughly global as supertankers, more properly known as ultra-large crude carriers, delivered millions of barrels of petroleum on a single voyage from the Persian Gulf to refineries in Europe, Japan, and North America. As oil-exporting countries deposited their surging receipts into banks in London, New York, and Tokyo, the financial markets lent generously to developing-country governments and helped multinational corporations plant their flags around the world.[4]

Yet this Second Globalization, like the First Globalization before it, was not truly global. Companies aggressively planted their flags abroad, but their identities were inextricably linked to their home countries, where almost all their top managers were born and bred. While foreign investment soared, most of it took place among a handful of wealthy nations, and so did most foreign trade. Less affluent countries, many of which fell deeply into debt, participated only tangentially, mainly by borrowing from rich-country investors and by exporting raw commodities like oil and coffee. Indeed, the harshest critiques of globalization during the four decades between 1947 and 1986 came largely from those who thought freer economic exchange enabled rich countries to exploit poor ones. Immigration was often deemed exploitative as well, as rich countries stood accused of causing a "brain drain" by enticing nurses and teachers to emigrate from poorer lands. Countries aspiring to overcome poverty and backwardness, critics claimed, would be better off doing more for themselves. Many large and populous countries, including China, India, and the Soviet Union, embraced autarky, tightly controlling trade, investment, migration, tourism, scientific exchange, religious ideas, and other sorts of international links their rulers thought dangerous.[5]

The ascent of free-market ideologies in the wealthier economies, emblemized by Margaret Thatcher's election to lead Great Britain in 1979 followed by Ronald Reagan's election as US president in 1980, opened the way to new economic relationships. When Honda Motor Company opened the first Japanese-owned auto assembly plant in the United States, in 1982, it shocked competitors with its ability to organize the timely delivery of engines and transmissions across thousands of miles of sea and land. By the late 1980s, such long-distance supply chains had become routine as a Third Globalization emerged. The nature of international trade changed dramatically, as it became practical for a retailer or manufacturer to have components designed in one country, made in another, and combined into finished products elsewhere still, moving the partially finished goods from place to place with little regard for national boundaries. The link between physical location and nationality was erased: when a Massachusetts-based manufacturer of industrial abrasives with plants in twenty-seven countries could be owned by a Paris-based corporation that counted Dutch pension funds, British investment trusts, and Middle Eastern governments among its major shareholders, who was to say whether the resulting entity was "French," "American," or just "international"? The fall of communism in 1989 seemed to signal the final victory of capitalism. As countries that had long been suspicious of market forces suddenly welcomed them, international trade grew nearly three times as fast as the world economy.

Once more, there were objections aplenty about exploitation—only now, instead of hurting workers in poor countries, globalization was said to devastate workers in rich countries. In 1994, Sir James Goldsmith, a wealthy British financier and scion of a thoroughly international family, criticized open borders in a best-seller called *The Trap*. Viviane Forrester, a French essayist, decried *L'horreur économique* in 1996. Three years later, as British sociologist Anthony Giddens warned of a *Runaway World*, tens of thousands of demonstrators, some anticapitalist, some environmentalist, some concerned about vanishing jobs, some prepared for a rumble, took to the streets of Seattle to protest a conclave of trade ministers from around the world. Economists' nearly unanimous argument that freer exchange would make the world more prosperous gained little traction, and the eagerness of poorer countries to open themselves to the world economy was largely ignored. When two British journalists published a book about globalization in 2000, their title, *A Future Perfect*, rang out of tune.[6]

World trade in manufactured goods rose 120 percent in the span of just seven years, from 2001 to 2008, as manufacturing surged in China—while during those same seven years, one in eight manufacturing jobs in Canada and the United States, and one in four in Great Britain, disappeared. It was hard not to draw a connection. The flight of factory jobs was followed by jobs in technology and service industries. As office buildings everywhere were cabled to the internet, a new industry called business-process outsourcing took hold: companies in Frankfurt and Paris moved their accounting work to lower-wage cities such as Warsaw and Prague, and agents in Manila answered customer-service calls for North American banks. By 2003, 285 of the 500 largest US companies were sending office work to India. "Thousands of white-collar jobs are going overseas," a US congressman warned in 2004, citing "incontrovertible evidence that the U.S. is on the verge of adopting the economics of third-world nations."[7]

The retreat of the Third Globalization began unrecognized, not long after *Emma Maersk* took to the seas. In the summer of 2008, amid a global financial crisis, the volume of international trade collapsed.

Cross-border investment in businesses, which had tripled over the previous five years, dried up just as suddenly. These trends were unhappy, but not surprising: in times past, trade and investment had ebbed during recessions only to rise afterward, and this pattern seemed likely to play out once again. But this time, as the world economy crept back from the depths in 2010, trade and investment did not rebound as they always had. The changes revealed by economic statistics and shipping data were gradually confirmed by the actions of international firms, which began retracting their supply chains and slimming down their foreign operations. Although angry opposition to globalization remained, now fueled mainly by anti-immigrant fervor in the United States and Europe, globalization itself was changing. By the time US presidential candidate Donald Trump inveighed against "radical globalization and the disenfranchisement of working people" in 2016 and the French politician Marine Le Pen criticized "the rampant globalization that is endangering our civilization" a few months later, these actions and reactions, this *sturm und drang*, pertained to an era that was already drawing to a close. When the viral disease labeled COVID-19 began to spread from Wuhan, China, in late 2019, leading to business shutdowns and household quarantines from Norway to New Zealand and disrupting commerce and travel on a global scale, the transformation of the Third Globalization into a very different set of international relationships was already well underway.[8]

———

Many trees have been felled in the effort to praise, condemn, or simply quantify globalization. This book does none of the above. It asserts that globalization, as it has developed over two centuries, is far from an inevitable consequence of capitalism. Globalization has transformed itself repeatedly over two centuries in response to technological change, demographic pressure, entrepreneurial ambition, and governmental action: someone speaking of globalization in 2020 was discussing an altogether different subject from globalization in 1980, much less in 1890. It treats the Third Globalization, the quarter-century or so between the late 1980s and the early 2010s, as a distinct stage in the world's economic history, a stage unlike what came before and what is likely to come after. It emphasizes the roles of transportation, communications, and information technology in enabling firms to organize their businesses around long-distance value chains, a fundamentally different type of economic relationship from any that existed before.

I have been writing about globalization as a journalist, economist, and historian for more years than I am eager to admit. My book *The Box: How the Shipping Container Made the World Smaller and the World Economy Bigger* showed how a seemingly simple innovation was the key to the lengthy supply chains that became the hallmark of globalization in the late 1980s. In *An Extraordinary Time: The End of the Postwar Boom and the Return of the Ordinary Economy*, I examined how governments responded to the global economic slowdown that began around 1973 by deregulating entire sectors of their economies and welcoming market forces, making it easier for firms to organize their businesses across national boundaries. *Outside the Box* builds on that earlier work, but also draws on new archival research, interviews, and a robust academic literature to explain why, in the early twenty-first century, globalization developed in ways that were counterproductive for many of the countries and many of the firms that eagerly embraced it. This historical perspective explains why, notwithstanding intense chatter about the impending end of globalization, I think globalization is far from dead. Rather, as it has on several past occasions, globalization is entering a new phase—one in which the world economy will still be bound closely together, but in ways different from what the experience of recent decades has taught us to expect. Understanding globalization's past may shed light upon its future, a future that will almost certainly not involve a return to the days when countries sought to prosper by fencing themselves off from their neighbors.

———

By and large, globalization has been good for the world. It has brought hundreds of millions out of dire poverty, turning the days when Americans told their children to eat their vegetables because people were starving in China into a distant memory. Consumers have gained access to an unimagined selection of products at very low cost, and some of the most isolated places on earth were linked to the world economy thanks to technologies that once would have passed them by. By allowing firms to specialize in their most productive activities at a global scale while relying on outside suppliers to meet their other needs, globalization has generated massive productivity improvements that have created immense wealth. International conflicts have not gone away, but they have been tempered by the fact that almost every country's prosperity depends more on its neighbors than ever before. When, as the coronavirus spread, hospitals around the world urgently sought ventilators to help critically ill patients breathe, efforts to build more were slowed by the need to acquire parts from a dozen countries—but also aided by a vibrant global market in which valves, tubes, and motor parts were to be had.[9]

But globalization has not been an unalloyed blessing. The rapid industrialization of countries that were only recently quite poor, especially in Asia, was matched by the brutal deindustrialization of communities across Europe, North America, and Japan. While the distribution of income among countries has become more equitable, inequality within individual countries has increased; people with access to capital have reaped great rewards from new opportunities, but workers reliant on wages often have found themselves competing directly with low-paid labor in distant places, and small towns have atrophied as big cities capture a disproportionate share of the growth. In the process, governments have lost much of their control over their economies. Minimum-wage laws and social protections became harder to enforce once firms could easily circumvent them by moving, or threatening to move, a particular activity abroad. The constant possibility of corporate relocation created an international contest to lower taxes on business, starving governments of the revenues to fund education and social programs intended to help workers cope with a world in which employment had become less stable. Over time, a relatively small number of firms came to dominate entire industries, a development that threatens to raise prices, retard innovation, and make incomes even more unequal.

The economic strains of globalization undermined the structures erected over decades to promote international cooperation, creating new uncertainties as nationalist narratives supplanted global ones.[10]

Through two centuries of history, globalization has not proceeded in a straight line. Wars and recessions have interrupted the flow of trade, investment, and migration, and individual countries have chosen to sever themselves from the world economy for extended periods—Russia from its 1917 revolution to the late 1980s, China for three decades after the Communist Party took power in 1949. Against this background, claims that "peak globalization" is past or that a globalized world economy is dissolving into regional blocs seem rather premature. Globalization is not going away. But by the second decade of the twenty-first century, as giant containerships sailed half empty around the world, it was taking on a very different form. The flow of metal boxes was its past. In the next stage of economic development, it would be the flow of ideas and services that would bind the world's economies more tightly together.

PART I

Coming Together

1

Global Dreams

IN 1764, a trader named Peter Hasenclever, fresh off the boat from London, embarked on an extraordinary venture in the mountain fastness of northern New Jersey. Hasenclever was a man of the world, a globalist by any measure. Born in the German Rhineland in 1716, he seems to have been fluent in German, French, Spanish, and English. In his youth, he wielded a hammer in a steel mill, purchased wool on behalf of German textile plants, and then sold their textiles as far afield as Russia and France. Later, he built trading houses in Portugal and Spain and advised King Frederick the Great on industrializing Prussia. In 1763, a successful and wealthy man, he moved to London, the center of a burgeoning transatlantic empire. Payment of seventy pounds sterling induced Parliament to grant him British citizenship, and with it the right to invest in the colonies. Then, he set out to fulfill an entrepreneurial dream, creating a partnership to supply the Royal Navy's dockyards, the world's largest industrial enterprise, with iron forged in America.

Neither Hasenclever nor his partners had ever visited America. On a map, the iron mines they acquired in New Jersey colony must have seemed ideal, located just twenty or thirty miles from the bustling port at New York. But as Hasenclever discovered after he finally crossed the Atlantic, the mines were dug into rocky, heavily forested hillsides in a region of valleys so steep and isolated that settlers had steered clear. The ore, a mass of dirt, stones, and iron, had to be extracted with picks and shovels, then loaded aboard oxcarts and hauled miles to ironworks near streams powerful enough to turn waterwheels. There, stamping mills crushed the ore, blast furnaces separated the iron from worthless tailings, and workers toiling in the immense heat of a hearth or a furnace melted off the iron and pounded it into bars, fourteen feet long and two inches on a side. Some of the wrought iron bars were melted down again so that fragments of charcoal could be hammered into the liquid iron, making carbon steel. Delivered to nearby villages, the iron and steel bars were useful only to blacksmiths shaping horseshoes and fire irons. Real profits would come from transporting the bars to the dockyards in England. Unlike most international traders of his day, who found buyers for foreign goods only after the goods arrived, Hasenclever envisioned a long-distance supply chain reliably furnishing the Royal Navy with metal vital for building warships. As side benefits, Britain's New Jersey colony would prosper and Hasenclever himself might be admitted to England's economic elite.

The Ramapo Mountains, though, had no roads or bridges over which to transport ore from mines to mills. Hasenclever's partnership, the American Company, had to build them itself. English colonists preferred farming to the dangerous, unpleasant work of making iron and steel in such a remote place; at great expense, the American Company imported experienced stonemasons and ironworkers from Germany, paying their passage in return for promised years of service. The company tapped its investors back in England to acquire thirty-four square miles of forest to meet the endless need for timber, which would be made into charcoal to fuel the blast furnaces and turn iron into steel. Then it tapped them again to build dams, reservoirs, and canals to keep the waterwheels turning.

The primitive state of transportation plagued the entire venture. As the forests were cut, the distance from each mill to the nearest remaining stand of trees increased year by year, requiring more roads and more oxen to get timber to the mills. The finished bars had to be carted away from the mills in the same way the ore was brought in, one wagonload at a time. In the winter months, the canals and rivers froze up and the roads became impassable. "The American iron turns out so dear," Hasenclever lamented. Ocean shipping was unreliable, and there was no telling when a consignment would reach the Royal Dockyards at

Deptford and Portsmouth. The Royal Navy apparently distrusted this erratic transatlantic supply line, for the American Company earned no profits and paid no dividends. The London partners soon ran out of patience. In 1768, the fourth year of operation, they ordered the iron-works closed. Hasenclever was held responsible for the partnership's debts, barely avoiding debtors' prison. When the mines reopened, they sold iron only nearby. The notion of a long-distance industrial supply chain already beckoned, but the developments that made it practical were yet to come.[1]

———

Goods have traveled vast distances since the earliest days of human civi-lization. Four thousand years ago, the Assyrians ranged hundreds of miles to establish trading colonies in what is now Turkey. Caravans laden with incense began trekking across Arabia once the dromedary was domesticated around 1000 BC, and Socotra, a tiny island off the coast of Yemen, became a hub for trade between India and Rome a mil-lennium later. Another thousand years on, at the start of the eleventh century, when Norse adventurers reached North America, they must have been disappointed at the lack of opportunities for trade. Marco Polo, his father, and his uncle had better luck when they set off from Venice on their famed journey along the Silk Road to China in 1271. The transatlantic slave trade, which began in the early 1500s, grew into a large and sophisticated business after 1750, with English merchants exporting guns, kettles, cloth, and shoes to their own trading posts on the coast of Africa, exchanging these wares for slaves, selling the slaves in the Amer-icas, and filling their ships with sugar and tobacco for the return trip to England. The African slave trade was extremely profitable and thor-oughly global, forcibly transporting an estimated 12.5 million enslaved people on at least thirty-six thousand transatlantic voyages and another half a million slaves shipped by sea within the Americas.[2]

These exchanges among distant peoples involved more than trade goods and slaves. They involved disease: the black death swept out of China in 1334, reached the Black Sea in 1346, and within seven years killed perhaps forty-eight million of Europe's eighty million people.[3] They involved ideas: Buddhism was imported from India into China two thousand years ago; Islam, founded in Arabia around 610, reached Spain by 713; and in the 1540s Portuguese priests brought Christian ideas to Japan. They involved economic dislocation: starting around the 1530s, the influx of silver from Spain's new American colonies fed inflation in Europe for 150 years, an event so disruptive that historians know it as the "price revolution." And they certainly involved the projection of political power, with country after country using trade as a means to expand its dominions with wealth and tax revenue extracted from colonies or vassal states.

In the current day, a casual tourist trip to Genoa, Amsterdam, or Istanbul, each a leading center of international commerce in its time, reveals that the exchange of people and goods created enormous wealth long before the age of computers and containerships. The fruits of that exchange are visible as well in the Persian rugs and Chinese porcelains that decorate châteaus and country houses across Europe. Yet these impressions also illustrate why economic relationships before the Industrial Revolution of the 1800s were a far cry from globalization as we understand that term today.

The famed Hanseatic League, a commercial alliance of cities in Northern Germany, monopolized trade around the Baltic Sea for three centuries until the late 1400s, but while this trade brought great prosperity to cities like Lübeck and Hamburg, it was tiny by modern standards: all the ships owned by Hanseatic merchants combined carried less cargo in a year than a single midsize twenty-first-century containership. Well after the Hansa faded into history, long-distance trade still involved mostly luxury goods, slaves, or essential commodities, such as wheat imported following a poor harvest in order to avert food riots. As recently as the turn of the nineteenth century, the average European family was unlikely to possess imported goods beyond a sachet of sugar and the occasional coin stamped from silver; imports of tea, one of the most widely traded commodities of the era, came to just a couple of ounces per person per year. China, probably the world's largest economy at the time, imported mainly silver bars and black pepper. India and Japan seem to have imported little of anything. In most societies, the international economy was of little consequence.[4]

Trade mattered greatly to merchants dealing in exports and imports; to sailors, carters, and packers who handled goods in transit; to artisans who made glass, fabrics, or other valuable goods for export; to workers forcibly conscripted to raise cotton or mine silver; and to rulers who saw trade as one more opportunity to levy taxes. In numerous European cities, on the other hand, guilds controlled the production of many goods from the eleventh century into the 1700s or 1800s, and blocking import competition enabled them to keep prices for their members' products high. In almost all countries, the vast majority of families lived on the land and on the margins of the cash economy, and to them the world mattered little. One indicator that the level of economic exchange was quite small: as late as 1820, the total carrying capacity of all the world's ships was around 5.9 million metric tons. The corresponding figure in 2018 was 322 times higher—and those ships, traveling much faster, were likely to complete many more voyages in a single year.[5]

———

Why was foreign trade so modest in premodern times? Mainly because trading was slow and expensive. When Venetian galleys started to ply the Mediterranean around 1300, each carried roughly 115 metric tons of cargo—approximately the contents of eight average containers aboard a modern oceangoing ship. Although some galleys were forty meters long, they were propelled by oarsmen as well as wind power, and feeding and housing the oarsmen took up a considerable part of their capacity. Shipboard space was so scarce that the vessels were permitted to carry only spices, silks, and other precious merchandise; less valuable products were not traded. Two centuries later, Venice used larger ships to import bulky commodities such as cotton and wheat from Syria and to transport barrels of wine from Crete, a Venetian possession, all the way to England. This involved impressive feats of organization, but surprisingly little cargo: the total capacity of the 107 merchant ships sailing for Venice in 1499 was less than twenty-six thousand tons of freight and people. In 2020, a single vessel could carry several times as much.[6]

A few years later, Portugal displaced Venice as the world's greatest maritime power by sailing directly between India and Europe, circumventing the middlemen who handled costly land transport across Iraq or Egypt on the way to the Mediterranean. Between 1500 and 1600, though, just seven Portuguese merchant ships, accompanied by armed caravels or galleons for protection, made the six-month voyage in the average year. All told, perhaps five thousand metric tons of cargo moved in Portugal's India trade each year—less than fits aboard one modern freight train crossing the North American plains. Admittedly, Portugal's population was barely one million at the time, but even so the small volume of its famed Asian trade is noteworthy. Portugal grew wealthy trading the pepper and other spices the fleet brought home, but for want of space, its ships on the Asia route carried almost nothing else.[7]

While bigger ships later crisscrossed the oceans, freight rates remained high enough that bulky or inexpensive goods were not worth transporting. Gold and silver were among the most widely traded commodities, because they were highly valuable relative to their weight and volume. Even in the late 1600s, when textile trade began to grow strongly, the products concerned were mainly high-quality Indian cottons exported to Europe and China and Chinese silks for wealthy European and Japanese buyers. The English weavers who blamed Indian cottons for destroying their livelihoods as early as the 1660s wore scratchy woolens and rough cotton clothing woven domestically precisely because there were no imported fabrics they could afford.[8]

Trading internationally was even costlier over land than across the seas. Freight moved by the wagonload where roads were good, but in seventeenth-century England, as economic historian Dan Bogart observed, "Packhorses were the superior technology on bad roads." The same was true in most other countries. Roads broad enough to accommodate wagons and firm enough to survive downpours were expensive to build and maintain. They existed only where there was enough traffic to justify private investment in turnpikes barricaded by toll gates, where local citizens could be conscripted for roadbuilding, or where military needs led the government to pay the cost. In 1800, after turnpikes had begun to ease travel between English cities, the cost of shipping a ton of freight just one mile by road equaled a farm laborer's wage for a full day's work. Transport was dear because while roads improved over time, the technology of horse-drawn wagons did not. Shipping by water, even along very circuitous routes, was almost always cheaper than shipping by land, but towns not on navigable waterways faced oppressive costs. China had faced up to this problem centuries earlier by constructing a wide-ranging network of canals, but it would be the early 1800s before canal systems spread widely within Europe, and even later in North America.[9]

The ubiquitous role of middlemen added to the cost of trade. Manufacturing migrated to rural areas, where costs were lower than in crowded cities and farmers had ample free time in the winter to tend hearths and looms, but most goods were produced by very small workshops. In Venice, a law from 1497—not always observed—prohibited a silk manufacturer from employing more than six weavers. Two centuries later the eighteen textile establishments in Clermont-de-Lodève, in the south of France, had only twenty-nine looms among them. Carriage making in New England was the work of small shops and independent craftsmen even in the late 1830s; a factory with one hundred workers proved too large to manage profitably. Manufacturers operating at this minuscule scale had no hope of exporting on their own. At best, they could supply a trader in the nearest village, who could sell the goods onward to a merchant in a larger town, who might know a merchant in a port city who consolidated shipments for export. Each dealer, of course, collected a commission that added to the price charged to customers abroad.[10]

Taxes had impeded foreign trade since the days when Greek city-states assessed a 2 percent duty on imports and exports. In 1203, King John of England, his treasury drained by war in France, created the first customs service, staffed by agents who required merchants to pay one-fifteenth of the value of imports or exports to collectors at each port. In many parts of Europe, local rulers and religious officials collected tolls each time freight crossed a river or entered a town. A Swiss trader in the late 1500s, when Germany was still a collection of duchies, counties, principalities, and independent city-states, reported paying thirty-one tolls between Basel and Cologne, and his descendants in 1765 would have faced duties imposed at almost five hundred locations in Bavaria alone. For more than two centuries, starting in 1635, Japan allowed European merchants to trade only in one place, Chinese merchants in one other; while this was intended to curtail the spread of foreign ideas, it also facilitated the collection of import taxes. China put a 20 percent duty on all imports in 1685, and in 1757 it required that all foreign trade pass through the customs office at the southern port of Guangzhou. Whether the trader paid those levies or went to extra expense to evade them, tolls and duties added to importers' bills.[11]

And then there was the matter of reliability. Stagecoaches usually ran on schedules; oceangoing ships did not. Sailing vessels typically cruised from port to port searching for cargo and headed overseas only when fully loaded. Severe storms, pirates, and hostile navies frequently damaged their cargo in transit. Inland journeys could be hazardous for traders as well as the freight they carried, owing to rapacious governments as much as to robbers; along the Loire River in France, "the poor sailors are often compelled in addition to make presents to the toll officials or the latter otherwise delay them as long as they please," one local official complained in 1701. During the Napoleonic Wars of the early 1800s, the British sought to block all sea trade with France; the French forbade their European client states to trade with Britain; and the United States cast a pox on both houses, banning Americans from trading with the warring parties and, in the process, throwing its own economy into depression. Whatever the circumstances, no importer anywhere could count on goods arriving on a particular day, or in a particular month, or at all. Market conditions in the importing country could be quite different than anticipated when the goods were shipped months or years before, destroying expected profits. Trading anything that could not be stored indefinitely was foolhardy.[12]

───────────

The economic orthodoxy that had reigned for centuries held that importing raw materials and exporting finished goods was the way to create wealth. In the 1700s this idea became known as mercantilism, but long before that Jean-Baptiste Colbert, finance minister to King Louis XIV of France, effectively translated mercantilism into law. In 1664, Colbert imposed a uniform import tariff across all of France in place of the disparate tariffs in effect in different regions. Three years later he hiked duties on stockings, wool cloth, and other products that competed with French-made goods. Other countries, including England and the Netherlands, responded in kind. British manufacturing flourished thanks to high tariffs, and by the late 1700s textile mills and potteries established to serve the protected British market were also exporting aggressively.[13]

Mercantilists saw international commerce as a competition with winners and losers. If a country exported more than it imported, it was victorious. If its trade was in deficit, it had met defeat. This way of thinking was not entirely irrational. The world economy, by and large, ran on silver. An importer generally had to pay for its purchases in silver; an exporter received silver in return. If a country consistently imported more than it exported, its stockpile of the precious metal would melt away, limiting its ability to import in the future and to buy armaments and hire soldiers in case of war. A consistent trade surplus, in contrast, would allow the country to build up its silver wealth. By those lights, Colbert's tariff increases were a great success because France's trade went from deficit to surplus, never mind that French nobles faced higher bills for foreign-made silk stockings and feathered hats. When Chinese emperor Qianlong wrote to Britain's King George III in 1793 to say, "I . . . have no use for your country's manufactures," he had more on his mind than the corrupting effects of foreign fashions. He knew that the British were much more eager to sell than to buy.

By mercantilist lights, wealth came from making things and exporting them. It followed that the only goods a country should import were those it did not make. Englishmen would have agreed unanimously that bringing in tea from India and sugar from Barbados made their country better off. But importing goods that competed with domestic products was to be avoided. The purposes of colonies in this scheme were to furnish raw materials and precious metals to the mother country, buy its manufactures, and provide it with tax revenue. The Wool Act of 1699, for example, protected British textile makers by allowing Irish wool to be exported only to England and Wales, guaranteeing manufacturers a steady supply of raw material, while barring colonists in North America from shipping woolen and linen yarn and cloth outside their own colony. Lord Cornbury, the British governor of New York, fully understood this purpose, advising London in 1705, "these Colloneys . . . ought to be kept intirely dependent upon and subservient to England, and that can never be if they are suffered to goe on in the notions they have, that as they are Englishmen, soe they may set up their same manufactures here as people may doe in England." Authorities of France, Spain, and every other colonial power would have said something similar.[14]

Little had changed sixty years later, in Peter Hasenclever's day. Mercantilism shaped the American Company's brief existence. The partnership existed only because Parliament granted Hasenclever British citizenship; as a Prussian citizen, his investment would not have been permitted because, by mercantilist lights, any profit he extracted would have diminished British wealth. The American Company could not have exported its iron and steel bars from New Jersey colony had not Parliament, aware that British ironmakers were desperately short of charcoal after depleting the forests near their mines, authorized imports under certain conditions. Even then, the company could ship only in British vessels and only to Great Britain. Despite its ambitions, the American Company could not escape the confines of its time.[15]

In a few countries, such as Great Britain and the Netherlands, international trade directly touched the lives of many citizens in the age of mercantilism, not always for the better. The innovations in spinning that helped British cloth conquer the global market in the late 1700s dramatically reduced labor costs—impoverishing thousands of English villagers who had earned part of their incomes at the spinning wheel. When Parliament dealt with the strains of war with France by prohibiting banks from redeeming paper money with gold in 1797, the credit crunch in Great Britain caused a recession in the United States. But most countries, from China and Japan to Russia and the vast Ottoman Empire, had weak international economic ties. The vast majority of the

world's population lived from subsistence farming, tenuously connected to the cash economy. Those remote from ports and major trade
routes hardly felt the effects of international commodity flows and
foreign loans. The work of British economist Angus Maddison, the
foremost historian of economic growth, offers a sense of scale. Maddison's estimate of international trade in 1813 was less than one two-
thousandth the volume in 2013.[16]

It would take three innovations to make globalization possible: the
oceanic steamship, the telegraph cable, and some dramatically different
ideas about international trade. All three came about with the unanticipated rise of capitalism.

2

The First Globalization

IT MAY HAVE BEEN no coincidence that the man whose thinking opened the way to globalization was himself a product of it. David Ricardo was a descendant of Sephardic Jews. His father's family, originally from Portugal, fled the Inquisition sometime in the early 1500s, found a haven in Italy, and then moved to Amsterdam, a burgeoning financial center, around 1662. Abraham Ricardo emigrated from Amsterdam to London in 1760 and married Abigail Delvalle, whose family had arrived in London shortly after Jews were permitted to live openly in England in 1656; her surname points to roots in Spain. By the time David, the third of at least seventeen children, was born in 1772, Abraham had become a British citizen and had grown wealthy trading stocks and bonds. He sent David off to Amsterdam at age eleven for two years of schooling before bringing him home to learn the family business.[1]

David Ricardo excelled in finance in his own right, becoming a prominent subscriber to government loans and joining the committee of proprietors of the stock exchange. He was a worldly man, conversant in several languages and steeped in the intellectual debates of his day. Foreign trade was among the most prominent topics, and Ricardo had unorthodox views. They became public in 1815, when he criticized proposed duties on grain imports—set out in legislation known as the Corn Laws—with the radical assertion that protecting Britain's farmers from foreign competition was unwise. It would be better, he said, to let in imports so grain prices would fall. As landowners' profits fell, they would shift their capital into the manufacturing sector. When that occurred,

Ricardo wrote, manufactured products could be exported to buy more grain than Great Britain could grow if it tried to be self-sufficient, making both the landowners and the country better off.

Two years later, Ricardo developed the point in *Principles of Political Economy and Taxation*. "Under a system of perfectly free commerce, each country naturally devotes its capital and labour to such employments as are most beneficial to each," he insisted. "This pursuit of individual advantage is admirably connected with the universal good of the whole." This was the theory of comparative advantage, the idea that was to earn Ricardo lasting fame. Foreign trade was not, as the mercantilists had insisted, simply a means of extracting wealth from other countries. Rather, England stood to benefit from importing as well as exporting, and its trading partners would benefit as well. Ricardo's arguments were perfectly suited to an era in which the flow of goods across borders would matter far more to average people than ever before, the era of industrial capitalism.[2]

———

Defining capitalism is a fool's errand, and assigning a start date is impossible. But the evidence is clear that in the 1820s and 1830s, larger enterprises under private ownership became more prominent, first in Great Britain and then, over time, elsewhere in Europe and North America. To be sure, the vast majority of industrial production still came from artisans' workshops, but factories occupying hundreds of workers were no longer unknown. Around the same time, governments, often cautiously, allowed greater scope for market forces to shape their economies. This transition played out differently in different countries, but by the time the term "capitalism" came into use in the 1860s, there was no dispute that something fundamental had been altered. Living standards, after falling steeply in the early years of industrialization as automation drove down wages and fetid slums burgeoned, began to improve as cities belatedly built water and sewer systems and funded primary schools to teach all children reading and arithmetic. Innovations in transportation and communications reduced the isolation of rural villages and allowed easier domestic trade. As economic historians Larry Neal and Jeffrey Williamson put it succinctly, "Whenever a country adopted its particular variety of capitalism in the nineteenth century, it also began to experience the onset of modern economic growth."[3]

Globalization went hand in hand with the rise of capitalism. Among the first signs was a law signed by King George IV of Great Britain in 1824, repealing no fewer than six separate acts prohibiting the "seducing of Artificers" to work abroad. Those restrictions, some dating to 1719, had been put in place to block other countries from building their economies with the help of British ingenuity. That was the mercantilist idea: the way to keep an economy strong was to keep other economies weak. Ricardo's argument that Great Britain would gain more from two-way trade than from trying to monopolize manufacturing cast these anti-emigration laws in a less favorable light, and mounting unemployment provided an added reason for repeal—to let workers displaced by new textile machinery find jobs abroad. Ricardo had died in 1823, but his ideas were steadily gaining adherents. They would influence a series of laws over the next two decades that gradually opened Britain's economy, and then other economies, to foreign goods.[4]

This was not a matter of altruism. Great Britain was far and away the world's leading industrial power, and its major industrial activity was processing cotton. Cotton goods, just 6 percent of British exports around 1784, made up 49 percent half a century later—when the volume was thirty times as high. Keeping Manchester's spinning, weaving, and dyeing mills busy required unprecedented supplies of imported cotton and unprecedented demand for exported cloth. Great Britain urgently needed to induce other countries to open their markets as well as opening its own, and Ricardo had furnished the intellectual case for its new free-market ideology. The ideology was powerful. At the time Ricardo wrote, international trade had stagnated for years as Europe's great powers waged war. Within a very few years, tariffs on imports were falling, the cost of trading among the countries of northwestern Europe was coming down, and the volume of trade was growing rapidly.[5]

The cotton supply chain was lengthy, stretching from Mississippi plantations to brokers' warehouses near the Liverpool docks to mills across the English Midlands and back out again to textile buyers around the world. Competition throughout this globalizing industry was intense, and incessant pressure to control costs meant that the working conditions of the people who farmed, transported, and processed cotton were dismal almost everywhere. In the United States, slavery expanded westward in the 1820s and 1830s to industrial-scale plantations in Alabama and Mississippi. In India, Brazil, Egypt, and elsewhere, small farmers who grew food crops for their own use were effectively turned into sharecroppers to meet Great Britain's insatiable demand for cotton. Circumstances were not much better for those who spun and wove in British cities, where height and life expectancy declined during the 1830s and 1840s as workers hired by the ever-expanding mills packed urban neighborhoods. Twelve-hour days in air thick with cotton dust were the norm, and the endless clacking of looms brought early deafness to many who survived. Charles Dickens memorably described working families new to urban life in the 1830s, packed into "rooms so small, so filthy, so confined, that the air would seem too tainted even for the dirt and squalor which they shelter." His description of life in South London would have described Manchester or Bolton equally well.[6]

Yet the pressure on costs served its purpose, giving Britain what would later be called a first-mover advantage. Starting in the 1820s, cheap British cottons displaced domestic textiles in Asia. India, long the largest producer and exporter of cotton cloth, was muscled aside by its colonial master, which drove it out of markets in the Middle East and North Africa in the 1820s and supplied two-thirds of the Indian subcontinent's textile consumption by the late nineteenth century. China grew no more cotton in 1840 than it had in 1750, by one estimate, while the population doubled; the added demand for cloth was met by imports. When France, Belgium, and other countries in continental Europe tried to follow the British example and build modern textile industries in the mid-1800s, they found their mills could not compete. The only way they could turn out cotton cloth at the same cost as Great Britain was to weave it with low-cost British yarn.[7]

————

Cheap transportation was the prerequisite for running the cotton industry on a global scale. Great Britain's insatiable appetite for cotton, in turn, drove investments that lowered the cost of moving American-grown cotton to English mills starting around 1830, just as British textile exports were taking off. Traditionally, raw cotton had been difficult to transport efficiently, because the loosely packed fibers occupied far more precious shipboard space per ton of weight than, say, wheat or coal. Shipowners took to "screwing" cotton with steam presses at US ports, packing it so tightly that a pound of cotton occupied barely half the shipboard space in 1860 that it had filled in 1810. Increased demand from exporters encouraged construction of larger ships; as with *Emma Maersk* nearly two centuries later, there was money to be saved by carrying more freight on each voyage. By the early 1840s, the cost of shipping cotton across the North Atlantic was one-fourth less than it had been two decades earlier—while exports from the Americas, mainly cotton shipped from the United States to England, roughly doubled.[8]

Robert Fulton's *Clermont*, the first commercially successful steamboat, had carried passengers from New York City up the Hudson River in 1807, but it was British engineer Isambard Brunel who adapted the steamship to make globalization possible. Brunel, engaged by the Great Western Steamship Company, challenged the orthodoxy that steamships were impractical on ocean voyages. His *Great Western*, laden with six hundred tons of cargo, crossed the Atlantic in 1838. Improved versions, using propellers rather than sidewheels and constructed of iron rather than wood, made the trip even faster. By the 1840s, steamships were crossing between Liverpool and New York on regular schedules, a major improvement over unreliable sailing ships.

The economics of steamships were difficult on longer voyages because the coal required to feed their voracious boilers occupied precious cargo space. In consequence, it took three decades after the first transatlantic steamship voyage before steam-powered vessels began to transform long-distance trade. The Suez Canal opened in 1869, creating a shortcut for ships steaming between Europe, India, and East Asia, but it would not have mattered without a network of British-controlled coaling stations in places like Gibraltar, Egypt, Aden, and Singapore that allowed ships to carry less coal, saving room for paying cargo. Even so, the route was profitable only because large sailing ships could not use the canal and had to make the long and arduous voyage around Africa. Sailing ships dominated on most long-distance routes until the 1870s, when the compound engine, a new technology that burned coal more efficiently, made steamships viable. The availability of cheaper steel plating made it practical to build much larger, faster vessels in the final decades of the nineteenth century, at which point cargo rates plummeted: in 1896, shipping Australian wool to Great Britain cost half as much per ton as in 1873—and shipping a ton of wheat across the North Atlantic cost about one-eighth what it had back in 1820.[9]

Steamships, with comparatively precise arrival and departure times, represented a radical change in the shipping business. By promising to sail on a particular date, oceangoing steamers made it possible for a manufacturer or a merchant to make better decisions about buying and selling and to plan around the arrival of imported goods. The key to effective use of the new steamship technology was the telegraph.

The electrical telegraph was undoubtedly the most important change in communications during the 1800s. As with the oceangoing steamship itself, there was a long lag between invention and practical innovation. The first commercial telegraph messages were sent in Great Britain in 1838 and, using Samuel Morse's famous technology, in the United States six years later. But it was not until the 1860s and 1870s that reliable telegraph services linked America, Europe, India, Australia, and Japan. The telegraph made it possible to know prices in other countries in real time. Exporters no longer needed to ship their goods into uncertain conditions, hoping to sell them months later at a profit; until the very moment a vessel weighed anchor, an exporter could change the destination of a shipment, demand a higher price from a customer abroad, or move the goods back into a warehouse in hopes prices would rise. Similarly, importers could make commitments based on up-to-date information about prices and supply trends, deciding at the last minute whether Russia, Australia, Argentina, or North America was the most sensible place to buy wheat for sale in Antwerp.

These two technologies, the steamship and the telegraph, combined to revolutionize long-distance international trade, making it possible for entrepreneurs like the Greek-born Vagliano brothers to coordinate the purchase, sale, and movement of hundreds of thousands of tons of grain and coal each year between Russian ports on the Black Sea, Constantinople, Marseilles, northwestern Europe, and London by the 1860s. A third factor soon came into play as well: by the late 1870s, most of the world's major trading countries had fixed the value of their currencies in terms of an ounce of gold. Before then, trade had usually involved what would later be called currency risk: importing from Germany would have cost a Swedish buyer 7 percent more in September of 1820 than in June simply because Sweden's currency lost value against Germany's during the intervening weeks. When a country moved to the gold standard, it automatically fixed the value of its currency against other currencies that were tied to gold. This rigidity came at a cost, making it hard for a government to fight an economic downturn by printing more paper money to stimulate spending, but it did remove the risk that exchange-rate changes would increase the cost of an import or reduce the value of an export after a deal was agreed.[10]

With transportation cheaper and exchange rates stable, the prices of commodities converged around the world: why would a French textile mill pay dear to import raw silk from India if similar silk was to be had more cheaply in Japan? The globalization of trade in raw materials, including greater ability to react to higher costs in one country by importing from another, tended to push prices down, giving a boost to manufacturers that used those commodities to make consumer goods.[11]

———

Like the changes that reshaped the world economy beginning in the 1980s, the First Globalization was disorienting. Industrial companies began bursting through borders. Singer, founded in New York in 1851 to sell the first commercially viable sewing machine, had an office in Paris in 1855 and a factory in Glasgow by 1867. Over the next half-century, textile, chemical, machinery, and consumer-products companies, mainly based in Europe or the United States, took their brands around the world: J&P Coats, a Scottish thread manufacturer dating to the late 1700s, made forty foreign investments between 1896 and 1913, mainly by purchasing factories in places as distant as Russia, Brazil, and Japan. Foreign competition became intense, prompting coal miners, glass makers, and cement manufacturers, among others, to form international cartels to keep imports from disrupting their markets.

The boom in international finance created new social distinctions by concentrating enormous wealth in a handful of places, of which London was easily the most important. Bankers and wealthy investors in France, Germany, and especially the United Kingdom lent vast sums abroad, while debtor countries such as the United States, Canada, and Argentina relied heavily on foreign lenders and investors to build railroads and expand industry: during the 1880s, the peak years of American railroad construction, around two-fifths of the total investment in US railroads was European money. By 1913, one-third of British wealth was invested abroad and half of all business assets in Argentina were owned by foreigners. Foreign-owned business assets may have been as important to the global economy as they would be half a century later, as companies used them to spread their technology and marketing prowess around the world. In almost every case, though, firms kept their important management, research, and engineering work in their home country; they were not international firms, but unmistakably British or German or American companies doing business abroad.[12]

Of course, just as would occur in the late twentieth and early twenty-first centuries, the First Globalization involved extensive movement of people. "Whereas formerly only the privileged few had ventured abroad, now bank clerks and small trades-people would visit France and Italy," the Austrian novelist Stefan Zweig recalled of the years before World War One. The true extent of "cross-border" migration is difficult to know: in an age of great empires, a family moving from Libya to Lebanon was not crossing the Ottoman Empire's international borders, and someone who relocated from Dublin to Liverpool remained within the United Kingdom. For that reason alone, figures showing that roughly one-fourth of the Irish population emigrated between 1841 and 1855 are probably an underestimate. But there is plenty of evidence from other countries. Roughly one-tenth of Norway's population left that country during the 1880s, and in the early twentieth century one out of every fifty Italians emigrated each year. On the receiving side, one in seven US residents was an immigrant in the late 1800s, and in 1914 nearly one Argentine in three had been born abroad, most likely in Italy or Spain.[13]

Less-studied waves of immigrants, just as large, reached other parts of the world. An estimated twenty-nine million Indians emigrated to such disparate places as Fiji, Guyana, and Kenya in the decades before 1914, and perhaps twenty million people from southern China went out to Burma, Singapore, the Dutch East Indies, and Indochina. Farther north, millions of ethnic Russians moved into central Asia and Siberia, and so did millions of Chinese. All told, over three million people moved across national borders annually in the first years of the twentieth century, many more than in any earlier time period.[14]

Yet what is often forgotten about the First Globalization is that Europe called the tune. Roughly three-quarters of international investment was funded by European capital, the bulk of it going into mines and plantations in poor regions of Latin America and Asia. The volume of goods trade grew explosively—by 1913, it was roughly thirty times higher than a century earlier—but at that date, 40 percent of the world's international trade still occurred among European countries. A thick web of railroads and inland waterways bound the continent's economies together, anchored by international agreements meant to keep trade flowing: the construction of the Gotthard rail tunnel through the Swiss Alps, which opened in 1882, was subsidized by Italy, Switzerland, and Germany, while the Central Commission for Navigation on the Rhine, an international body, supervised so many projects to deepen and straighten the river's main channel that the cost of barge freight between the Netherlands and Germany fell by three-fourths between 1890 and 1914. Links were tight enough that in some industries, manufacturers regularly did business in multiple European countries, routinely shipping sewing machines from Great Britain to Italy and chemicals from Germany to France.[15]

Another 37 percent of the world's trade, more or less, moved between Europe and other parts of the world. Much of this was the fruit of colonialism, with European countries using foreign outposts to provide minerals and agricultural products they could not produce at home and then to import the colonial power's exports to keep factory hands back in the home country employed. Among the most egregious examples was the Belgian Congo, a colony privately owned by King Leopold between 1885 and 1908 and thereafter controlled by the Belgian government, where men were forced to collect rubber in the jungle for export and brutally punished if they failed to meet their quotas. The remainder of Europe's overseas trade in 1913 was mainly with the United States. About two-thirds of US exports went to Europe, principally natural resources such as cotton, wheat, and copper, with a smattering of machinery and farm equipment. Unlike Europe, the United States raised its tariffs repeatedly to protect domestic factories in the nineteenth century, during which manufactured goods actually accounted for a steadily declining share of its imports.[16]

Less than one-fourth of international trade at the peak of the First Globalization moved between non-European countries. Even after foreign powers led by Great Britain forced a defeated China to accept greater imports—including opium from India—in the 1840s and 1850s, East Asia's role in the world economy was small and shrinking. The same was true of India. Japan, which was opened to trade by US Navy gunboats in 1853, was an exception, but the rapid expansion of its foreign trade after the 1860s began from near zero; by 1913, its exports were barely one-eighth those of the United States. Latin American countries had negligible trade with one another, and purchased only a tiny share of US exports.[17]

And roaring trade itself can be a deceptive indicator of the ways in which economies, and workers' lives, were linked to the global economy. Nearly two-thirds of the calories consumed in Great Britain, from Jamaican sugar to Russian wheat to Danish butter, were imported, but the corresponding figure for China was probably close to zero. As a share of the world's total output, economists estimate, exports plus imports grew from less than 3 percent in 1815, when Napoleon's defeat at Waterloo brought peace to Europe, to between 8 and 12 percent by 1913. But while fast oceangoing steamships now linked ports around the world, it was still the case in 1913 that most of those vessels' cargo was primary products—the same minerals, fibers, and foodstuffs that had dominated trade flows for ages past. In many cases, a country's trade was dominated by one or two commodities: bananas in Nicaragua, wool and gold in Australia, rice in Thailand. Individual families were exposed less to the world economy in general than to the price of a specific product. If the price of cocoa was down, whether because of weak demand in Europe or excess supply in Africa, a cocoa-exporting country faced trouble. Globalization aside, many countries had placed too many of their economic eggs in a single basket long before capitalism came on the scene.[18]

Only a handful of countries—Japan, the United States, and a few European nations—exported more manufactured goods than raw materials in the early twentieth century. Supply chains, in the modern sense of a factory in one country supplying a specialized part, component, or chemical to a factory in another, existed hardly at all. When the US government looked for such relationships, it valued "Imports of Articles Partially or Wholly Manufactured for Use as Materials for Manufacturing" at approximately $113 million in 1906. The value of all materials used by the country's 216,262 manufacturing establishments was $8.5 billion, so imported manufactures, by the government's measurement, were only 1.3 percent of the inputs US factories used to produce their goods.[19]

Perhaps, over time, the rapidly industrializing world economy would have evolved in a way that created more complex linkages among industries in different countries, leading to more complicated supply chains. That did not occur. Instead, in 1914, the First Globalization crashed to a halt.

3

Retreat

THE END of the First Globalization can be dated with some precision. On June 28, 1914, the heir to the throne of the Austro-Hungarian Empire was assassinated in Sarajevo, in what was then the Austro-Hungarian territory of Bosnia-Herzegovina. After a month of threats and troop movements, with other powers intervening to support their allies, war erupted across Europe. On July 28, as Austria-Hungary declared war on Serbia, the Montreal, Toronto, and Madrid stock exchanges closed their doors. By July 30, as Germany and Russia mobilized their armies, exchanges from Vienna to Paris were shuttered. On July 31, with German troops poised to invade Belgium and France, the London Stock Exchange ceased business. A few hours later, as brokers milled about the trading floor just before ten in the morning, the man charged with sounding the brass bell to open the New York Stock Exchange was told to wait.

The cause of that decision, the exchange's president wrote later, was that with the rest of the world's stock markets closed, "the resumption of business on that morning would have made New York the only market in which a world panic could vent itself." That was not the whole truth. The secretary of the treasury, William McAdoo, was intimately involved in the decision to shut down trading in New York. McAdoo feared that if the bell sounded at 10 a.m., foreigners would dump their stocks and bonds, use the proceeds to purchase gold, and take the gold back to Europe to pay the cost of waging war. In the United States, as in most of Europe, gold underpinned the entire financial system, and US banks were required to exchange paper dollars for gold at an official price upon request. If US gold supplies were sucked across the ocean, banks would no longer be able to meet this obligation, causing what was vividly called a "panic." Bank lending would dry up, businesses would struggle to pay their workers, and the economy would grind to a halt.[1]

Once, it would have been possible to solve that problem by reducing the amount of gold a dollar bill could buy, or by redeeming dollar bills with silver rather than gold. But the fixed exchange rate of the dollar against Europe's main currencies, set in terms of gold, had drawn foreign investment to the United States by removing an element of risk. All told, foreign-owned businesses were worth about 5 percent of the US economy's output. Foreigners owned textile fiber plants, tire factories, some $2.7 billion of railroad bonds, and one-fourth of the shares of United States Steel Corporation, the country's largest company. Such investments had transformed the US economy since the 1870s. The only way to keep these funds from fleeing was to keep the gold standard in place, and that required a temporary halt to the globalization of finance. Foreign-exchange trading was suspended. The New York Stock Exchange, one of the most important vehicles of globalization, would not resume normal operations for nearly nine months.[2]

The disruption of the financial markets was only the first blow to the vision of a world in which goods and money moved freely across borders. The second came with the dramatic decline of international trade. Disrupting trade was the major strategic goal of both the Central Powers—initially Germany, Austria-Hungary, and the Ottoman Empire—and the Entente allies, France, Russia, Great Britain, and Japan. The moment the war started, the British Royal Navy blockaded Germany. Germany-bound vessels were seized. Ships bound for neutral countries such as Norway and the Netherlands were forced into British ports, where officials confiscated anything that might be transshipped to Germany. Much of the German merchant fleet was trapped in the harbors at Bremen, Hamburg, and Lübeck for the balance of the war; as a high-ranking British maritime official explained later, the Germans "had no shipping problem, for they had no shipping opportunities." Germany countered by threatening to sink any merchant vessel bound for Great Britain, a transparent attempt to stifle trade by making it more expensive to insure ships and cargo. Great Britain, Norway, and the United States quickly provided state-sponsored insurance for ships to keep commerce flowing.[3]

Great Britain, by virtue of geography and its larger navy, had the better of the situation. In the first months, its blockade was not watertight. German textile mills managed to import Australian wool via the United States and Sweden, both neutral at the time, and the United States insisted on its right to import German textile dyes. But by 1915 the blockade was drastically constricting the commerce of the second-largest trading nation in Europe, even as Germany's war against Russia cut off its grain imports from the east. The British tightened the noose further by threatening to halt coal shipments to the Scandinavian countries unless they stopped exporting food and iron ore to Germany. Under this relentless pressure, Germany's foreign trade fell by nearly three-quarters between 1913 and 1917.[4]

The lack of merchant shipping was felt far from the bloody trenches of the Western Front. Great Britain controlled nearly half the world's oceangoing shipping in the summer of 1914. British-owned ship lines, such as Peninsular & Oriental, the largest steamship operator, and China Navigation Company, which moved freight and passengers throughout Southeast Asia, carried a very large share of Asia's international trade. The British government requisitioned many of those vessels for military needs, while a new agency, soon to be designated the Ministry of Shipping, took charge of the rest. Under this arrangement, the Ministry of Shipping effectively controlled the foreign commerce of Great Britain, and also of France and Italy. Merchant vessels were told where to sail and what cargo to carry. Only approved products could be imported into Great Britain, lest precious shipping capacity be taken up by nonessential cargo.[5]

In 1915, the first full year of the war, the volume of international trade worldwide was 26 percent lower than in 1913. Europe's exports fell by half, while exporters in Latin America, thousands of miles from the field of battle, struggled to find ships to move their coffee and meat to market. Very few new vessels were to be had. British shipyards, which had built two-thirds of the world's new merchant tonnage in 1913, could not maintain production with their workers off to war. Although the United States cranked up shipbuilding in 1916, it needed those new ships to move troops and military supplies once it declared war on Germany in April 1917; they were not available for commercial trade. The shortage of tonnage worsened as German submarine attacks inflicted staggering losses on the merchant fleets of neutrals as well as the Allied countries. British authorities pretended that the problems were minor. In early 1917, they tried to boost morale by declaring that 2,500 ships were arriving in British ports each week. They did not reveal that 2,360 of those were boats too small to cross the ocean, leaving only 140 bringing wheat, beef, or other critical supplies. Shipping was so scarce that China's imports fell 34 percent from 1913 to 1918, Italy's 62 percent, Persia's an astonishing 75 percent. Around the globe, international trade decreased by approximately one-third over the four years and three months of the war.[6]

———

An armistice ended the war in November 1918. It was signed in the midst of a global flu epidemic that may have left a hundred million dead, at a time when revolutions across Europe were seeking to overthrow the old order and across a heavily indebted continent that faced years of reconstruction. The victorious European countries gave priority to acquiring additional colonies, rebuilding their gold reserves, and annexing territory from the ruins of the collapsed German, Austro-Hungarian, and Ottoman empires. Restoring trade and investment ranked very low on the agenda. Eventually, as historian Michael B. Miller has pointed out, the war would boost globalization by so weakening Europe that Japan and the United States would take on key roles as organizers of the world economy. But those effects lay well in the future.[7]

In a sense, limiting globalization was the goal of postwar diplomacy. The peace negotiations in Versailles, near Paris, were seen as the beginning of the end of empire, or at least of certain empires. For Woodrow Wilson, the US president, "self-determination," a vague concept that presumed that a common language or a common ethnicity should be the basis of political sovereignty, was the most important aim. "The war undoubtedly had the effect of over-exciting the feeling of nationality," Italian foreign minister Sidney Sonnino explained. "Perhaps America fostered it by putting the principles so clearly." Nationalistic ideas came to dominate economic policy. Trade barriers rose anew, foreign investment became suspect, and domestic control of merchant shipping was treated as a strategic imperative. As they consolidated power in the new Soviet Union, the Bolshevik Communists who had overthrown the Russian Empire embraced similar policies, if not for the same reasons. Their goal was to keep foreign capitalists at a distance.[8]

One measure of globalization is how "open" a country's economy is to world trade. Such calculations are inevitably subject to dispute: how, for example, does one adjust for the fact that a shipment from Prague to Vienna moved within a single country until 1918 but crossed an international border thereafter? But despite such technical issues, the underlying trends are very clear. In 1913, the final year before the war, exports came to about 12 percent of the world's total economic output. After a brief postwar upturn, international trade slumped badly as much of the world fell into recession in 1920 and 1921. Although economic growth, and trade with it, picked up around 1924, exports in the second half of the 1920s equaled only 10 percent or so of global output, well below the prewar level. The world economy was less open than it had been.[9]

This outcome was deliberate. Country after country increased tariffs in the 1920s to help its own manufacturers and farmers recover. In Great Britain, for a century the leading advocate of freer trade, Parliament passed the Safeguarding of Industries Act in 1921, levying duties that made optical equipment, instruments, organic chemicals, and other products from outside the British Empire one-third more expensive. That law also authorized penalties against imports that the government thought were being sold below the cost of production—a provision that violated treaties with no fewer than twenty-six countries but pleased industrial trade unions. The United States increased tariffs in 1921 and again in 1922; while two-thirds of US imports faced no duties, average tariffs on the rest raised the cost of a $100 import to $139 before it left the dock. Spain's average import tariff went from 33 percent in 1913 to 44 percent in 1925, British India's from 4 percent to 14 percent. Often enough, one country's new import restrictions led other countries to retaliate in kind. Between 1925 and 1929, twenty-six European nations hiked their tariffs, as did Australia, Canada, New Zealand, and many countries in Latin America.[10]

Had shipping costs resumed their prewar decline, cheaper freight might have counteracted the effects of higher tariffs. Productivity had grown much faster in shipping than in other industries starting in the late 1800s, mainly because the use of steel in place of iron allowed larger vessels that could carry more cargo. As a result, international trade by sea became cheaper: one ship line calculated that its average cost to carry one ton of cargo fell by 60 percent between 1885 and 1914. But in the 1920s, costs stopped declining. The reasons are debated among historians, but whatever the cause, average shipping rates in the 1920s, adjusted for inflation, were barely lower than they had been back in 1913, so lower transport costs provided no stimulus to trade.[11]

The hesitant growth of foreign commerce was accompanied by a retreat from foreign investments. Before World War One, the value of foreign-owned assets around the world, from government bonds to manufacturing plants, had come to about 18 percent of the world's economic output. That figure declined through the 1920s, hitting 8 percent by 1930. There were, of course, many highly visible foreign investments. Ford Motor Company, which had assembled cars from US-made parts in Great Britain and France before the war—an early example of long-distance manufacturing supply chains—owned thirteen plants in Europe by the end of the 1920s. But Ford's expansive footprint revealed the limits of globalization in the interwar period: it required plants even in small countries, such as Denmark, because high tariffs made it impractical to serve all of Europe from one or two larger, more efficient plants. While IBM factories in France and Germany assembled tabulating machines from parts imported from the United States, many foreign companies licensed foreign plants to make their products rather than importing parts or ingredients, the better to avoid paying tariffs on imports: US automakers exported from Canada to gain duty-free access

to the British Empire, but their Canada-made vehicles required a specified percentage of Canadian content to avoid high Canadian duties on
US-made parts. Overall, finance and manufacturing became much less
international during the 1920s. Faced with the constant need to negotiate around tariffs, currency controls, and other obstacles, investors preferred to bring their money home.[12]

Migration waned as well. The United States, the largest destination
country, had received more than one million immigrants a year six times
between 1905 and 1914. After it enacted tight restrictions in 1924, annual
immigration averaged about three hundred thousand, nearly a third of
it from Canada rather than more distant places. Another one-time mag-
net for European immigrants, Argentina, had drawn around two hundred thousand annually before the war but averaged about half that
many in the 1920s. China became the main source of cross-border emigration, sending millions of people to Southeast Asia and millions more
to the increasingly Japanese-dominated region of Manchuria.[13]

––––––

The Great Depression put an end to any hope of restoring freer movement of goods, investment, and people quickly. October 29, 1929, the
Tuesday the New York Stock Exchange cratered amid trading so pan-
icked that the tickers printing out share prices ran hours behind, has
gone down in popular imagination as the start of the Depression. But
that was the stuff of tabloid headlines. Well before Black Tuesday, deflation had taken root across much of the world. Inept economic policy
lay at its heart. Governments held to their commitments to fix their
currencies in terms of gold at a time when gold was scarce, driving up
their domestic interest rates, strangling economic growth, and leaving
banks to struggle with portfolios of loans to insolvent borrowers. By
1930, evidence indicates, every major economy, from Japan to Italy to
Canada, was in the grip of an extended price decline.[14]

Deflation tends to undermine economic growth. Businesses put off
buying equipment and consumers stop spending: Why purchase something today when it will be cheaper tomorrow? As this occurred around

the world in the early 1930s, joblessness became endemic. Data for most countries are fragmentary in this period, but according to official estimates, the US unemployment rate, roughly 3 percent in the generally prosperous economy of 1929, jumped to 9 percent in 1930. Conditions on US farms were so critical that the average daily wage for farmhands, $2.15 without room and board, was one-third less than it had been ten years earlier. Europe had it no better, as governments worried more about balancing their budgets and preserving their gold supplies than about putting people back to work. It would take eight years for the Dutch economy to again be as large as it had been in 1929, nine years for Canada's, ten years for France's. The Dow Jones Industrial Average, the best-known gauge of prices on the New York Stock Exchange, would require fully twenty-five years, until November 1954, to regain its pre-crash level, and considerably longer if the average were adjusted to reflect inflation in the interim.[15]

The economic downturn itself reduced international trade. With consumers scared to spend money, exports and imports dropped a startling 8 percent worldwide in 1930. But worse was to come. In April 1929, the US Congress responded to cries of hardship in the farm sector by starting work on a new tariff law. What began as a modest effort to help farmers quickly spiraled out of control. The Smoot-Hawley tariff, as the Tariff Act of 1930 has been known ever since its enactment eight months after the stock market crash, increased the number of products subject to tariffs and raised rates. The law set many tariff rates in terms of dollars per unit or per pound, rather than as a percentage of the import's value, so as deflation took hold and prices fell, duties came to account for a larger share of the value of imports. By 1932, the Smoot-Hawley tariff would add 59 percent to the cost of bringing many minerals, farm products, and manufactured goods into the country.[16]

The United States was already the world's largest trading nation in 1930, accounting for about one-seventh of all international trade. The new tariffs infuriated its trading partners, whose exports were effectively blocked even as their manufacturers were already facing weaker demand. Canada and European countries struck back by raising their own tariffs on US exports. Then, as a banking crisis spread across Europe in the summer of 1931, governments unlinked their currencies from gold so their central banks could inject more money into struggling economies. The gold standard collapsed, and exchange rates went wild. One after another, countries introduced controls on foreign exchange, making it hard to obtain the foreign currency needed to pay for imports.

Adjusted for price changes, the volume of world trade fell nearly one-third between 1929 and 1933 and then mounted only a feeble recovery. Trade in manufactured goods fell 42 percent over the same years. Foreign investment came nearly to a stop, as one country after another limited citizens' ability to move money abroad. When the League of Nations looked at matters, it found that in the sixteen months after September 1, 1931, twenty-three countries increased tariffs across the board, fifty raised them on selected items, and thirty-two imposed import quotas or licensing systems. A League report warned, "By the middle of 1932, it was obvious that the international trading mechanism was in real danger of being smashed as completely as the international monetary system had."[17]

The long-lasting economic crisis, made far more severe by the collapse of international trade and foreign investment, had major political consequences. Amid stubbornly high unemployment and worsening living standards, national governments in the United States and Canada took more aggressive measures than ever before, aiding farmers; building public works; providing assistance to the poor, elderly, and unemployed; and vastly expanding the role of the state. No more would economic well-being be treated as merely a private-sector concern. In Europe, the crisis destabilized elected governments, as partisans of authoritarian nationalist movements marched through London and Paris and brought dictatorial regimes to power in Germany, Hungary, Portugal, and elsewhere.

Places that mainly exported commodities, including many of the European powers' colonies in Africa and Asia, had a particularly difficult time. High trade barriers in the wealthy countries of Europe and North America meant that commodity exporters had no prospect of developing manufacturing. Their only alternative, selling the output of their farms and mines, became hazardous. After the price of copper collapsed in 1929, the value of Chile's exports, expressed in US dollars, plummeted 88 percent in three years. Brazil, with a big export trade in coffee and sugar and no manufactured exports to speak of, saw the value of its exports fall by two-thirds. Rubber, wool, palm oil, tin: all fell sharply in price during the early 1930s, so that each ton of exports bought fewer manufactured imports than before. The prices of many commodities remained depressed for years, until preparations for World War Two created new demand. Living standards in the poorer parts of the world lagged farther behind those in Europe, North America, and Japan.[18]

By the late 1930s, the world was breaking into a series of trading blocs, in which some countries gave special preferences to favored partners while using tariffs to fence others out. The British Empire stood apart: most of the exports of Canada, India, Australia, and South Africa were sold within the empire, where they faced no import duties. Japan, which already controlled Korea, occupied Manchuria and parts of eastern China in the 1930s and turned them into the main market for Japanese exports; Chinese trade with other countries was largely cut off. As Germany's trade with North America collapsed, its commerce was redirected to Europe, including countries it hoped to turn into vassal states. Italy, too, traded more with its colonies in Africa, principally Libya, and less with others. Foreign investment dried up and cross-border lending ground to a halt as the unwinding of international economic relations paved the way to war. On September 1, 1939, 1.5 million German troops marched into Poland, unleashing a bloody conflict that would devastate much of the world.

4

North and South

IN JULY 1944, World War Two, the most destructive conflict ever waged, was about to enter its sixth year. With Allied troops squeezing Hitler's Germany from east and west and pressing north across the Pacific towards Japan, economic experts from forty-four countries met at Bretton Woods, a resort in the White Mountains of New Hampshire, to lay plans for the postwar world. The question before them was how to restore trade and cross-border investment without creating economic crises like those of the decades before the war. That required, above all, finding a way to manage exchange rates.

The Depression-era experience deeply influenced the negotiators at Bretton Woods. The benefits of a more open world economy were widely acknowledged, save by the Soviet Union. At the same time, though, it seemed obvious that tying exchange rates to gold had made the Great Depression worse, leaving governments unable to inject money to reinvigorate their economies in the face of mass unemployment, worsening living conditions, and social unrest. While the possibility of unstable exchange rates was worrying, a return to the era when the price of gold mattered above all else was not in the cards.[1]

The solution reached at Bretton Woods was a more flexible sort of gold standard. Each country would announce its exchange rate in terms of US dollars. The United States, in turn, promised to convert foreign central banks' dollars into gold at the rate of $35 per ounce. Thus, all the major currencies were fixed in terms of gold and in terms of one another. But two loopholes were built into the new system. One allowed a government to change its exchange rate by up to 10 percent from the starting point. That permitted it to modestly adjust interest rates to manage its domestic economy. The other loophole provided that if a country was in "fundamental disequilibrium"—a phrase that was never defined—the government could modify its exchange rate, but only with the permission of a new international organization, the International Monetary Fund (IMF). The underlying notion was that a flexible gold standard would create confidence in the stability of a country's currency while at the same time allowing exchange rates to rise or fall when the country faced serious economic problems.

Some countries proved to be paragons of stability. The Swiss franc, for example, traded within a hair's breadth of 4.3 to the US dollar from 1946 until 1970, and 5.18 Swedish kronor, give or take a percentage point, were worth one dollar for more than two decades. On the other hand, countries with troubled economies were forced to devalue; in inflation-prone France, one dollar bought 119 francs in 1945 but 490 at the start of 1960, when the French government tried to stabilize the currency by creating a "new franc" that was worth 100 old ones. The thing countries were meant not to do, except in dire circumstances, was restrict imports to help control their currencies. Indeed, freer trade was the point of the whole Bretton Woods system. But to make the system work, there was one product that could not be traded freely: money. If investors could sell British pounds for French francs at will, their transactions could upset the pound–franc exchange rate; therefore, capital flows needed to be controlled. "Private owners of wealth have no right to the liberty to move funds around the world according to their private convenience," British economist Joan Robinson asserted in 1944. What this meant, in practice, was that governments kept tight rein on the financial industry, limiting cross-border investment and even determining which of their citizens had access to precious foreign currency. Finance could not be allowed to globalize.[2]

———

For the negotiators at Bretton Woods, expanding international trade was more than a matter of economics. Having lived through two catastrophic world wars, they saw closer economic ties between nations as fundamental to avoiding a third. But they also knew that family-owned farms and businesses lay at the heart of most countries' economies. Trade barriers and investment restrictions kept small, inefficient enterprises alive but made it hard for successful ones to expand abroad. Especially in Europe, where a factory in one country might be a short drive from potential customers in another, making it easier to operate across borders might result in larger firms that could spend more to buy the latest equipment and to fund research, improving their productivity and boosting living standards across the entire continent.

The Bretton Woods agreement was meant to start this process by creating the International Trade Organization to govern world trade. The idea that an international body might regulate US trade policies, though, raised hackles in the United States, and the new entity was stillborn. In its place, twenty-three countries established an organization with much weaker powers, the General Agreement on Tariffs and Trade. The GATT's ambition was to reduce import duties by consensus. In four negotiating rounds between 1947 and 1956, each member country offered to lower its tariffs on certain products, in return for commitments by the other countries to do likewise. The end result of each round was a list of thousands of tariff reductions, some knocking 20 percent or more off the price of an important foreign-made good, forcing domestic producers to become more efficient if they hoped to compete. The GATT was often derided as a talking shop, and negotiating tariff reductions became slower and more cumbersome as additional countries claimed seats at the table. It succeeded in pushing down tariffs on industrial products, in some cases all the way to zero, but tariffs on agricultural products barely fell at all. The obstacles to trade in services, which usually took the form of licensing requirements or other restrictions rather than tariffs, were so daunting that the GATT barely touched them.

Despite its many shortcomings, the GATT introduced two innovations that would dramatically affect the course of globalization. One was to make tariff cuts binding: once a country had agreed that imported truck axles would face a duty of only 5 percent instead of 15 percent, it could not increase the duty again. This provided an insurance policy for businesses, assuring them that some future government would not suddenly upend their plans by making a particular import dearer. The other innovation was that a country's commitments applied equally to all the other members. Until that point, trade agreements had generally involved two countries—the United States and Nicaragua had signed one in 1936—or a restricted group, such as some countries within the British Empire. The tariff reductions agreed in the GATT, though, applied to imports from any country that joined. Countries could strike more favorable trade agreements with one another only if such arrangements covered "substantially all" of the trade between them or if two-thirds of GATT members approved. This provision opened the way to a remarkable series of treaties that would eventually turn much of Europe into a single market.[3]

———

Prosperity was slow to return to the postwar world. The first years after the end of the war in 1945 were difficult in North America and miserable in many parts of Europe and Asia. Import restrictions left over from the 1930s—the first tariff cuts under the GATT would come in 1948—were only one of the obstacles to economic recovery. The cost of waging war had exhausted many countries' reserves of gold and dollars, leaving them without the wherewithal to import tractors and factory machinery, meat, grain, and coal—and leaving the United States and Canada, whose factories had survived undamaged, without key export markets. Years of price and wage controls had undermined workers' buying power, triggering labor unrest and demands for state takeovers of private industry: France lost more than twenty-two million workdays to strikes in 1947. In that same year, farmers in Europe and Asia produced far less food than a decade earlier, and manufacturers postponed investments because they found the permissible prices unfair. Economic growth was tenuous, to the point that in many countries, income per person, adjusted for inflation, was still lower in 1948 than it had been before the war.[4]

It took aid from the United States to break the dam. The Marshall Plan, approved by Congress in 1948, channeled nearly $13 billion to European countries over four years, so they could import the machinery, raw materials, food, and feed needed to restart their economies. The fundamental purpose was strategic: the United States, easily the dominant power in the postwar world, was eager to assemble a coalition of states strong enough, both politically and economically, to stand up to the Soviet Union, which it saw as the greatest threat to peace. The Soviet Union and its client states rejected Marshall Plan aid and wanted nothing to do with greater trade and foreign investment. With the Soviets fencing themselves off, the three western occupation zones were amalgamated into the Federal Republic of Germany—West Germany—and given a new currency, the deutsche mark. These moves sparked the revival of what had been the largest and most industrialized economy in prewar Europe.[5]

Help from the Marshall Plan came with strings. All seventeen countries that joined up had to promise, among other things, to end price controls and to encourage private initiative. Thus, they committed themselves to economies based on free exchange at prices determined by supply and demand, unlike the state-run economies being set up to the east.[6] The Americans also required the Marshall Plan countries to act collectively. Cooperation did not come easily to nations that had fought one another twice within the memory of most living adults. The first concrete step was taken in 1951, when six countries bound themselves to eliminate all discriminatory practices affecting coal, the main fuel for electricity and industrial power, and steel, a key industrial product. The European Coal and Steel Community opened the door to greater trade, allowing the most efficient mines and steel mills to expand and sell their products across Western Europe, thereby pressuring less efficient ones to close down. The Community's governing body, known as the High Authority, was to guide such decisions, handing out loans to update mills and grants to help displaced workers, funded by a tax on every ton of coal and steel.

More than jobs were at stake. The underlying purpose, as French foreign minister Robert Schumann said, was to tie the countries closer together to "make war not only unthinkable but materially impossible." The idea of national governments handing control of part of their foreign trade to an international body was radical—so radical that the French diplomats who developed the scheme kept it secret even from their own government as long as possible. Belgium, France, Italy, Luxembourg, and the Netherlands signed on because, while they knew that Europe's revival required a healthy West Germany, they wanted assurance that Germany would not again use its economic might to wage war.[7]

Strictly speaking, the European Coal and Steel Community violated the rules of the GATT, because it did not cover "substantially all" trade. But the United States, the most powerful GATT member, did not object to this legal defect; it wanted the Community to succeed, because its concern that the Europeans would discriminate against US exports weighed less than its desire to build a bulwark against communism. Communist parties with pro-Soviet sympathies were strong in Italy, France, and elsewhere. Raising workers' living standards was seen as the best way to defeat them, and if that meant that Europeans might buy more from one another and less from the United States, that seemed a small price.

This strategy was wildly successful. With lower tariffs, more stable currencies, and strong demand for manufactured goods generated by the Korean War, Europe's economies shifted into high gear. Between 1950 and 1952, West Germany's exports to other European countries rose 87 percent, Sweden's 45 percent, Holland's 36 percent. By 1953, nine-tenths of West Germany's imports entered free of customs duties. Foreign investment took off, as European firms invested heavily outside their home countries and US manufacturers opened factories across Europe. The productivity payoff from greater trade and investment was immediate. By 1955, the average Dutch worker produced one-fourth more than in 1950, the average West German worker two-fifths more. Living standards rose apace: as Italy's exports of manufactured goods more than doubled between 1950 and 1957, adjusted for inflation, millions of impoverished peasants moved from isolated villages in the south to the burgeoning cities of the north, where factory jobs offered steady wages, indoor plumbing was common, and store windows showed the latest fashions. There was a reason Italians knew the postwar era as *il miracolo*, the miracle.[8]

Some European leaders had even greater dreams, of erasing the borders that had caused two world wars. In 1956, in the Treaty of Rome, the European Coal and Steel Community was rebaptized as the European Community, within which members would eliminate restrictions on all imports from other member countries, not just on coal and steel. This was totally novel: never before had national governments freely surrendered all power over trade policy. Free trade within the European Community forced European manufacturers to become international companies, whether they wanted to or not. The bet was that as stiffer competition put outmoded factories out of business, the more modern ones would add new jobs at higher wages to replace what was lost. It was a bet that would pay off handsomely.

———

A Second Globalization commenced as the first GATT agreement took effect in 1948. The volume of world trade rose rapidly, but the pattern of trade was similar to that of the First Globalization. Goods, as well as foreign investment, flowed mainly among Western Europe, North America, and Japan, which had been the most highly industrialized regions before World War Two. In the language of the time, these were known as the "North," the "center," or the "developed" economies, depending upon the political leanings of the speaker. International trade was generally popular in the North, as manufacturers added relatively well-paid jobs by the millions.

The rest of the world, though, participated in the Second Globalization mainly by supplying raw materials to these "advanced" countries. In the "South," the "periphery," the "less developed" economies, the average person consumed significantly fewer manufactured goods than the average person in Europe or North America, and domestic factories produced little aside from clothing. Poorer countries were unable to move up the economic ladder, processing their cotton into fabric and their ore into iron bars, because of the high cost of shipping their goods and because the wealthier countries raised barriers to their industrial exports. Few jobs offered more than a subsistence wage. One statistic graphically captures the divide: In 1959, Latin America, Africa, and Asia, added together, were responsible for less than 10 percent of the world's manufacturing output.[9]

To be sure, these countries, many of which broke free from their longtime colonial masters in the postwar years, did a robust business exporting minerals, foods, and fibers. Primary products, from coffee to jute to petroleum, made up nine-tenths of Brazil's exports in 1955 and three-quarters of India's and Turkey's. In almost every case, though, these exports were limited to products that the wealthier countries either did not produce in sufficient volume or lacked altogether: there were foreign markets for Chilean copper and Indian tea, but Colombian sugar was unwanted in the United States and rice from Thailand could not be sold in Japan. What's more, most countries were extremely dependent on just one or two commodities, so a sharp decline in the price of rubber or tin could be cataclysmic. The people of these poorer countries thus saw themselves as losers for whom foreign trade and investment brought penury, not prosperity. This comported with the strongly nationalistic sentiments in lands eager to break free from European control.[10]

The Argentine economist Raúl Prebisch laid out an alternative route. The head of his country's independent central bank, Prebisch was driven from office following a military coup d'état in 1943 and eventually forced into exile. In March of 1949, with few other options, he signed on as a consultant to an obscure United Nations organization, the Economic Commission for Latin America, based in Chile. His first assignment was to prepare an economic survey of Latin America. His report, presented to a conference that May, was a bombshell. He asserted that while freer trade had benefited the large industrial countries, it had failed those "on the periphery of the world economy." David Ricardo's claim, that each country would be best off if it produced those goods it turned out most efficiently and traded them for its other needs, would not allow these peripheral countries to improve workers' productivity and raise living standards, Prebisch insisted. Instead, he argued, the countries on the periphery were running on a treadmill, needing to export more and more raw materials in order to buy the same quantity of manufactured imports. Rather than welcoming free trade, he said, the peripheral countries should bring in machinery and factory equipment while discouraging imported consumer products. Consumer goods could be made locally in factories protected by high tariffs and exported to the wealthy countries. Over time, Prebisch asserted, this strategy would raise productivity in countries on the periphery, allowing them to gradually open their economies.[11]

Prebisch's vision, known as import substitution, found a welcome reception in much of the world. For Latin American countries, it presented an alternative to economic domination by the United States and Great Britain, while for Asia and Africa it offered a guide for ex-colonies to escape the economic control of their former colonial masters. From newly independent India, which set up a planning commission in 1950, to the British colony of Gold Coast, which created a planning ministry even before it became the independent country of Ghana in 1957, governments assigned experts to determine which industries they should develop and how those industries should be fostered. The idea that import substitution offered a "third way" of economic development, distinct from both state-dominated Soviet communism and the capitalist system advocated by the United States, was endorsed by the leaders of twenty-nine African and Asian countries who convened for the first meeting of nonaligned nations in Bandung, Indonesia, in 1955. Almost unanimously, these rulers felt that their countries were mired in an unequal relationship with the wealthier parts of the world.

The way to rectify this imbalance, they thought, was to put an end to the drastic swings in commodity prices that wracked their economics. In 1958, a group of prestigious economists engaged by the GATT concluded that the commodity-exporting countries had a point, and that limiting the brutal volatility of the international markets might make sense. Commodity price stability was so alluring that seventy-seven countries—immediately tagged the G-77—asked the United Nations to help bring it about. Over European and American opposition, the UN set up an organization to look after the developing countries' concerns, the United Nations Conference on Trade and Development (UNCTAD), in 1964. Prebisch, named its leader, called for radical change in the relationship between the wealthy countries and the poorer ones, including cooperation to stabilize commodity prices, support for import substitution to strengthen manufacturing in the developing countries, and greater foreign aid. This package of proposals, and several more, would become known as the New International Economic Order.

In theory, these ideas were alluring; in practice, less so. Stabilizing the price of a commodity such as coffee required, first, that the producing countries each limit their output, which meant controlling the amount each grower could harvest. Second, an international fund would need to buy, store, and sell as much coffee as required to keep the global market price at the agreed level. This would require huge amounts of money as well as the wisdom to know when the current price was too high, justifying sales of coffee from storage, or too low, in which case the fund should buy up coffee. Neither the money nor the wisdom to manage such a system was easy to find. As for import substitution, empowering officials to award import licenses and subsidies left endless opportunities for corruption, while creating industries that were hopelessly inefficient precisely because they lacked foreign competition. Only a handful of the countries that tried it, notably Korea, Taiwan, and, years later, China, used import substitution successfully. Many followed UNCTAD's advice to create merchant fleets and guarantee them a share of the country's maritime trade; these badly managed ventures were costly both for the governments that sponsored them and the exporters who were forced to use them.[12]

As of the end of the 1960s, many poorer countries were still barely connected to the world economy. The developing countries of Asia— torn by the war enveloping Vietnam and Laos, repeated hostilities between India and Pakistan, an armed face-off on the border between South and North Korea, and the turmoil of the Great Proletarian Cultural Revolution in China—provided less than 1 percent of the world's exports of dry cargo in 1967, according to UNCTAD. Africa's economies were stagnant, and Latin America had little to show from import substitution save a mountain of foreign debt. Much of the world understood international trade to be a plot by the "North" to control the "South," and most of the poorer countries wanted no part of it. A few years later, those positions would be reversed.[13]

PART II

One World

5

The Container Revolution

IN THE LONG SWEEP of history, 1956 was a significant year on two counts. It was the year in which international trade in manufactured goods first exceeded trade in commodities. It was also the year in which a radically new method of moving freight, container shipping, first came into use. Neither event earned much notice at the time. Both were landmarks of the Second Globalization, and would open the way to dramatic changes in the world economy during the Third Globalization.

The cost of transporting goods was a major obstacle to international trade after World War Two. The great advances in merchant shipping—the replacement of sailing ships with oceangoing steamships, the replacement of iron hulls with steel, the development of efficient compound engines for steamships—lay decades in the past. Moving goods internationally by rail was slow and costly: in Europe, passenger services had priority over freight, which was neglected by the state-owned railways; in North America, regulation of freight rates dragged down railroads' profits to the point that they slashed investment in their tracks and freight yards; and in Asia, few tracks crossed borders. Innovations such as larger tanker ships and the use of forklift trucks on docks had not been enough to keep the cost of moving freight from rising steadily.

Exporting bulk commodities was simple enough: conveyor belts deposited wheat or iron ore into the hold of a bulk ship, and crude oil or gasoline was pumped aboard a tanker, requiring little time or labor in either case. But exporting what was known as "breakbulk freight"—discrete items packaged separately, such as a washing machine, a bag of coffee beans, or a carton of plastic dolls—was an arduous process. Goods left factories or processing plants in every variety of packaging, from wooden crates or metal drums to burlap bags or paperboard cartons. Each item had to be loaded individually onto a truck or a railcar. If the export was to go by sea, it was hauled to a port, where it would be removed from the truck or train and carried into a warehouse, to be stored, perhaps for several weeks, until the ship was ready to depart. Loading the ship required bringing each shipment onto the dock, placing it alongside other pieces of cargo in a net or on a wooden pallet board, and using a winch to lift the load into the hold. There, dockworkers would separate each item from the assembled load and determine where it should be stowed. Thus, every barrel of chemicals or carton of shoes was handled several times even before a ship set sail.[1]

A typical transatlantic ship in the 1950s could carry perhaps two hundred thousand separate items, from tightly packed bales of cotton to four-door sedans. Merely loading the vessel could take two weeks and involve a hundred or more dockworkers. Discharging the ship at the end of the voyage and then transporting the goods to their final destinations were just as cumbersome. All told, shipping goods from a US factory to a customer in Europe, the main destination for US exports, could take three months and cost 10 to 20 percent of the value of the goods, with a high risk of theft or damage. Factories often clustered near the docks in port cities to minimize transportation time and cost; for this reason, major ports such as London, Hamburg, and New York City were also manufacturing hubs. Holding down the expense and complication of moving goods from one place to another was a major consideration in deciding where to locate a factory.

Stuffing freight into containers to reduce shipping costs was not a novel idea. The concept had first been tried out with detachable cargo compartments aboard canal boats in the 1700s. French and British railways moved wooden shipping containers in the nineteenth century, using cranes cranked by hand to transfer the boxes between rail flatcars and horse carts. In the United States, various railroads put freight into small steel boxes positioned side by side on specially designed railcars during the 1920s. Containers, though, did not sit well with the railroad regulator, the Interstate Commerce Commission, which had long required that each commodity being transported by rail have its own rate. The commission ruled that railroads could not charge less for a container than for the equivalent weight of the most expensive commodity inside the container. To comply, a railroad would have to open each container and inspect every parcel inside. This was hardly a recipe for speeding shipments or cutting costs.

More experiments with containers began after World War Two. Ships designed for amphibious landings on Pacific island beaches were turned into "roll-on/roll-off" vessels to transport trucks along the US Atlantic coast. The International Container Bureau, originally established by European railroads in 1933, resumed its efforts to encourage the use of small wooden containers aboard freight trains. The US military adopted small steel boxes, known as Conex boxes, for soldiers' personal belongings, and several US railroads developed containers to be transferred between specially designed trucks and railcars. Small numbers of steel containers were sent by ship.

None of these efforts reduced the cost of shipping goods internationally. Railroads' container systems did not mesh with those of ship lines. To load a container aboard a ship, a dockworker first had to use a ladder to climb atop it and attach hooks at each corner, and after a winch lowered the container into the hold, another docker had to climb atop it to remove the hooks before shoving the container into place alongside other cargo. Vessels were not designed for large metal boxes, which wasted precious shipboard space. "It is certain that the goods would occupy far less space if they were stowed individually instead of in containers," the head of the French stevedores' association said in 1954. The cost of sending an empty container back where it came from outweighed any savings from using the container in the first place. It was widely agreed by the middle of the 1950s that the cost of handling cargo had become a major impediment to international trade. Yet change was painfully slow in coming.[2]

———

The container era began in April 1956, when the *Ideal-X*, a converted tanker left over from the war, carried fifty-eight aluminum containers on its deck from Newark, New Jersey, to Houston, Texas. No one imagined this concept would turn the world economy upside down. It was conceived with an entirely different purpose in mind: to shave a few dollars off the cost of moving trucks between North Carolina and New York.

The *Ideal-X* was the brainchild of a trucking magnate named Malcom P. McLean. McLean, born in rural North Carolina in 1913, had become a trucker in the depths of the Great Depression, earning a few extra dollars by using a rusty trailer to bring in motor oil for the gas station he managed. By 1945, after expanding rapidly during World War Two, McLean Trucking owned 162 trucks, hauling textiles and cigarettes from North Carolina to Philadelphia, New York, and New England. Regulations made it difficult for motor carriers to serve new routes, so McLean Trucking bought up smaller trucking firms as a way to enter new markets. By 1954, it had become the eighth-largest US trucking company by revenue and the third-largest by after-tax profit.

The rates charged by truck lines, like those of railroads, were subject to approval by the Interstate Commerce Commission. To offer lower rates than its competitors and thereby attract new customers, a truck line had to prove that the proposed rates would be profitable. An obsessive focus on cutting costs in order to justify lower rates was the key to McLean's success. And it was this that led him, in 1953, to come up with a novel idea for moving freight. Thanks to the postwar boom in auto sales, worsening traffic jams were delaying trucks and driving up costs. McLean proposed to build waterfront terminals in North Carolina, New York City, and Rhode Island at which trucks would drive up ramps to deposit their trailers aboard ships. The ships would sail along the coast, avoiding the worsening traffic. At the port of arrival, other trucks would collect the trailers and deliver them to their destinations.

Further research convinced McLean that it made more sense to detach the trailer bodies from their steel beds, axles, and wheels, and to move only the bodies aboard ship. To carry out his scheme, McLean proposed to buy a tiny domestic carrier, Pan-Atlantic Steamship Corporation, which already had the authority to operate between ports along the Atlantic and Gulf of Mexico coasts. Regulators, though, frowned on a trucking company owning ships. To win approval of the transaction, he sold McLean Trucking and then took over Pan-Atlantic, which would run containerships on its existing routes. Pan-Atlantic's revenue came mainly from sailing between the US mainland and Puerto Rico, a US island territory, on routes where trucks and trains offered no competition. Despite resistance from the longshore unions that rightly feared the container would eliminate most of their members' work, other US ship lines gradually introduced containers on routes to Hawaii and Alaska.[3]

There was one factor common to these early forays into container shipping: each ship line used the containers it deemed best suited its own business. Pan-Atlantic's containers were thirty-five feet long because, at the time, that was the maximum length trucks were allowed to haul on important highways leading to its New Jersey terminal. Other companies tried containers that were eight, seventeen, or twenty-four feet long. Some containers had slots beneath for transport by forklift. Others lacked slots but had eyes on the top to which longshoremen could attach hooks for lifting. Some had doors at the rear, others at the side; some had internal supports to allow for stacking, others had none. Conforming to a single industry standard, each ship line felt, would mean using containers that were less than ideal for its particular business. The US Navy, which had the right to commandeer subsidized ships in times of war, fretted that incompatible container systems would complicate logistics. Under government pressure, the shipping industry formed committees to set standards for container length, strength, lifting mechanisms, and so forth. After three years of intense bargaining, the committees agreed in 1961 on the most controversial issue. Containers, it decided, should be ten, twenty, thirty, or forty feet in length, so that some combination of smaller containers—say, one twenty-foot box and two ten-footers—could occupy the same space aboard ship as a single forty-foot container.

Then the International Organization for Standardization (ISO) became involved. In September 1961, delegates from eleven countries came to New York to start talking about containers, with observers from fifteen more in attendance. Debate over container sizes, internal structure, door placement, and the like, which had consumed three years in the United States, was now repeated at the international level. The importance of new rules was obvious to all: international container shipping would make sense only with purpose-built vessels, but no one would invest in vessels designed to carry containers of a particular size if there was a chance that some other size might become the international standard. The most contentious issue was the method for lifting containers and locking them to a truck chassis or connecting them to one another. Each container manufacturer wanted its way of doing this to become the international standard. Not until 1965 did the committee reach agreement on a single design for the steel fitting at each corner of a container, so that a standard forty-foot container could be handled at any port or rail terminal anywhere in the world. Finally, container shipping could go global.

———

In March 1966, two ships converted to carry containers alongside mixed freight made their first voyages between the United States and northern Europe. This, though, was not an economical proposition: if a vessel then had to spend days in port to unload other cargo in addition to containers, the cost advantage of container shipping was lost. The first ship designed to carry only containers, operated by Malcom McLean's company, renamed Sea-Land Service, arrived the following month in Rotterdam, where truckers were waiting to deliver its 226 containers across Europe. Thereafter, Sea-Land's ships crossed the Atlantic weekly. Competitors were close behind. By 1968, just two years after that first transatlantic containership voyage, ten containerships a week were crossing the North Atlantic, and traditional breakbulk ships had all but abandoned the route.

Things went more slowly in the Pacific. The experts said transpacific container shipping was not financially viable: because of the long distance between North America and Asia, ships spent more time at sea than at the dock, so there was less money to be saved by speeding up loading and unloading. In any event, Asia was not a particularly promising market in the 1960s. Only Japan was a major trading nation. China,

in the throes of the Cultural Revolution, prohibited foreign investment and privately owned businesses and had very little foreign trade.
South Korea, still very poor, was just beginning to industrialize; it exported mainly labor-intensive products such as neckties and shoes and
kept imports to a minimum. Vietnam, divided in half and convulsed by
war with the United States, had almost no foreign commercial relations
at all.

Unexpectedly, the US war in Vietnam would bring the breakthrough
of intermodal shipping. South Vietnam, seven hundred miles long from
north to south, was hugely unsuited to modern military operations. It
had just one deepwater port, in Saigon; one aging railroad line, largely
inoperative; and a rudimentary highway system, mostly unpaved. Its
infrastructure strained to accommodate the twenty-three thousand US
troops who at the start of 1965 were "advising" the South Vietnamese
military in an unending war against both domestic guerillas, known as
the Viet Cong, and their backers, the socialist government of North
Vietnam. When President Lyndon Johnson decided in April 1965 to
commit large numbers of US troops, the navy's Military Sea Transportation Service was hard-pressed to supply them with boots and building
supplies, much less communications gear and weapons. Incoming cargo
piled up on the docks at Saigon while troops in the field lacked basic
equipment. As matters went from bad to worse, magazine articles made
the logistical mess in Vietnam into an embarrassment in Washington.

Desperate to solve the problem, a military study team recommended
basic changes in shipping procedures in December 1965. The team's first
recommendation was that all shipments to Vietnam should come in
"unitized packaging," a long-winded name for containers. After extended resistance within the military, in March 1967 Sea-Land was
awarded a contract to operate containerships between the US mainland
and a new port it would create in a Vietnamese harbor called Cam Ranh
Bay. It opened service later that year, with the first containership delivering 609 containers—as much cargo as could be carried on ten average
breakbulk ships hauling military freight to Vietnam. Sea-Land's route to
Cam Ranh Bay settled all doubts about whether containerships could operate profitably across the wide reach of the Pacific. The first containership

service between Japan and the United States began in 1967. Within three years, containerships were calling at Hong Kong, Australia, Taiwan, and the Philippines, tying them more closely to an international trading system that had been dominated by Japan, the United States, and Western Europe.

Container shipping helped turn globalization into a worldwide phenomenon, supercharging international commerce. The United States imported more than one million vehicles for the first time ever in 1967, most of them from Germany. Those cars did not move in containers, but parts required to service them did. US imports of tires and tubes increased at a rate of 25 percent per year during the first decade of international container shipping, led by products from France and Japan, while US imports of cameras from Japan and Germany grew at a similar rate. In 1972, the United States imported more manufactured goods than it exported for the first time since the nineteenth century. US companies' investments in foreign factories more than doubled between 1968 and 1978, while the value of foreign-owned manufacturing assets in the United States tripled—including a new Volkswagen assembly plant in Pennsylvania, made practical by the containerships that ferried engines and transmissions across the Atlantic at low cost.[4]

Containerization enabled Japan to become an export superpower, and as its increasingly advanced manufactured goods penetrated markets in Europe and across Asia, overseas investments followed: Japanese companies, traditionally inward looking, would have ten times as much investment in the United States in 1978 as a decade earlier. Japanese companies began using factories in Taiwan and Korea, no longer isolated by erratic transportation links, to assemble Japanese components into low-cost radios and alarm clocks for sale in other developing countries, while American corporate giants used plants in Malaysia, Singapore, and the Philippines to build subassemblies from US-made parts to supply factories back in the United States. By 1980, exports from Asia, excluding Japan, were eleven times as high as at the start of the decade, and the region's imports had grown almost as fast, as foreign assembly began to create the international supply lines that would bring globalization to a radically new stage.[5]

6

Hot Money

FOR A QUARTER-CENTURY after World War Two, stable exchange rates were the cement that held the world economy together. That cement began to crumble at the end of the 1960s. The ensuing economic chaos demonstrated that national governments could not cope with the strains and stresses of a globalized financial system—but that finance would globalize regardless, at considerable cost to the public.

The arrangements agreed at Bretton Woods in 1944 sought to minimize exchange-rate fluctuations. This required strict controls on the financial sector to contain the flow of money across borders. Many governments kept banks' foreign lending on a tight rein, required importers to obtain licenses to spend precious foreign currency, and even specified how much cash travelers could take abroad. A firm acquiring a foreign company might need one government's permission to export the money to clinch the deal and another government's promise that the new subsidiary would be allowed to remit dividends abroad. Running a factory reliant on imported components was risky, because the dollars or yen needed to purchase those inputs might not be available. The financial obstacles to operating a business across borders were high.

The entire exchange-rate system depended upon the United States. As the United States helped with postwar rebuilding and paid for its troops stationed in Western Europe and Japan, its dollars ended up in the vaults of foreign central banks. Holding those dollars to help finance their countries' imports and foreign investments involved no risk for the central banks, because the United States had promised it would buy their gold at any time at the price of $35 per ounce. But in every year save one during the 1950s and early 1960s, more dollars flowed out of the United States than flowed in. Buying back those dollars slowly drained US gold stocks, to the point that other governments and central banks held more dollars than the United States had gold. If all of those foreigners sought to exchange their dollars, the gold would run out, leaving the system without its anchor. As a practical matter, keeping dollars out of foreign hands was impossible so long as the dollar was the world's main currency. Without a surplus of dollars, it would have been hard to finance the international trade and investment that were fueling the world's impressive economic growth.[1]

Under this contradiction, the Bretton Woods system began to fracture. Its breakup was encouraged by critics such as French president Charles de Gaulle, who threatened in 1965 to redeem French-owned dollars for US gold in a deliberate effort to shake US hegemony. The US government took some half-hearted measures to stanch the outflow of dollars. A 1961 law reduced the amount of purchases American tourists could bring back from abroad without paying import duties, while a 1964 law put a tax on foreign stock and bond issues in the United States. For good measure, Washington asked US banks to cut back their foreign lending. Each such announcement strengthened the conviction among bankers and investors that fixed exchange rates could not survive. In 1967, Great Britain, running short of foreign currency because of perennial trade deficits, shook the markets by unexpectedly devaluing the pound sterling. Then, in 1971, President Richard Nixon renounced the US promise to exchange dollars for gold. In one emergency summit meeting after another, world leaders struggled to find a new way to stabilize exchange rates. In 1972, they gave up, agreeing to let the whims of the market set the values of their currencies.[2]

The shift to floating exchange rates undermined the case for keeping a tight lid on international finance. In 1973, the US government declared free movement of capital to be just as important in shaping an open world economy as free movement of goods. Other countries disagreed strongly. "Is it reasonable that such speculative movements should influence the flow of international trade, and hence the jobs of millions of persons throughout the world?" Belgian finance minister Willy de Clercq rejoined. As the home of the largest financial market and the most important currency, the United States carried the argument. Over the next few years, one regulation after another would fall away as countries opened up to foreign investors, foreign bankers, and foreign companies seeking to issue shares, build factories, or acquire local firms. Although trade in goods was still hindered by a raft of restrictions and complications, trade in money became all but free.[3]

———

The end of the Bretton Woods system came just as oil-exporting countries in the Middle East agreed to cut production and demand higher prices. Oil was bought and sold worldwide in US dollars. As prices jumped in 1973, exporters such as Saudi Arabia and Libya suddenly found themselves with huge quantities of dollars and little idea of how to manage them. Bankers in London, New York, and Tokyo were delighted to come to the rescue. But with the spike in oil prices driving their own economies into recession, they had to put the oil producers' "petrodollar" deposits to work elsewhere. For the first time since the start of World War One, banks began lending large amounts to poorer countries in Latin America, Eastern Europe, Africa, and Asia. The less developed countries, widely referred to as LDCs, vacuumed up long-term loans at low interest rates to pay for the roads, dams, and factories they thought would jump-start their economies.

In many instances, a big bank arranged the loan and sold off pieces to other banks that often knew little or nothing about the borrowers, to the point that the fortunes of banks in places like Atlanta and Düsseldorf depended on borrowers in Buenos Aires and Jakarta making payments on time. The volume was so large that LDCs were responsible for one-sixth of all loans owned by US banks. At the same time, companies in the wealthy countries were taking advantage of floating exchange rates to borrow in foreign currencies, introducing yet more complications into global finance. To cope with the influx of money, 169 new foreign bank branches opened their doors in the major European financial centers between 1971 and 1974. As historian Harold James observed, "The 1970s was the decade when internationalization really took over banking."[4]

Bankers gave little thought to the novelty of the risks they were taking. They knew how to evaluate business borrowers, but exchange-rate risk—the possibility that a bank that used dollar deposits to fund loans in Italian lira or Japanese yen might be unable to repay depositors if exchange rates moved the wrong way—was unfamiliar. Loans to businesses located in LDCs could go bad because of an unexpected currency devaluation or import restriction, even if the borrower's business strategy seemed sound. Rich-country governments had encouraged banks to lend to LDCs, and bankers naturally expected to be bailed out if these loans got them into trouble. After all, institutions such as the International Monetary Fund and the World Bank had been created for just that purpose. Walter Wriston, the head of New York-based Citibank and the most prominent banker of his day, insisted that banks had become so proficient at international lending that they were unlikely to suffer large losses. Besides, Wriston famously pronounced, "Countries don't go bankrupt."[5]

Bank supervisors, charged with keeping their countries' banking systems safe, watched the foreign lending warily. They all oversaw domestic banks, but international banking was a different story. Swiss secrecy laws kept American authorities from examining US banks' operations in Zürich—but in any event, the US Federal Reserve Board had no bank examiners abroad. No supervisor had the power to make sure that a borrower's inability to service a loan from a Japanese bank in New York would not endanger the parent bank in Tokyo: neither US nor Japanese authorities had a full understanding of the bank's finances. There was no international agreement about how much capital—shareholders' funds—banks should be required to maintain to ensure that they could repay depositors even if borrowers or trading partners defaulted on their obligations. The likelihood that thinly capitalized banks would undercut well-capitalized banks in the competition to make loans threatened a race to the bottom that could leave banks vulnerable in a sour economy. And there was no attention at all to the risk of contagion, the possibility that a problem in one country would infect others.

All of these risks burst into public view in the spring and summer of 1974. First, investigators discovered that Franklin National Bank, a mid-sized institution based near New York City, had suffered undisclosed losses from unauthorized currency trading. Franklin had engaged in hundreds of trades with other banks around the world, and if it were declared insolvent and closed down, some of its trading partners might fail as well. US authorities were forced to keep Franklin alive, pumping in cash as they gradually unwound its positions. One month later, a little-known German bank, Bankhaus Herstatt, was revealed to have suffered huge losses on currency trades that circumvented internal controls. German supervisors quickly shuttered it, without considering that Herstatt traded heavily with banks abroad. Its outgoing payments to banks in other countries were blocked, undermining those foreign banks' finances. Herstatt's failure, in turn, exposed problems at other banks that had evaded national regulations by moving money among their subsidiaries in different countries, turning banking into a game of three-card monte. Supervisors had known nothing about any of these problems at relatively small banks, raising the worrying question of whether they were on top of matters at far larger and more complex institutions.

In the face of the first international financial crisis since the 1930s, banking supervisors from Europe, North America, and Japan began meeting regularly to discuss how to make cross-border banking safer. The politics were daunting: some supervisors lacked legal authority even to share information with their counterparts in other countries, and all wanted to make sure that any new standards did not place their own country's banks at a disadvantage. The result was an international agreement that dodged the most difficult issues, such as deciding what country would have ultimate responsibility to supervise financial institutions operating across international borders. "It is not possible to draw up clear-cut rules for determining exactly where the responsibility for supervision can best be placed in any particular situation," the supervisors concluded. There were no new rules to prevent crises like those caused by Franklin and Herstatt. The issue of whether banks in different countries should be required to maintain similar levels of shareholder capital was so politically sensitive that the supervisors' committee decided in October 1976 not to discuss it. When it came to international finance, there would still be no one in charge.[6]

The longer the banking supervisors talked, the more dollars poured into the oil exporters' accounts, to be lent out around the world. Commercial loans to the less developed countries, $17 billion in 1972, reached $209 billion in 1981. The banks' impressive growth, though, masked increasingly fragile foundations.

In October 1979, the Federal Reserve Board decided to push interest rates as high as needed to slow the US economy and put an end to stubbornly high inflation. Rates on one-year bonds issued by the US Treasury, which had been 9.4 percent the previous June, reached a remarkable 17 percent by 1981. Given the size of the US economy, the Fed's move spread pain worldwide. In the United States, the housing market shut down and auto sales crashed, bringing the highest unemployment rate since the Great Depression. Japan and Europe were hit hard as interest rates rose and as US consumers bought fewer Toyotas and BMWs. But as the aftereffects rippled across the globe, it was the less developed countries that faced the greatest distress. Many of their loans carried floating interest rates; every time US interest rates ratcheted higher, so did the payments they owed their bankers. When the finance ministers of countries like Poland, Uruguay, and Indonesia inquired about refinancing their debts, they found that the bankers who had so eagerly lent to them a few years earlier were no longer willing. Their central banks' reserves of dollars, essential for making loan payments, ran low.

———

International debt crises were not a new phenomenon. The First Globalization had seen many of them. Perhaps the first came in 1890, after a sharp rise in British interest rates put a sudden end to enthusiasm in Great Britain, then the world's leading financial power, for investing in Argentina. As the Argentine economy stumbled, the government's default on its bonds undermined the British merchant bank Baring Brothers, the leading lender to Argentina, and caused chaos across Latin America until the Bank of England supported Barings to end the crisis. The Panic of 1907, which began with an attempt to corner the copper market in New York, led to a deep recession in the United States and widespread bank failures and economic downturns in countries as widely separated as Sweden, Japan, and Chile. Unexpectedly, it was the central bank of France that came to the rescue. The financial crisis that erupted with World War One in August 1914 spread to fifty countries as far apart as Japan, Peru, and India, all of which relied for financing and export markets on European countries that were engulfed in the war.[7]

During the Second Globalization, restrictions on the international flow of money meant that financial crises of this sort, transmitted from country to country like a viral epidemic, were at first rare. Few economic policy makers in the 1970s had ever experienced a financial crisis at first hand. But as cross-border flows broadened from a trickle to a flood, the risk of crises reemerged in a virulent form. In 1981, eleven countries on three continents sought to renegotiate their foreign loans. Then, on August 12, 1982, the Mexican government informed the US Treasury that it could not pay $300 million due the following Monday, much less the $2 billion a month required to service its foreign debt over the coming year. Commercial bank lending to less developed countries ceased immediately; although Brazilian officials insisted that "Brazil is not Mexico," financiers now spotted similarities that had previously escaped their notice. The bankers' skepticism was well founded. Brazil had no hope of making timely payments on its foreign debt, and neither did Turkey, Argentina, Indonesia, or Poland. By the end of 1982, with the LDCs collectively owing over $700 billion in foreign-currency debt, forty countries were in arrears.[8]

The LDC debt crisis lasted into the 1990s. It would prove extremely costly, in both economic and human terms. In the debtor countries, living standards collapsed, and malnutrition and infant mortality increased. Imported consumer goods vanished from the shelves, and wage increases were deliberately kept below the rate of inflation in an effort to make exports cheaper abroad. "Those who pay are primarily workers whose real wages are cut," US economist Rüdiger Dornbusch observed. It would take the better part of two decades until average incomes in Peru and the Philippines regained the purchasing power they had enjoyed in 1982. Rich-world governments insisted that the LDCs embrace austerity in order to accumulate the sums needed to pay foreign creditors, which meant slashing outlays for health, education, housing, and other social needs. Even so, only one highly indebted country, South Korea, succeeded in boosting exports fast enough to accumulate the dollars required to repay its debts. Elsewhere, servicing debts from the past would weigh heavily on the countries' ability to have healthier, better-educated workers able to compete in a fast-changing world economy. Not without reason have the 1980s been called the "lost decade."[9]

The cost of the crisis to the wealthier economies is harder to calculate. In part, the cost took the form of slower income growth and higher unemployment. Banks, crippled by their delinquent loans to foreign borrowers, could not fulfill their normal role of helping businesses replace old machinery, build new facilities, and finance customers' purchases. Several of the world's largest banks teetered on the verge of failure, and taxpayers' money was used to rescue them. "There already has been a constant transfer of risk from private to public lenders," Toyoo Gyohten, a former Japanese finance ministry official, observed in 1992. Commercial banks, Gyohten noted, held 62 percent of developing countries' debts in 1984 but only half by 1990; the rest had been handed off to governments or international organizations. Eighteen countries with $191 billion of outstanding debt negotiated forgiveness of at least a portion between 1989 and 1994, aided by the World Bank, the Inter-American Development Bank, and other organizations ultimately supported by national governments. Taxpayers in the wealthy economies were effectively called upon to subsidize the globalization of finance.[10]

One of the aftereffects of hot money would be longer lasting. The economic crises in the less developed countries depressed their currencies relative to those of wealthier economies, especially the United States. These favorable exchange rates helped the LDCs run trade surpluses by making their exports more attractive abroad and their imports dearer. Trade surpluses, the International Monetary Fund counseled, would enable the LDCs to amass foreign currency to pay their bankers. "US imports from Asia and European developing countries increased by some 80 percent between 1980 and 1984," the IMF reported proudly in 1985, adding that "exporters of manufactures achieved remarkable success." US workers felt the consequences. The US trade deficit with developing countries in East Asia increased from $4 billion in 1980 to $30 billion in 1986. Apparel plants, shoe factories, and steel mills laid off workers by the tens of thousands. Employment in US factories, which had averaged nearly nineteen million over the four years before the debt crisis erupted, would never approach that level again.[11]

7

Kindling

FOR THE HISTORICALLY INCLINED, the globalization of finance that began in the 1970s seemed to be a rerun of an old movie. There had, after all, been plenty of money sloshing around the globe in the years before World War One, when 71 foreign banks boasted offices in London, German-owned Deutsch-Asiatische Bank financed trade across Asia, and New York's National City Bank touted its relationships with 132 foreign banks that could arrange payments of any size in any city within twenty-four hours. Yet the resurgence of cross-border lending that occurred after 1973 was not simply a return to the days of old. Even as banks were rediscovering foreign markets, many of the rules that had restrained them from entering new businesses and taking new risks were being stripped away in the name of deregulation.[1]

Banking was only the beginning. A worldwide movement to deregulate business activity dramatically changed the way the global economy functioned in the final decades of the twentieth century. The narrative of its advocates was inevitably the same: government regulation favored entrenched interests, impeded innovation, and burdened the public with unnecessary costs. Deregulation, it was said, would bring greater efficiency, livelier competition, and lower prices as market forces worked their magic. In some cases, deregulation performed as advertised, in others not at all. But even where it was successful in stimulating competition, deregulation undermined consumer protections, enfeebled labor unions, and left many workers to struggle with lower wages and poorer working conditions. Ill-designed deregulation in the financial sector contributed to crises from Korea to Argentina. Most of all, deregulation weakened the power of national governments to manage their countries' economies as they surrendered traditional powers and outsourced responsibilities. As two Italian central bankers described the key development of that age, "Markets became the unifying factor of the global economy." Deregulation provided kindling for the Third Globalization, which unfolded in the late 1980s.[2]

————

The extent of business regulation in the postwar world boggles the mind. In the Soviet Union, China, and the socialist countries of Eastern Europe, of course, setting limits on the private sector was not an issue; almost all economic activity was under direct government control, and private businesses were very small or nonexistent. Elsewhere, although most enterprises were privately owned, rules large and small dictated what they could do, how and when they could do it, and what price they could charge for it. Not all these rules were set directly by national governments: in some places, mayors and provincial governors had great authority over commerce, and many private groups were empowered to regulate businesses and professions and, at times, to fix prices. Each country had a different historical legacy, but all were determined to use the law to keep unrestrained competition in check.

The social purposes behind many types of regulation were clear. Laws setting minimum wages or maximum working hours were designed to redress the imbalance of power between employers and workers, and laws governing workplace safety recognized that competitive pressure might lead employers to cut corners unless the government intervened. But in many other cases, regulations served mainly to protect the interests of some businesses against others. Banks in the state of Illinois could have only a single office, as mandated by the state constitution, so that big-city bankers from Chicago could not annihilate small-town banks. Stock-trading commissions in London were fixed by the stock exchange to preclude competition that might harm established brokers. India's "license raj" required dozens of approvals before starting a business, coddling existing firms while also keeping foreign competitors out. A Japanese law from the 1950s prohibited stores larger than five hundred square meters unless nearby merchants approved, and West German regulators sought to control barge and truck freight rates in order to drive business to the state-owned railway.[3]

These types of rules often ran head-on into economic reality. Some regulations were shaped to force one customer to subsidize another, while others codified a particular interpretation of "fairness" by requiring that small customers and large customers be treated exactly the same even if it cost more to serve one than the other. Customers who saw no reason to bear such burdens sought ways to evade them. In the early 1960s, to take but one of many examples, one-sixth of the freight shipped from US factories went out in trucks owned by the manufacturers themselves. This occurred not because manufacturers wanted to be in the trucking business, but because factory-owned trucks were exempt from the regulations facing truckers who offered service to the public. Those regulations meant that if a factory in Des Moines wanted to hire a trucking company to deliver an order of wooden doors to Paducah, it needed to locate one that had the legal right to carry doors between those two points and pay the officially authorized rate. It was often simpler and cheaper for the factory to use its own trucks instead, even though they might have to make the return trip empty.[4]

Such contradictions between the demands of regulation and the marketplace created occasional calls to ease or eliminate regulations. A deregulation movement was fanned by American scholars, supported by foundation grants, who churned out dissertations, journal articles, and books attacking the regulatory state. In individual cases, deregulation proceeded in small steps, with no larger purpose. Legal rulings dismantled regulation of interstate trucking in Australia in 1954, but the country's state governments continued to regulate truck rates and routings within their borders for another two decades. A 1968 British law made it easier for truckers to enter the industry, but price controls remained in place. When, in 1969, the US Federal Communications Commission first allowed a start-up company to transmit voice calls and data using microwave antennas, no one imagined that the nationwide monopoly of the American Telephone and Telegraph Company would be un-wound within a decade and a half. The political pressure to pare the government's oversight was minimal. As American political scientists Martha Derthick and Paul J. Quirk observed in 1971, deregulation "re-mained a solution in search of a widely perceived problem."[5]

A suitable problem soon appeared. In the early 1970s, many of the railroads serving the northeastern and midwestern United States de-clared bankruptcy, threatening the economies of hundreds of communi-ties. The railroads' distress was due, in part, to regulations that had forced them to continue operating money-losing passenger trains and low-volume branch lines. In a 1976 law restructuring the bankrupt com-panies, Congress granted railroads greater freedom to set freight rates in hopes they might recapture lost freight traffic and find a more stable financial footing. That proved to be only the first step in loosening the reins. The political consensus shifted 180 degrees; improbably, voices across the ideological spectrum agreed that excessive regulation had made the US transportation system inefficient, harming consumers and retarding economic growth. An emboldened Congress passed nine dif-ferent laws deregulating transportation between 1976 and 1986, elimi-nating the federal government's power to decide which airlines should fly between Los Angeles and Seattle, what fares an intercity bus could charge passengers, and what commodities a trucker might carry. One of the most consequential effects of deregulation, though, was hardly noticed at the time: transportation companies were allowed to carry freight under contract.[6]

For decades, in almost every country, transportation regulators' pri-mary job had been to assure that all customers received identical rates and services. The principle of nondiscrimination meant that a ship line had to offer every toy manufacturer the same rate per ton between Hong Kong and Hamburg, and that a railroad could not let one customer keep a freight car for several days while insisting that another return it promptly. Contracts governing rates and services were anathema to regulators pre-cisely because they involved discrimination: whoever signed a contract was getting a deal that others were not. But complying with thick vol-umes of rules and legal precedents had made freight transportation expensive and unreliable. It could take weeks to move a boxcar a thousand miles and months to move freight across the ocean; carriers were indifferent to such delays, because they earned no bonus if a shipment was delivered on time and faced no penalty if it appeared late. Claims of lost or damaged freight were frequent, and farmers wanting to ship their wheat often found that empty railcars did not show up when promised. Shipping goods internationally was so costly that many products were not worth shipping. Manufacturers and retailers kept their warehouses stuffed with parts and finished goods, a costly form of insurance against business disruption, to manage the risk that vital shipments would not arrive on time.[7]

The contracts permitted by deregulation allowed transportation companies and their customers to negotiate prices and service standards. One of the first provided that Ford Motor Company would send a daily trainload of autos and parts from Salt Lake City, in Utah, to San Jose, California, via the Western Pacific Railroad. The railroad agreed to deliver the train by 2:30 each morning and to pay Ford a penalty for each fifteen minutes the train was late. Ford, in return, agreed that it should not pay the same for each freight car, but rather a low rate per car for a sixty-car train and a much higher rate per car when its train was shorter. Ship lines could strike similar deals, stuffed with commitments, contingencies, and penalties for nonperformance, starting in 1984. As other countries followed the US lead, contract freight became the norm in international trade. By 1986, more than four-fifths of the cargo from Japan to the US Pacific coast, the largest route for US imports, moved under contract.[8]

Contract freight provided the decisive impulse to the globalization of factory production. Conveniently, it arrived just as deregulation of telephone service for business was getting underway. With competitors challenging its long-standing monopoly, American Telephone and Telegraph cut rates for international phone calls by 40 percent in 1981 and 1982; as the cost of calling tumbled, the number of overseas calls from the United States increased sixfold between 1980 and 1990. Similar changes unfolded in Europe, where governments introduced competition into communications services for businesses and began privatizing national telephone monopolies, starting with British Telecom in 1984. The combination of more reliable transportation and inexpensive communications made it feasible for manufacturers and retailers to create intricate long-distance supply chains, engaging a plant in one country to make inputs that could be sent for further processing in another and then to consumers elsewhere still, coordinating the production process from afar by telephone, telex, and fax machine.[9]

————

The deregulation movement fueled globalization in another way as well. Deregulated industries were ripe for private investment—often, by foreign capital. Amid the sweeping 1986 financial market deregulation known as "Big Bang," almost all of Great Britain's major brokerage houses and merchant banks were snapped up by foreign banks seeking global scale. Scores of state-owned electric, gas, and water companies were auctioned off, often to foreign buyers, and foreign corporations acquired telephone franchises from Indonesia to Ireland. Once Japan's Large-Scale Retail Stores Law was revised in 1992 to allow larger stores and longer store hours, major US and European retailers entered the market. Even state-owned companies became global enterprises, bidding to operate "privatized" rail lines, airports, and port terminals around the world.[10]

Through the 1980s and 1990s, many developing countries discovered that deregulation was the price of foreign money. The experts promised that sluggish state-owned enterprises drowning in red ink would become efficient and profitable in private hands. Letting market forces rather than government edicts shape their economic development would help less advanced countries put international assistance to good use in building prosperous and modern economies, it was said, so deregulation became mandatory for countries that sought aid funds from foreign governments and low-interest loans from international organizations such as the World Bank.[11]

This counsel was blind to history. No country had ever climbed from poverty to prosperity by leaving economic development to market forces. The eighteenth-century Industrial Revolution that made Great Britain the world's greatest economic power would not have occurred without deliberate government policies to suppress imports of textiles, block the emigration of artisans who might share their knowledge of textile machinery abroad, and enclose common lands to push displaced laborers into the emerging industrial cities. The growth of manufacturing that made the United States wealthy in the late nineteenth century relied not only on protection against imports but also on regulations, notably court rulings that held labor costs down by repressing trade unions and blocking state laws to limit working hours and improve factory conditions. The remarkably rapid growth of Western Europe's economies after World War Two involved a large dose of government planning, with officials often determining which firms could borrow money or obtain foreign currency, and the economic blossoming of Japan, Korea, and Taiwan in the late twentieth century was based on state guidance about which industries should be fostered with import protection, low-cost credit, and cheap land. The notion that market forces alone can turn poor economies into rich ones is a myth.

Additionally, few less developed countries were up to the mundane bureaucratic tasks of managing deregulation. Although the heavy-handed regulation of the postwar era often served political interests rather than the public, making deregulation and privatization work required creating and enforcing regulations rather than eviscerating them: without detailed rules as to how it must switch phone calls and share billing information with other players, a former state telephone monopoly could simply act like a private telephone monopoly, with no economic benefit to anyone save its new owners.

The lack of administrative capacity proved disastrous when it came to deregulating the financial sector. Countries such as Russia, Malaysia, and Indonesia bowed to international guidance that they should make it easier to open banks, supervise them with a light hand, and allow domestic companies to borrow freely abroad. This meant in practice that well-connected entrepreneurs took over their countries' banking systems, lending recklessly, while central bankers and bank supervisors struggled to keep the financial system stable. In all three countries, the deregulation of finance led to severe economic crises in 1998, devastating the living standards of millions of people who only recently had begun to enjoy the benefits of globalization. Even the World Bank, that high temple of economic expertise, belatedly acknowledged that much of its advice had been flat wrong. As its experts admitted contritely, "The 1990s experience shows how difficult both privatization and regulation are."[12]

———

Deregulation resonated around the world. The value of world trade in manufactured goods, after stagnating amid the recession of the early 1980s, rose 130 percent between 1983 and 1990. This tidal wave of freight, almost all of it moving under contracts negotiated between shippers and carriers, encouraged investment in larger ships, in high-tech distribution centers, and in railcars on which containers could be stacked two high, doubling the amount of goods a single train could haul. Deregulated telecommunications led to innovations that enabled manufacturers, retailers, and transportation companies to manage this complex system. The internet would not have transformed the world in the twenty-first century had strictly regulated national telephone monopolies not been forced to face competition in the twentieth.[13]

These innovations, the fruits of deregulation, did not benefit all businesses in equal measure. The winners were large corporations, which could cut costs by operating on a global scale, and whose constant involvement in the freight market gave them up-to-the-minute information that they could use to demand the best terms from transportation and communications companies. Consumers, who had access to an unimaginably large selection of goods at lower prices than before, were winners as well. Workers and small businesses, on the other hand, fared less well in this increasingly deregulated world. Workers in industries facing import competition saw their wages squeezed or their jobs vanish altogether. Small firms, companies that had been the bedrock of local economies for decades, had no leverage in head-to-head bargaining with railroads and ship lines, so as inexpensive imports swamped their markets, they were frequently forced to sell or simply close down. When it came to reaping the benefits of deregulation, size and scale mattered immensely. Those without them usually lost out, while those who achieved them warmed to a world in which national borders were far more porous.

8

"A Giant Sucking Sound"

DURING THE QUARTER-CENTURY that began in 1948, the noncommunist countries of Europe enjoyed flourishing economies. Prosperity brought telephones, refrigerators, and indoor plumbing to almost everyone, thanks in good part to the free-trade area formed in 1957 in the Treaty of Rome. By 1969, when the countries in the European Community finally abolished all tariffs on one another's exports, income per person had more than doubled in France and tripled in Germany in the eighteen years since the creation of the European Coal and Steel Community put the region on the path to a common market. Germany's exports mushroomed to nearly one-fourth of its economic output in 1973, four times the share in 1950, creating millions of jobs in the process, and the story elsewhere in the European Community was similar. Unrestricted access to a larger market allowed producers to take advantage of economies of scale and become more efficient. Their higher productivity—the average amount EC residents produced in one hour of work roughly tripled during those years—supported impressive wage increases. Three countries outside the tariff-free zone, Denmark, Great Britain, and Ireland, saw much slower growth in foreign trade—and in their citizens' incomes. The disparity was so evident that all three eagerly joined the European Community in 1971.[1]

The oil crisis that began in October 1973 was a breakpoint. Economic growth plummeted as sharply higher oil prices drained consumers' wallets and decimated business profits. Unemployment, nearly invisible in Western Europe for two decades, climbed in every country. With rising inflation eroding the value of workers' wages, there was a sense that Europe's precious social market economy, in which private enterprise and an activist state combined to assure full employment, generous social benefits, and steadily rising living standards, was in crisis.

To placate voters, Europe's leaders boosted spending on social programs, from housing assistance to grants for children. They lowered the retirement age on the theory that this would free up jobs for the young: by 1980, most women in Western Europe were out of the labor force by age sixty-one, most men by sixty-three. They offered subsidies to avoid mass layoffs at unprofitable factories, a self-defeating strategy that hurt better-run competitors by keeping zombie plants alive. European governments handed out more money to support new information-technology industries than the United States or Japan, without creating viable enterprises. When industrial subsidies fell short, they encouraged "crisis cartels," asking industrialists to agree among themselves which plants should close while the state offered long-term payments to the workers whose jobs were axed.

But nothing could bring back the good times Europeans had enjoyed through 1973. Long-time coal and steel towns were devastated, as one in five steelmaking jobs vanished between 1978 and 1981. By the middle of the 1980s, a quarter of young adults were unemployed in France, a third in Italy. More than 40 percent of Europe's unemployed workers had been out of work for over a year. As Gaston Thorn, the European Community's top official, asked in 1984, "Is it surprising that the people of Europe should wonder whether the Community is capable of reviving growth and reducing unemployment?"[2]

The underlying problem was one that had no ready solution: the rapid productivity growth of the 1960s and early 1970s was over. Almost every nation in Europe felt the squeeze. Between 1963 and 1973, the most basic measure of productivity, the amount of output produced by one hour of the average worker's labor, had nearly doubled in Italy; between 1973 and 1983, the increase was less than one-third. Belgium's productivity growth, 86 percent over the decade from 1963 to 1973, fell to 37 percent over the following decade. Europe's dynamism had disappeared. By 1984, the term "eurosclerosis" entered the vocabulary, suggesting that Europeans' unwillingness to let old industries fade away and to embrace new ones was stifling growth. As the free-market economist Herbert Giersch diagnosed the problem in 1985, "Essential members of the body economic have become too rigid to permit a quick and painless adjustment."[3]

While the Treaty of Rome had invigorated Europe's economies by eliminating tariffs on trade among the member states, it left other matters under the full control of national governments. Each country still had its own technical standards: toys from West Germany could not be sold in France unless they met French safety rules, and a detergent manufacturer might need to mix a different formulation for Rome than for Amsterdam. Transportation and service industries were not covered by the Treaty of Rome at all. The treaty's benefits had been real, but they had reached their limits. According to one survey, nine out of ten European corporate executives saw the fragmentation of Europe as a barrier to efficiency.[4]

Not knowing what else to do, Europe's leaders doubled down. In 1985, they agreed to go beyond eliminating tariffs and create a single market stretching from Greece to Ireland. Under the Single European Act, which took effect in 1987, border posts went away, truckers and airlines were free to move freight and people anywhere in the European Community, and uniform standards were applied to everything from veterinary medicines to passenger-car emissions. People from one country could work in or emigrate to any of the others, and their vocational training and university degrees were valid across all twelve member countries. Responsibility for assessing the effects of large corporate mergers, dealing with pollution from ships, regulating broadcasting, and hundreds of other matters shifted from national capitals to EC authorities. In a way never seen before, elected governments voluntarily surrendered much of their sovereignty in favor of a united Europe, and businesses started treating Europe not as a dozen markets, but as one.[5]

———

North America seemed unlikely to follow Europe's lead. While the United States and Canada had close relations—a special agreement had allowed automakers to send engines, parts, and finished cars back and forth across the border without formalities since 1965—Mexico was far more defensive. Over half of the country's territory had been ceded to the United States in the nineteenth century, and fear of further intrusions from the north lay behind Mexico's sky-high tariffs and its constitutional ban on foreign investment in the oil industry. Many imports required licenses, which the government rarely granted when similar products were made domestically, and new cars for sale in Mexico had to be assembled there, mainly from Mexican parts. Thanks to such policies, manufacturing in Mexico was backward by international standards; at Volkswagen's plant in Puebla, the last plant in the world to make the old-fashioned Beetles widely used as taxis in Mexico City, workers performed tasks that had been automated in Germany years before. While manufacturing had expanded rapidly since the 1950s, very little was sold abroad, save for goods assembled in factories along the border that received transistors or pieces of cut fabric from the United States, soldered or sewed them into finished products with cheap Mexican labor, and shipped them north. Mexico had declined to join the GATT, as that would have required it to reduce its tariff rates. Instead, it wanted the United States to welcome Mexican exports, with Mexico offering nothing in return. As José López Portillo, its president from 1976 to 1981, liked to say, trade agreements should "treat the equal equally and the unequal unequally." Needless to say, the US government did not agree.[6]

Mexico's import substitution policies yielded solid economic growth until the 1970s, when discoveries of massive oil reserves drew new attention from Washington. US president Jimmy Carter, who took office in January 1977, sought closer ties. In particular, the United States was obsessed by fears of an energy shortage, and it wanted Mexico to let US companies drill for oil in hopes that more Mexican crude might lower gasoline prices and help bring down inflation. Control of the oil industry, however, was an explosive issue in Mexico; the Mexicans were willing to borrow abroad to fund wells, pipelines, and refineries, but they were not prepared to let foreigners participate in any way. They did agree to create joint committees to address major issues in US-Mexican relations, including trade and immigration, but refused to open their economy. After persistent US prodding, López Portillo agreed in 1979 to reduce tariffs so Mexico could enter the GATT, but in the face of an uproar in Mexico he then backed away.[7]

At the time, his retreat seemed unimportant, because Mexico's economy was hot. Flights from New York to Mexico City were booked out by bankers eager to lend money to the government, to big private companies, and to Pemex, the state-owned oil company. Mexico's foreign debt, $18 billion in 1975, hit $78 billion in 1981, just as oil production by Pemex, the country's main source of foreign currency, undershot projections. The bubble burst when Mexico's insolvency hit the headlines in August 1982. López Portillo added fuel to the fire, suddenly nationalizing every bank in Mexico. Because the banks held shares in many companies, nationalization put the government in command of much of the country's private sector. By the time the International Monetary Fund, the US government, and Mexico's foreign bankers cobbled together a rescue package in October, the peso had lost three-quarters of its value and the economy was crippled.

The Mexican economy flatlined for seven years. Even those workers lucky enough to keep their jobs saw their buying power destroyed. The need to earn ever more pesos to buy a dollar bankrupted companies that had borrowed abroad, even if their Mexican businesses were healthy. Although manufacturing output rose only slowly during the 1980s, non-oil exports quadrupled within a decade as companies desperately sought dollars to service their debt: everything that could be sold abroad was exported. With every spare dollar going to pay creditors, Mexico had nothing left to invest in machinery, education, or infrastructure.

The nationalization of the banks snapped the cozy ties between the government and Mexico's industrialists, who had been quite willing to accept a heavy state hand so long as they earned fat profits in an economy with little competition. Now, many Mexican executives saw exposing the economy to market forces, including international trade, as the only way to get the government out of their businesses. Working through a joint US-Mexican business committee, they cautiously floated ideas that still verged on heretical, such as welcoming foreign investment and removing barriers to trade. President Miguel de la Madrid, who took office in late 1982, responded carefully. Some tariff rates were reduced in 1984, and fewer imports were subject to licenses. At a breakfast with business leaders in 1985, he hinted that Mexico might join the GATT and seek a trade agreement with the United States. The ensuing agreement set out nothing more than procedures and guidelines, few of them binding on either country. Nonetheless, it proved so controversial that both governments had to reassure their publics that a single market like the one being formed in Europe was not in the works.[8]

————

For the United States, Mexico was not the only game in town. President Ronald Reagan had made no secret of his belief in laissez-faire economics, based on free trade and private enterprise, and Mexico was only one of several cards his government was playing to diffuse that doctrine around the world.

The biggest was something called the Uruguay Round, a negotiation aimed at remaking the GATT. Since the late 1940s, the GATT had succeeded repeatedly in increasing trade by lowering tariffs on manufactured goods. But the agreement had large holes. It did not cover trade in agricultural products, a sensitive topic in every country, or trade in services. Shipments of textiles and clothing were controlled with high tariffs and extensive use of import quotas under an arrangement outside the GATT. The GATT was of little use when one country accused another of subsidizing exports or claimed that imports were damaging domestic industries. When it came to enforcing its own rules, the GATT was widely regarded as a paper tiger, which is why dozens of trade ministers convened in Punta del Este, Uruguay, in September 1986, in an effort to fix it.[9]

Those talks, which would eventually involve 123 countries, did not move quickly, so the Reagan administration made an unexpected move of its own: it bargained a pact with the largest US trading partner, Canada. Since the two countries had freed up movement of automotive products back in 1965, thousands of trucks a day had moved parts and finished cars between auto plants in Ontario and Michigan. The new

US-Canada Free Trade Agreement, ratified in 1988, went several steps beyond, eliminating all tariffs on each other's exports, easing travel for businesspeople, allowing companies in one country to bid for government business in the other, and promising to treat each other's service providers the same as their own. But the real purpose of the US-Canada deal was less economic than diplomatic. Negotiating over trade, according to one popular theory, was like riding a bicycle: if the rider could not keep moving forward, the bike would fall over. If other countries would not sign a single large agreement to open their borders, the United States was asserting, it would maintain the momentum for freer trade by signing smaller deals with one country at a time.

Such a close arrangement with their big and powerful neighbor was not what the Mexicans had in mind. They were very aware that the many border plants assembling goods for US customers brought Mexico little economic benefit. Employing unskilled labor and using almost no Mexican content or technology, they provided no opportunity for Mexico to move up the ladder to more valuable manufacturing work. A new generation of Mexican officials dreamed of more sophisticated foreign investments. But in 1990, when President Carlos Salinas tried to interest European bankers and industrialists in Mexico, he found few takers. Countries across Eastern Europe were shaking off Communist rule and seeking connections to the West, and no one in Europe had time for Mexico. With no other option, Salinas decided that Mexico would have to embrace North America. Once he said the word, it took just two years to expand the US-Canada Free Trade Agreement into a treaty among all three countries, the North American Free Trade Agreement, signed in 1992.

Despite its name, the 1,700 pages of NAFTA said nothing about free trade. Many provisions were narrowly tailored to favor specific interests in one of the three countries, and some of the most controversial topics under discussion in Europe, such as free movement of workers and steps toward a common currency, were not even on the table. NAFTA did eliminate tariffs on trade among the three countries—a step that required Mexico, which had much higher tariffs, to make steeper reductions than Canada and the United States. Yet many barriers stayed in place. Mexican truckers could not move goods between points in the

United States, and vice versa. Canada maintained its quotas on dairy imports, and Mexico's energy sector was still off limits to foreign investors. But the details mattered less than the vision. By protecting foreign investors against radical changes in Mexican economic policy and granting Mexican goods nearly unlimited access to northern markets, the treaty sent Mexico down an unexpected path. Instead of exporting oil and cheap goods made with unskilled labor, it could attract multinational corporations that might bring skilled jobs and up-to-date technology. For good measure, Salinas ordered all eighteen of the banks that had been nationalized amid the 1982 financial crisis to be sold off to domestic buyers in 1991 and 1992; that move was not required by NAFTA, but was an additional signal of Mexico's eagerness to join the modern global economy.

That prospect was not universally welcomed. In Mexico, the abrupt abandonment of autarky came as a shock. Impoverished corn farmers tending two-acre mountainside plots and small manufacturers with antiquated machinery feared they would be washed away in the flood of imports from the north, and economic nationalists raged against the prospect that the newly privatized banks might eventually end up in foreign hands. Labor unions in Canada and the United States protested that manufacturers would shift production south, environmental groups foresaw corporate polluters settling on the Mexican side of the US border, and vociferous nationalists objected that national sovereignty was being infringed. Full-page ads in leading US newspapers decried "SABOTAGE! Of America's Health, Safety, and Environmental Laws," while Ross Perot, a wealthy and conservative businessman who ran for president in 1992, predicted, "You're going to hear a giant sucking sound of jobs being pulled out of this country." After President Bill Clinton submitted NAFTA to Congress in 1993, most members of his own Democratic Party voted against it. Only when opposition Republicans came out in support did Congress consent.[10]

———

The separate moves toward freer trade within Europe and then within North America achieved their purpose. As the North Americans were ratifying NAFTA, the European Community was expanding to fifteen nations and transforming itself into an even closer communion, the European Union, some of whose members wanted to replace their national monies with a common European currency. Despite the endless squabbles over policy and the legendary complaints about the bureaucracy in Brussels, the benefits of a united Europe were so alluring that countries across Eastern Europe and the Mediterranean queued up to join. Clinton, fresh off his successful drive to ratify NAFTA, pushed the Europeans to bring the Uruguay Round talks to an end. Weeks of round-the-clock negotiations ensued, with the United States and the European Union in the leading roles, before the many parts of a complex deal fell into place. The agreement was formally signed in April 1994, eight years after the negotiations were launched in Punta del Este. At that point, as an official explanation admitted delicately, "negotiation-fatigue was felt in trade bureaucracies around the world."[11]

Of the many issues on which the nations involved in the Uruguay Round finally agreed, from reducing farm subsidies to welcoming trade in services, two would prove particularly consequential in shaping globalization. The wealthy countries promised to open their markets to clothing made in poor countries at long last; by 2005, most of the rich countries' import quotas on clothing and textiles would be gone, allowing countries that had barely been connected to the world economy, such as Bangladesh and Cambodia, to develop large garment industries. At the same time, poor countries as well as rich ones agreed to slash their import tariffs, particularly for manufactured goods, with many products facing no tariffs at all. Coming on top of the expansion of the European Union and the adoption of NAFTA, the Uruguay Round agreement changed the calculations for multinational companies. Now, by and large, they could manufacture goods in one country and ship them to another with little worry about how tariffs would affect their costs. International supply chains, which had taken root in the 1980s, could stretch ever farther around the world.[12]

This is exactly what occurred. Trade patterns changed markedly. By the end of the 1990s, parts and components accounted for 29 percent of international trade as producers cut a roll of fabric or etched a semiconductor in one country and then shipped it on for further work in another.

What's more, after 1990 a steadily greater share of the wealthy economies' imports came from less prosperous ones. The traditional trading
centers of Europe, North America, and Japan no longer dominated.
Dozens of deals between pairs or small groups of countries did away
with tariffs, simplified import formalities, and removed other obstacles
to foreign trade and investment. In 1990, when the United States, Canada, and Mexico first sat down to negotiate NAFTA, there had been
nineteen such agreements in force around the world. By 2000 there
were seventy-nine, from a modest pact easing trade among four Pacific
island nations to an ambitious agreement between Canada and Chile
addressing trade, foreign investment, environmental and competition
policy, telecommunications, and a dozen other subjects.[13]

Lower tariffs, cheaper and more reliable transportation, and falling
telecommunications costs brought the world economy to a new stage,
the Third Globalization. After stagnating between 1980 and 1985, when
many countries suffered recessions, global trade in manufactured goods,
measured in dollars, doubled between 1985 and 1990, then again between 1990 and 2000, and once more between 2000 and 2010. Foreign
investment rebounded as well. Large companies, almost all of which
were identifiable by their country of origin during the 1970s and 1980s,
began to take on an international character, locating high-priority research abroad and filling the corner offices at their headquarters with
executives from all over the world.[14]

Yet the effects of creating a single market in Europe, a free trade area
in North America, and a low-tariff regime around the world turned out
to be very different than anticipated when those arrangements were
hammered out in the early 1990s. Thanks to advances in information
technology, culminating in the internet, a customer in one country
could closely supervise a supplier in another, while suppliers could gain
real-time access to customers' inventory records and change production
plans on short notice. But while containerships and computers made it
feasible for manufacturers and retailers to extend their supply chains to
almost any location with good access to a port and a phone line, that is
not what happened. Instead, companies' value chains mainly linked the
wealthiest economies with a mere handful of lower-wage countries—

principally China, Mexico, Turkey, Bangladesh, Vietnam, and some East European states—which emerged as large-scale producers of manufactured goods for the world market. The rest of the world participated in the Third Globalization mainly by supplying commodities—just as in earlier decades—and by seeing cheap Chinese goods wipe out their inefficient domestic industries.

Yet for all the talk about free trade in goods, the free flow of foreign investment, and the disappearance of national borders, the Third Globalization was not simply a market-driven phenomenon. Governments shaped it at every turn—often, in ways that were contradictory to the goals their political leaders espoused.

PART III

Tales of Excess

9

Dentist Ships

LOWER TRADE BARRIERS, the free flow of finance, and advances in transportation, computing, and communications all helped make the world smaller. But it was not only such fundamental changes that caused businesses to stretch their supply chains around the globe. Decisions about where to make things and how to deliver them were colored by the fact that transporting goods across the oceans was highly subsidized while transporting goods domestically often was not. Shipyards, owners and operators of ships, canals, and port terminals were among the beneficiaries, able to provide their services at an artificially low cost because of the aid they received, either directly or indirectly. Ironically, many of those subsidies were provided by the governments of high-wage countries that were hit hard by the loss of factory jobs due to the low-cost imports that inexpensive shipping made possible.

Some countries had subsidized passenger ships with contracts to carry mail in the nineteenth century, but subsidized shipping was not the norm in the years after World War Two. In the decades before the war, the vessels produced by the world's shipyards in an average year had been able to carry less than three million tons of cargo. Wartime ship production had been several times that, and despite the loss of thousands of ships at sea, many of the merchant vessels hurriedly constructed by US shipyards during the war were still in service in the early 1950s. Those ships, though, had deliberately been built small to minimize the loss of armaments and food if one were hit by a torpedo. Oil companies and commodity traders wanted larger vessels to handle the fast-growing commerce in petroleum, grain, and iron ore at lower cost. Their orders filled shipyards to capacity; the Greek shipowner Aristotle Onassis alone purchased thirty new tankers from US, German, and French yards between 1948 and 1954. The capacity of newly launched vessels topped five million tons in 1954 and ten million a decade later, as supertankers displaced World War Two tankers a tenth their size. By the early 1970s, with containership construction in full swing, vessels with a total capacity of more than thirty million tons—ten times the prewar average—were gliding down the slipways each year.[1]

The lion's share of the postwar world's commercial shipbuilding—nearly two-thirds in 1960—occurred in Europe, most of the rest in Japan. Governments invariably considered shipbuilding a critical industry. Shipyards building oceangoing vessels routinely employed thousands of workers and were major consumers of steel. World steel output nearly quadrupled between 1950 and 1973, and a substantial share of that metal was shaped into hulls, beams, and deck plates that were welded into oceangoing vessels. Japan specialized in building oil tankers, usually to standard designs, while orders for passenger liners, general cargo ships, and then containerships kept European yards busy. "Japanese shipyards refined their production techniques during this period to the point that their productivity was more than double that of European and American yards," a study for the US Navy concluded, while their labor costs remained low. Government aid for ship construction was relatively minor except in the United States, where subsidies were used to induce US companies serving international routes to build in US yards, and in Japan, where the export-import bank provided low-cost financing to foreign shipowners during the 1960s.[2]

The oil crisis of 1973 changed matters overnight. Demand for tankers plummeted, and trade in other goods was hit hard by the spreading recession. Many shipowners refused to accept delivery of vessels they had ordered but no longer needed. Orders placed with Japanese shipyards fell 90 percent between 1973 and 1978, and the decline was nearly as steep in Europe. At a moment when the industry's outlook already seemed dire, South Korea muscled in. South Korea's rapid industrialization over the previous decade had depended on exports of labor-intensive products such as clothing and footwear, but as wages rose, government economic planners set a course for heavy industry, in which labor costs mattered less and workers could earn more. They laid out a series of major state investments. The first, Pohang Iron and Steel Company, which opened in 1972, was perhaps the most highly subsidized industrial venture in history up to that point. The move into steelmaking was followed by a shipbuilding development plan, which proposed to build nine shipyards by 1980 and five more by 1985.

Korean shipbuilders previously had made only small vessels for fishing and coastal trade, mainly out of wood. No shipyard in the country was capable of building modern tankers or containerships. The government pressured companies such as Hyundai, South Korea's largest industrial conglomerate, to build and operate the new yards, granting them tax holidays, access to scarce foreign currency, low-interest loans from state banks, and loan guarantees that let them borrow cheaply overseas. Hyundai's first yard was at Ulsan, where it could obtain steel cheaply from the new mill at Pohang, thirty-five miles up the coast. Hyundai began with a foreign ship design that called for building an oil tanker in two halves, but it was so inexperienced that the completed halves did not fit together, causing the shipyard to miss the promised delivery date. When the buyer refused to accept the ship, the government helped start a new ship line to take the unwanted vessels off the shipyard's hands. That company, Hyundai Merchant Marine, soon ranked among the world's major ocean carriers.[3]

As a job-creation strategy, the shipbuilding development plan proved wildly successful. Subsidies to the shipyards and to the Pohang steel mill, along with South Korea's low wages, allowed Korean yards to underprice competitors in Europe and Japan. As a result, ship lines around the world were able to obtain vessels at bargain prices. State financing even enabled shipyards to charter newly built vessels to carriers so troubled that no commercial bank would lend them money—a strategy that kept shipyards busy, but further subsidized shipowners.[4]

By 1990, South Korea's ship production was eight times higher than it had been in 1975, while every other major shipbuilding nation was producing far less tonnage than before. In Japan, the country hardest hit by the shipbuilding crisis, the government orchestrated an "anti-depression cartel," which shut down 50 of Japan's 138 dry docks by the end of 1980, eliminating 119,000 jobs. European governments were less decisive. Subsidies for new ships ran rampant, to the extent that a 1987 European Union directive limiting "production aid" to 28 percent of a vessel's cost was deemed a great accomplishment. With ready access to cut-rate financing for new ships, ship lines eagerly added to their containership fleets in a market that was already oversaturated.[5]

———

Subsidies were not only for shipyards and steel mills. Investors in shipping got on the gravy train as well. Traditionally, merchants and financiers invested in merchant vessels with the goal of making a profit. As container shipping burgeoned, though, much of the money that went into the sector was intended to make losses. Through the labyrinth of the tax code, the government of West Germany encouraged prosperous citizens seeking tax shelters to invest in oceangoing ships. By doing so, it turned Hamburg, the country's largest port, into the Wall Street of the shipping industry—and provided another way for a globalizing world to transport its goods at artificially low cost.

Hamburg, located on the Elbe River about seventy miles from the North Sea, has been an important shipping and trading center since the Middle Ages. The division of Germany after World War Two hurt the city, as the Iron Curtain between Western Europe and the Soviet-dominated countries farther east meant that its port no longer handled cargo for Berlin, Prague, and other places once served by barges on the Elbe. Nonetheless, Germany's second-largest city remained home to major shipbuilders, numerous ship lines, and a sizeable community of bankers, insurers, engineers, brokers, and lawyers who specialized in maritime matters. But by the early 1970s, Hamburg's livelihood was under threat. A change in Greek tax law had led German shipowners to shift 631 ships from German to Greek registry in a two-year span. In the short term, reflagging under the Greek flag threatened German tax revenue. Looking further ahead, it seemed possible that the activities involved in owning, managing, and financing those ships might move away as well.[6]

The German government's response was to offer more generous tax write-offs to shipowners. Around 1973, bankers seized on the change in the tax law to craft an ingenious way to finance ships. Rather than directly buying a share of a vessel, which only the very rich could afford, people of middling wealth were invited to put their money into limited partnerships, each created to finance a single ship. With this cash in hand, the partnerships, known as ship funds, could borrow the remaining sums required to build the ship. This let shipowners acquire new tonnage while putting up little money of their own. Financial wizardry ensured that the new ships would be unprofitable, at least for a decade or so. The funds then passed those losses through to the individual partners, who could deduct up to two and a half times their investment when they reported their income to tax authorities. It was an unbeatable deal. More than fifty German financial institutions created ship funds, which generated hefty management fees for them and commissions for financial advisors who promised their customers large returns with no risk. As historian Erik Lindner explained, "The traditional idea that a fleet owner should make a profit disappeared into the background."[7]

The tax break was wildly successful—so successful that the government scaled it back in 1984 and again in 1995. Even so, it met objections from the European Commission, the executive body of the European Union. The commission found in 1997 that by subsidizing new vessels, certain tax measures "have tended to create or maintain overcapacity," which, of course, enabled ship lines to acquire vessels on the cheap. It directed that tax relief for shipping should be granted only where the "strategic and commercial management of all ships concerned" occurred within the European Union and the companies complied with European rules on safety and working conditions.[8]

Vessels owned by partnerships often didn't meet these standards, and the fact that their investors could report tax losses larger than their investments also ran afoul of the rules. But while taking away that tax break, the European Commission gave its blessing to a different one, known as a tonnage tax. No matter where a ship was built, as long as it was registered in Europe and engaged in international trade, it could be taxed on the basis of its size rather than its actual profit or loss. The attraction for German dentists and doctors was even greater: now, instead of credit for a tax loss, they would expect a lightly taxed dividend payment each year. Record amounts poured in to ship funds. At the peak of the market, in the early 2000s, the funds supported €20 billion, or roughly $26 billion, of annual investments in shipping, enough to build hundreds of ships each year.[9]

Many of these "dentist ships" were owned by the Hamburg companies that organized the partnerships, which built them to the specifications of major ship lines and then operated them under contract. The fleet manager E. R. Schiffahrt, controlled by a venerable Hamburg shipping family, was a case in point. As of 2008, it had eighty-two containerships in its fleet or on order. All were financed through a sister company, Nordcapital, which had raised €1.6 billion from partnerships that had a total of forty-one thousand investors. With that money in hand, Nordcapital could turn to banks that specialized in shipping, such as HSH Nordbank and Commerzbank, for loans to cover the remainder of the construction costs. Other companies sponsored similar funds to finance tankers and bulk ships, usually built in Korea or China. Buoyed by thousands of relatively small investments—a typical investment in a ship fund was around €25,000 (about $35,000 at the time)—the German-owned fleet ballooned. HSH Nordbank, based in Hamburg, claimed to be the world's largest ship lender, with a whopping €40 billion of ship loans making up half its total loan portfolio.

———

Thanks to the ship funds, one of every three containerships built in the first years of the twenty-first century was ordered by a German owner and operated with a German government tax subsidy. Carriers based in Taiwan and Chile, France and Japan, took the opportunity to charter German-owned ships on favorable terms. Many of those new vessels, ordered in 2007 and 2008, were delivered as the fallout from the financial crisis depressed trade in 2009 and 2010, bringing highly subsidized capacity on to the market at the worst possible time.

The result was catastrophic for ship-fund investors. The supposedly risk-free partnerships suffered staggering losses as their ships sailed half empty or were laid up altogether, leaving their investors in the lurch. Hundreds of partnerships declared insolvency, as did some of the fleet managers who sponsored them. German taxpayers, having subsidized the construction of the vessels in the first place, had to ante up again to rescue the tottering banks. The state governments of Hamburg and Schleswig-Holstein, owners of HSH Nordbank, were on the line for roughly €14 billion of losses and eventually had to sell the bank. Commerzbank received a €16 billion federal bailout in return for handing the federal government a quarter of its shares. Many of the dentist ships were sold off to raise cash; Germany's share of the containership charter fleet fell from two-thirds in 2010 to one-third in 2017. But while fewer ships were in German hands, they remained available to carry cargo, their vast capacity driving down freight rates and making it artificially cheap to trade goods by sea.[10]

China stepped into the market as German investors withdrew. In 2006, the government in Beijing identified shipbuilding as a "strategic industry" and set a goal of China becoming the largest shipbuilding nation within a decade. It backed this up with heavy state investments: thanks to an estimated $4.3 billion of subsidies, two state-owned companies, China Shipbuilding Industry Corporation and China State Shipbuilding Corporation, added more than one hundred dry docks large enough to build commercial vessels within seven years. Chinese shipowners—many of them state-owned companies—went on a demolition spree, replacing their older tankers, bulk ships, and containerships with new, highly subsidized ships built almost exclusively in Chinese yards.

China quickly dominated the market for bulk ships, used to transport raw commodities such as coal and ore: between 2006 and 2012, 57 percent of new bulker tonnage worldwide was produced in China. Breaking into the market for containerships, much more complex vessels, was tougher. As late as 2005, almost all large containerships were built in South Korea and Japan, as vessel owners judged that China lacked the skilled workers for such complicated projects. But with ample state aid, China quickly moved up the learning curve. Building in a highly subsidized Chinese yard cost 20 to 30 percent less than building in a highly subsidized Korean yard. It was no wonder that between 2006 and 2012, China built about two-fifths of the world's new containership capacity.[11]

The economic implications of subsidized shipping went well beyond the cost to taxpayers. With the public sector bearing part of the expense of building and operating ships, the global merchant fleet expanded far more quickly than would have occurred without the subsidies. This contributed to chronic overcapacity. With too many ships chasing too little cargo, shipping rates fell so low that ocean carriers' receipts from voyages barely covered their fuel bills. Carriers' massive financial losses worked to the benefit of companies that sent their cargo by sea—the shippers. Thanks to subsidies for ship construction, shippers were able to pay less than the full cost of moving their goods by sea and therefore could sell their exports for prices that did not reflect the true cost of transportation. Those taxpayer subsidies played an important role in making long-distance value chains financially viable.

The competitive implications are worth considering. Around the world, government subsidies for surface transportation were generally smaller than those for ocean shipping. In many countries, truckers had to pay substantial taxes on diesel fuel and highway tolls to boot. Railroad freight was usually priced to make a profit; where railways were owned by government, the profits from freight often served to subsidize passenger service. Lax regulations governing the environmental cost of ocean shipping were a form of subsidy as well, as was a postal-rate structure that favored packages from developing countries to wealthy countries over domestic shipments. Because companies shipping to domestic customers by truck or rail paid something closer to the full cost of transporting their goods, they faced comparatively higher transport costs than importers who shipped by sea. Even as domestic producers fought against import competition, shipping subsidies gave an edge to the importers. It was an industrial policy of a very odd sort.[12]

10

Hand on the Scale

SUBSIDIZED SHIPPING helped make globalization financially viable. Subsidies to international business helped make it contentious.

When it comes to international trade, the term "subsidy" has no precise definition. Some subsidies, such as a government grant to entice a company to build a factory in a particular place, are blatant. Others, such as a government guarantee of a bank loan that enables a foreign customer to purchase an export, may escape notice unless the borrower defaults and taxpayers are stuck with a bad debt. Special breaks buried deep in the tax code, state grants for an industry research program, and import restrictions that enable domestic producers to raise their prices are all forms of subsidy, but so are less obvious measures such as a requirement that a military purchase only equipment made domestically. The common thread is that a government in one country is distorting competition in ways that affect the imports, exports, or investments of another.[1]

In a world in which almost all commerce was domestic, the fact that a government aided farmers or manufacturers mattered little to other countries. Traditional economic thought justifies this indifference, holding that subsidized exports are a blessing: if someone wants to sell you something for less than the cost of producing it, why look a gift horse in the mouth? Until the 1960s, claims about unfairness in international trade revolved not around subsidies but around differences in wages. For example, when US manufacturers took strong exception to clothing imported from Japan in the 1950s, they protested "cheap-labor foreign competition" until Japan, then a low-wage country, agreed to limit its exports of cotton apparel in 1957.[2]

Subsidies became a sensitive issue only in the 1960s, as the US government doled out contracts to US companies for military and space projects. European countries objected that the Americans were drawing on government-subsidized research to gain an unfair edge in building passenger jets, computers, and thousands of other products for the civilian market. With European aircraft manufacturers struggling to survive, companies in France, Germany, the Netherlands, Britain, and Spain— mostly state owned—were painfully fused into a pan-European corporation, Airbus Industrie, in 1970. The United States promptly complained about the large subsidies being channeled to Airbus. The Europeans returned the fire, alleging that commercial planes from US-based aerospace firms such as Boeing and Lockheed were equally subsidized. The dispute would drag on for decades, periodically erupting as one or another company won a sale over its competitors.

Under the rubric "structural adjustment," the European Union tried to manage the shrinkage of troubled industries such as steel, shipbuilding, chemicals, and paper in hopes of creating companies strong enough to withstand international competition. If industries were simply allowed to collapse, European politicians worried, the survival of the European Community could come into question. The US government was less generous with cash handouts to individual companies, but state and local governments commonly used grants and low-interest loans to lure new companies and retain old ones. Other countries complained loudly about the United States' aggressive use of trade barriers to keep troubled industries afloat and its requirements that many goods procured with government funds be produced domestically, not imported. The large US defense budget also funded development of leading-edge technologies for aircraft, computers, and other products that were easily repurposed for civilian use. California's microelectronics industry emerged as the world's leader, in part, because the US military pumped large sums into companies located in what became known as Silicon Valley; prior to 1967, more than half of US output of integrated circuits went into missile systems, giving US manufacturers a scale no other country's chipmakers could match. Whether these public expenditures amounted to unfair subsidies benefiting US exporters would be a point of contention for years to come.[3]

————

Subsidies for capital-intensive industries such as steel and chemicals were flashpoints as early as the 1950s. For historical reasons, a large part of the world's capacity was concentrated in one-industry towns like Youngstown, in Ohio, and Ludwigshafen, in southwestern Germany, where leading companies had set up shop many decades earlier. Those regions' high wages mattered little, as labor represented only a small share of production costs, and the large scale of existing plants provided such a cost advantage that new factories in other countries would have difficulty gaining a foothold. When Asian and Latin American governments determined to build up domestic steel and chemical industries of their own, they had no chance of success unless they subsidized the factories and guaranteed domestic sales by keeping imports out.

This strategy of import substitution, as we saw in chapter 4, frequently misfired. In countries such as India and Argentina, many of the new factories were white elephants, making things that could have been imported at much lower cost and doing nothing to drive economic growth or reduce poverty. In Japan, however, import substitution proved wildly successful. Strongly supported by import restrictions and subsidies, Japanese manufacturers advanced from labor-intensive work, like sewing clothes and soldering circuit boards, into large-scale production of machinery, autos, chemicals, and metal products. A key reason Japan succeeded where other countries failed was that while the government kept foreign competitors at bay, it forced domestic companies to compete vigorously with one another and to export. Firms not up to the challenge were allowed to fail. Those that succeeded became as productive as the best companies abroad.[4]

Japan's imports had exceeded its exports for two decades, but in 1965 it began running a trade surplus that would endure, with only brief interruptions, for forty-six years. Inexpensive Datsuns and Toyotas appeared on the streets of US cities, and Japanese steel made inroads in California, where transportation costs favored steel coils arriving by ship across the Pacific over those moved by rail from Pittsburgh and Chicago. Once containership service opened in 1968, lowering transport costs and reducing cargo damage, the shelves of US and Canadian appliance stores groaned under the weight of Japanese-made televisions, stereos, and microwave ovens. By 1970, Japan had become a highly industrialized and extremely prosperous country, producing 45 percent of its national income on the factory floor. Meanwhile, a variety of obstacles, official and unofficial, made it difficult for foreign manufacturers to sell in Japan. In 1966, the country assembled around 2.5 million cars—and imported just 15,244.

In 1968, after the steel industry cried foul, the US State Department demanded that Japan and Europe "voluntarily" limit their steel exports. A few months later, US makers of color televisions claimed Japanese TVs were undermining their industry, even as presidential candidate Richard Nixon promised to curb imports of textiles from Japan. Shortly after Nixon took office in January 1969, he told reporters that he would "prefer to handle this on a voluntary basis." With Japan depending on the United States for both export markets and military defense, its government took the hint. The powerful Ministry of International Trade and Industry, MITI, put a lid on textile exports and issued new guidance to Japanese companies. "The concept that, 'No matter what may be involved, we must expand exports' can no longer be considered appropriate," it announced in 1972. "Depending on the circumstances, such a policy tends to cause dissatisfaction on the part of other nations."[5]

––––––––

It was the oil crisis that began in October 1973 that turned export subsidies into a tool of open commercial warfare. A precipitous rise in the price of oil, resulting from production cuts by oil-exporting countries in the Middle East, brought recession in the rest of the world. No country was more endangered than Japan, which produced no oil of its own. To raise the dollars needed for oil imports, the government in Tokyo desperately wanted to power up exports. But Japan was no longer a cheap place to make things: oil, now dear, provided three-quarters of Japan's energy, and the average factory wage, in dollars, had risen 38 percent between 1971 and 1973. MITI determined that for Japan to prosper, industries relying on cheap energy or cheap labor should give way to "knowledge" industries. In MITI's vision, Japan would grow wealthy selling cars, advanced electronics, and precision machinery, not toys, clothes, and transistor radios.

MITI had the power and the money to put its vision into effect. It encouraged competitors to decide among themselves which aluminum smelters, paper mills, and shipyards should close. So many textile plants were shuttered that Japan's 1972 promise to limit exports of synthetic fibers to the United States turned out to be irrelevant. Companies that complied with MITI's recommendations might receive grants and subsidized loans to expand in new lines of business, and, of course, protection from import competition, while generous assistance eased the pain of the eight hundred thousand manufacturing workers who lost their jobs owing to industrial restructuring between 1973 and 1979.[6]

High on the list of favored industries was auto manufacturing. While Japanese vehicles were small and not particularly comfortable, they were perfect amid an oil crisis that had made fuel-guzzling Cadillacs and BMWs expensive to drive. Japan's annual car exports nearly trebled between 1973 and 1980, and truck exports rose even faster. Japanese models accounted for one-fourth of car sales in the United States in 1980, but in Japan, workers who wanted to spend their rapidly rising incomes on automobiles were very unlikely to buy a Chevrolet or a Volkswagen. Tariffs added 30 or 40 percent to the cost of foreign-made vehicles, and registration fees were far higher on large imported cars than on small Japanese-made ones. In any event, few auto dealers in Sapporo or Fukuoka were willing to handle foreign models.[7]

As MITI's planners had envisioned, the credo "lighter, thinner, shorter, and smaller" captivated Japanese executives. By 1975, machinery and transportation equipment accounted for half of Japan's exports, four times the share two decades earlier. Thanks to MITI's support for research and development, computers, cameras with advanced optics, numerically controlled machine tools, and high-capacity color photocopiers began pouring out of Japanese factories. Not everything MITI touched turned to gold: despite its urging, Japanese companies failed to produce a commercially viable jet engine. But Japan's success at promoting exports while fencing out imports helped generate enormous trade surpluses with countries whose sophisticated industrial products competed with Japan's. Its new trade pattern rapidly became an international problem. Politicians and trade unionists across the United States, Canada, and Western Europe were outraged. As factory closures spread across import-devastated industrial communities in the US Midwest, the English Midlands, the German Ruhr, and the north of France, a new word entered the economic lexicon: "deindustrialization."[8]

Japan's push into advanced manufacturing, coming as economic growth downshifted around the world, challenged the Bretton Woods arrangements that had played such an important role in globalization since World War Two. The men who negotiated those agreements had not been starry-eyed. They were aware that every government faced pressures to assist workers, firms, and communities, but they did not envision subsidies would grow so large as to undermine support for a more open world economy. Now, though, Japan stood accused of flooding the world with subsidized high-value exports while keeping its own market off limits. MITI's heavy hand on the scale, critics charged, meant that trade harmed other countries while benefiting only Japan.[9]

A 1960 agreement among seventeen of the largest trading nations was designed to address such a situation. Under that pact, if subsidized exports threatened "material injury" to an industry in the importing country, that country could retaliate with import duties equal to the amount of the subsidy, taking away the foreigners' cost advantage. This provision proved a useful threat. The Japanese government did not want to be singled out as a violator of international rules, so it repeatedly agreed to "voluntarily" restrain its exports, much as it had done with synthetic fibers to placate Richard Nixon in 1972. In 1977, it limited Japanese companies' exports of cars to Great Britain and color television sets to the United States. In 1978, it imposed "intensified monitoring and guidance" on exporters of automobiles, motorcycles, steel, televisions, ships, photocopiers, watches, and cameras, and it set minimum prices for exports of machine tools to the United States and Canada so companies could not offer discounts to gain market share. The following year, the United States slapped a 15 percent tariff on bolts, nuts, and screws in order to "save" a US industry threatened by Japanese competition, even though the industry being saved was known for its archaic, inefficient factories.[10]

That same year, 1979, saw the near collapse of Chrysler Corporation, the third-largest US automaker. Amid warnings of mass unemployment, the US Congress agreed to guarantee up to $1.5 billion of loans to keep Chrysler afloat. Other car companies were on the brink, as 1980 became one of the worst years in the history of the US auto industry. Although high interest rates and a lack of small cars were killing off sales, politicians and union leaders loudly blamed Japan. During that year's presidential campaign, Ronald Reagan, known as a free trader, told workers at a Chrysler plant in Detroit that the US government should "convince the Japanese that in one way or another, and in their own best interest, that deluge of cars into the United States must be slowed while our industry gets back on its feet." Japan accepted "voluntary" restraints on auto exports to the United States in 1981, along with tighter controls on exports of cars to Western Europe and Canada. By 1983, Japan had agreed to control exports of videotape recorders, quartz watches, lathes, forklift trucks, and several other products to Europe, in each case acting "voluntarily."[11]

The results proved disappointing. Each new "voluntary export restraint" seemed to expand Japan's trade surplus, not shrink it, as its manufacturers, limited in the number of autos and televisions they could export, shipped more sophisticated goods at higher prices. The added profits gave Japanese firms the money to build factories in North America and Western Europe, strengthening the perception that Japanese-style capitalism was conquering the world. Only later would it be clear that in its enthusiasm to develop advanced manufacturing, Japan had forgotten its remarkably inefficient service sector. Changing money in a bank required signatures from several underemployed bankers, and the department stores on Tokyo's glitzy Ginza engaged young women dressed in kimonos to bow politely to arriving customers. Over-all, productivity in services—that is, output per hour worked—was lower in 1980 than it had been in 1970. In the years ahead, Japan's stulti-fied service sector would come to be seen as a drag on economic growth, but in the 1980s, with Japanese manufacturers flourishing, the stagna-tion of service industries barely drew notice.[12]

———

Japan was not the only country upsetting its trading partners at a time when the world economy was in a funk. No country learned more from Japan's experience than South Korea. Although its population was con-siderably smaller, South Korea would follow Japan in using subsidies successfully to reshape the patterns of international commerce.

Until the 1960s, the Korean economy was stagnant. The Korean pen-insula had been occupied from 1910 to 1945 by Japan, which used it mainly as a source of rice and tungsten, and then was divided at the end of World War Two into a northern zone, controlled by the Soviet Union, and a southern zone, originally controlled by the United States. The Korean War between 1950 and 1953 destroyed most of the peninsula's infrastructure and industry, leaving more than one million people dead. When it ended, the government in the South committed to rapid indus-trialization. The first step was to put masses of people to work making clothing and shoes. But its economic policies looked inward. Barriers to imports were high, and as late as 1963, exports were negligible.

In 1965, President Park Chung-hee decreed a new course. "We, too, can successfully compete with others in the international export race," he announced to the nation in 1965. The government pushed down the value of South Korea's currency, the won, to make Korean products cheaper abroad; granted generous financing for exports; and offered tax exemptions on inputs used to make exports. It set annual goals for ex-ports of specific commodities and used the Bank of Korea, the central bank, to provide low-cost credit to help companies meet those goals—but in order to encourage competition among exporters, firms that had met export targets the previous year were given favored access to the loans. South Korea's economic experts were convinced that size mattered, so they encouraged the growth of diversified industrial groups, known as *chaebol*, that would be large enough to compete globally with multinational corporations based in Europe, Japan, and North America. Government planners used import tariffs and loans from state-controlled banks to direct the chaebol to invest in specific sectors, such as auto and electronics manufacturing. As the American economist Alice Amsden wrote, "Every major shift in industrial diversification in the decades of the 1960s and 1970s was instigated by the state."[13]

Unlike many poor countries, South Korea invested heavily in education, giving it an unusually literate workforce. This proved a huge advantage as Korean companies, aided by the government, went looking for new products to export at a time when the world economy was languishing. In 1962, before the export drive began, food and raw materials accounted for four-fifths of South Korea's exports, and seaweed counted as a major export product. By 1980, South Korea's manufacturing sector was fourteen times larger than it had been in 1962, and foreign trade, mainly in manufactured goods, accounted for more than two-thirds of the country's economic output, a much higher share than in Europe, North America, or Japan. This was not welcomed abroad: nearly half of South Korea's exports to high-income countries in the early 1980s faced restrictions meant to deal with unfair trade. After a pause during the global economic slowdown of the early 1980s, the government tried to shift South Korea's export-led growth onto a different track, emphasizing innovation and advanced technology. Investments by Japanese companies, frowned upon in earlier years, helped the chaebol make cars, color televisions, and pharmaceuticals.[14]

This state-directed economic policy revolutionized a country that had previously looked inward. In 1986, South Korea's chronic trade deficit turned into a surplus for the first time in decades. By 1988, South Korea had become the world's tenth-largest trading nation, and its income per person, adjusted for inflation, was eight times what it had been in 1960. The country had 996 private research and development centers in 1990, up from 54 a decade earlier, as businesses heeded the government's calls to hire engineers and stop relying on cheap labor. Complaints about subsidies, import barriers, and a deliberately undervalued currency did not go away—but now, the claim was that South Korea was unfairly stealing market share in advanced technology. Among the success stories was the semiconductor industry. Semiconductors had been largely an American preserve, but by 1990, South Korea was the second-largest supplier of computer memory chips in the US market. When the US International Trade Commission ruled in 1993 that several Korean companies were injuring the US industry by selling memory chips for less than fair value, it had to admit that customers found Korean chips more reliable and faster to obtain than those produced in the United States.[15]

South Korea's push into high-value production was carefully planned. Under a five-year "Plan for Localization of Machinery, Materials, and Components," announced in 1992, the government helped Korean companies reduce imports of four thousand products, from auto parts and machinery to semiconductors and computer components. Previously, South Korea had relied on Japan for many of these goods, but government money financed factories to make them at home. Once more, subsidies had a dramatic effect on trade patterns. In the targeted sectors, South Korea's trade surplus soared from $3 billion in 1997 to $108 billion in 2014. For the first time, it became a large-scale exporter of intermediate goods. A large share of them moved through international supply chains to factories in China, which relied more on Korean semiconductors and optical devices than on those from any other country.[16]

11

The China Price

CHINA, AT THE start of the 1980s, was scarcely a presence in the international economy, much less in global affairs. The political turmoil of the Cultural Revolution had turned the country upside down through most of the 1970s. The chaos, along with the ruling Communist Party's insistence on party control of a planned economy, had kept China poor. Change had begun in 1978, after paramount leader Deng Xiaoping visited Japan and Singapore and then declared, "We must acknowledge that we are backward, that many of our ways of doing things are inappropriate, and that we need to change." But there was a considerable distance to go. The economy was primitive, and millions of the students who might have helped modernize it had been forced to abandon their educations to perform physical labor on collective farms. China had negligible military or diplomatic influence, because it was too impoverished to project power.[1]

In popular memory, China's rise to strength and prosperity after decades of instability is recalled as a story of success upon success. But in the first years after its opening to the world in 1978, China was by no means a great power, economically or otherwise. "Through autarky, China failed to develop a single industrial product with which it could compete internationally," the British journalist Joe Studwell observed. As in most socialist economies, state planners had long emphasized building up heavy industry. The first ten-year plan under Deng's leadership called for a crash effort to double steel output by 1985 and build smelters, coal mines, oil fields, harbors, power plants, and railroads. This ambitious program was well beyond China's means. It was quickly replaced by a more realistic plan to ramp up production of consumer goods. Making shoes, cosmetics, and transistor radios for China's vast population demanded far more labor than making steel, offering a way to soak up the tens of millions of rural workers who were sure to be displaced as China's archaic farm sector was modernized, and also provided consumer goods to improve Chinese households' living standards.[2]

Starting in 1979, after Deng traveled to the United States, the Chinese government cautiously opened a few Special Economic Zones where foreign trade was encouraged. Taking advantage of extremely favorable labor costs—by one estimate, manufacturing wages in Hong Kong were twenty times as high as in China in 1981—manufacturers from Hong Kong and Taiwan began opening factories in southern China. The chemicals, plastics, fabrics, and components were made elsewhere, shipped to Shenzhen and Guangdong to be assembled into dolls, dresses, or power drills, and then exported via Hong Kong to customers around the world. China's contribution was a cheap, obedient workforce that was accustomed to working long hours.

The wealthy countries strongly supported China's opening by granting China the same tariff rates most other developing countries received, removing a large competitive disadvantage. These lower tariffs on exports to North America, Japan, and Europe made it practical for China to again become a trading nation. Its Western trading partners were more concerned with the balance of power than the balance of trade; their tariff reductions were intended to drive a deeper wedge between China and the Soviet Union, which was not treated as kindly in the West. But this gift came with strings attached. The United States made its favorable tariff treatment for China subject to an annual review, with the constant threat that it might be discontinued.[3]

China's international trade doubled in the two years between 1978 and 1980, but then hit a wall. The government's insistence that foreigners invest only through joint ventures with firms owned by local, provincial, or national governments repelled foreign manufacturers. But while it distrusted foreign investment, China was unable to create modern industries on its own. The state-owned companies that dominated the economy produced according to planners' directives, not customers' preferences. There were no private businesses earning profits that could be reinvested in research and development, because there was no place for entrepreneurs to find capital: stock markets did not exist, and banks, which had been permitted only since 1978, were clueless about lending to private firms. Even for government-owned enterprises, borrowing money was difficult; a 1980 foreign bond sale to finance a joint venture with a Japanese company to make textile fibers proved so controversial that the government was hesitant to repeat it.

As late as 1986, China was producing a minuscule fraction of the world's manufactured exports, and its market share was not growing. Becoming a hub of the international economy was a distant dream.[4]

———

The Republic of China, which had fought on the Allied side during World War Two, had been a founding member of the GATT in 1947. When the Communist Party took control of the mainland in 1949 and proclaimed the People's Republic of China, the leaders of the former Republic of China fled to the island of Taiwan. From there, in 1950, the Republic of China announced its withdrawal from the GATT. The People's Republic did not recognize the legitimacy of this action, but it wasn't much bothered. The Communist Party was struggling to establish a new government in a country wracked by decades of war, and its orientation was inward. Besides, China had a long history of unhappy relations with colonial powers, and European countries still occupied Chinese territory in Hong Kong and Macao. Opening China to the international economy was not high on the new government's list of concerns.[5]

Three decades on, an outward-looking China was acutely aware of its need for foreign technology, investment, and markets, and its absence from the GATT suddenly took on huge importance. Not belonging was risky. The GATT was where countries wrote the rules that governed international trade. If, for example, a country claimed that Japanese polyurethane was harming its chemical industry, it had to follow certain procedures before it could restrict shipments of the offending products from Japan. As a nonmember, China was not protected by such rules. Joining the GATT would make it harder for other countries to interfere with its trade.

China's newfound interest won it an invitation to sit in on various GATT meetings, starting in 1981, but only as an observer. Other countries were dubious that China was suited to be a member. When it asked to resume membership, in 1986, it was rebuffed. After all, a country in which most industry was owned by governments, in which decisions about importing and exporting were matters of state and law enforcement was arbitrary, did not seem to fit into a trading system designed with market economies in mind. Over the next few years, as other developing countries—Botswana, Costa Rica, Morocco, Venezuela—accepted that freer trade at market prices would benefit their economies and negotiated entry to the GATT, China was left on the outside, looking in.[6]

In the late 1980s, as the economic reforms that had begun in 1978 ran their course, China's economic growth slowed to a crawl. "China is walking at a snail's pace, while the rest of the world is galloping," asserted an American buyer quoted in *Business Week*. Wage hikes were no longer so generous, and the inflation rate reached double digits. Outrage against corruption and demands for a more democratic political system led to protests across the country, culminating in an army operation that killed hundreds, or perhaps thousands, of protesters in Beijing's Tiananmen Square in June 1989. The June Fourth Incident, as it was known in China, spooked foreign investors. After an internal struggle, party leaders rejected any changes that might weaken the leading role of the Communist Party but followed Deng's advice to push on with reforms to open China's economy. "Without reform and opening our development stops and our economy slides downhill," he warned top party leaders. "Living standards decline if we turn back. The momentum of reform cannot be stopped."[7]

Deng stepped down from his main official post in November 1989. Although he remained an influential voice behind the scenes, his policies of encouraging private enterprise and giving market forces greater sway—even allowing stock exchanges to open in Shenzhen and Shanghai—came under fire from more orthodox Communist Party leaders. Accused of undermining the party and promoting capitalism, Deng fought back publicly. In January 1992, he unexpectedly emerged from retirement and embarked on a month-long trip through southern China. In speech after speech, he called on provincial and local leaders to break free of old ideas and adopt policies that could improve productivity and living standards, regardless of whether they sounded capitalist. Visiting the Special Economic Zones he had approved eight years earlier as test-beds for market-oriented reform, Deng declared the experiment a success.

Deng's "southern excursion" proved to be a turning point in globalization. In March 1992, the political bureau of the Communist Party Central Committee agreed to stay the course of market-oriented reform. In October, before the full party congress, Communist Party general secretary Jiang Zemin reaffirmed the party's leading role, but called for the party "to quicken the pace of the reform, the opening to the outside world and the drive for modernization." Deng's views had won out.[8]

By the end of that year, the government eased rules on foreign investment, and money from Hong Kong, Japan, and the United States began to pour in. In 1991, when China's direction had still been in doubt, foreigners had spent a mere $4 billion on factories, buildings, or business ventures. The figure was six times higher in 1993, as the Chinese economy took flight. While some of this investment was aimed at making goods to sell in the fast-growing Chinese market, most of it went into producing for international retailers like Uniqlo and Carrefour and for manufacturers like Hewlett-Packard and General Motors.[9]

China's exports of manufactured goods rose fivefold during the 1990s, with much of the growth in products that China had barely exported before: chemicals, machinery, telecommunications equipment. By 1998, 45 percent of China's exports were produced in foreign-funded plants. Lower tariffs on inputs led to higher productivity in manufacturing as more Chinese plants used those inputs to make goods for export.

The central government provided decisive help by forcing the bloated state-owned sector to slim down. Local and provincial governments were instructed to "Grasp the Large, Let Go of the Small": small state-owned enterprises were sold off to private entrepreneurs, but many larger ones were consolidated into market-oriented firms, several in each industry, that were to compete with one another even as they remained under state control. Perhaps twenty million industrial workers were laid off as state-owned companies cut costs to become competitive in the global market—the first Chinese victims of the Third Globalization.[10]

———

The long Uruguay Round negotiations led to creation of a World Trade Organization to replace the GATT as the overseer of international trade. The WTO was formed without China's involvement, but from the moment it opened its offices in the Centre William Rappard in Geneva— the building previously occupied by the GATT—at the start of 1995, China wanted in.

To enter the WTO, China needed to strike deals with each of the member states, addressing their concerns about its economic policies and laying out how it would treat their exports. Some of these talks were contentious, above all those with the United States and the European Union. Opposition to China's accession was strong, with many US and European experts warning that China would flood foreign markets with its exports while never giving foreign firms equal access to its own market. There were also complaints that China deliberately tried to depress the value of its currency, the renminbi, to make its goods artificially cheap in other countries. On the other side of the argument, though, China's rapid economic growth and the vastness of its potential market were an irresistible lure to executives of multinational corporations, which pressed hard for China's entry. The resulting agreements went into great detail. China would reduce tariffs on cars from over 80 percent to 25 percent, on European pasta from 25 percent to 15 percent, on American frozen pork from 20 percent to 12 percent. Foreign firms would not be required to transfer technology to Chinese enterprises or to use Chinese content in their products. China would allow private firms to import and export without government approval, would let foreign banks conduct domestic business in China, would let foreigners own up to 49 percent of joint ventures in telecommunications, and so on.[11]

In return for making thousands of such promises, often reflecting the priorities of particular commercial interests in other countries, China gained guaranteed access for its exports to customers in 142 nations. Manufacturers, wholesalers, and retailers, whether Chinese or foreign, were henceforth able to route their supply chains through China without worrying that another country would suddenly raise tariffs or place quotas on Chinese-made products and thereby upset their plans. China also succeeded in being classified as a "developing country" for WTO purposes, a status that entitled it to restrict imports and trade-related investment in ways that developed nations could not.[12]

The impact of China's entry into the WTO, in December 2001, was instantaneous. Now, manufacturers in other countries demanded that their suppliers source from China unless their plants in higher-wage countries were able to meet the "China price." In 1985, Walmart Stores, which then operated modestly sized discount stores in small American towns, had committed to selling US-made goods. In 2002, now the world's largest retailer, Walmart took advantage of China's new WTO membership by moving its global purchasing headquarters to Shenzhen, from where it managed relationships with thousands of Chinese factories that supplied supercenters from Brazil to Japan. Hundreds of other retailers followed Walmart's lead. In January 2005, just after the final US quotas on apparel were eliminated, 18.2 million Chinese-made cotton knit shirts arrived in the United States, nineteen times as many as in the previous January. Knowing that shareholders would approve, an executive of Liz Claiborne, a US-based apparel maker, told the *Wall Street Journal*, "China is going to be the most important country in our sourcing strategy." At the time, China was providing less than a third of US imports of textiles and apparel; eight years later, it supplied more than half.[13]

China's emergence as an economic power proved particularly troublesome for the world economy because of the way its trade developed. In the early 1990s, as party leaders were debating whether to maintain the economic reforms advocated by Deng Xiaoping, China's foreign trade had been relatively balanced; in 1993, its imports exceeded its exports. But starting in 1995, China's trade shifted in a mercantilist direction. Its hungry factories swallowed up unprecedented volumes of imported copper, coal, and iron and used them to generate an enormous trade surplus in manufactured goods. By 2005, exports from China's factories accounted for nearly one-third of its entire economic output. Those exports were far more sophisticated than typical for a country with low incomes and a poorly trained workforce. China's income per person, adjusted for differences in living costs, was below those of Tunisia and the Dominican Republic well into the twenty-first century, but while those countries were shipping clothing and electronics assembled from imported materials, China was making engines, kitchen appliances, and photovoltaics. Often, the foreign manufacturers claimed that their technology had been purloined; laws protecting the rights of foreign patent holders were rarely enforced, and foreign companies complained of rampant theft of designs and formulas, in some cases by their own Chinese joint venture partners.[14]

———

Subsidies were essential to China's emergence as a major player in the world economy. In 1980, when the Communist Party had just begun to open the economy to market forces and foreign investment, its exports of goods and services accounted for less than 6 percent of the economy, well below the global average. A quarter-century later, China's exports equaled 35 percent of its economic output, well above the norm for the rest of the world. High tariffs and other obstacles made it hard for producers in other countries to sell in China, but tariffs on imported components were reimbursed if the manufactured goods were exported, so it was cheaper for a factory to produce for export than to make the identical product for the domestic market. A more blatant subsidy to exporters was hard to imagine.[15]

Between 1995 and 2005, according to one study, the Chinese government spent $310 billion on industrial subsidies, with state-owned enterprises, often controlled by provincial or local governments rather than by officials in Beijing, claiming nearly half. That $310 billion, equal to one-fourth of China's total economic output in 2000, includes only amounts paid directly toward firms; it does not take in tax rebates on exports, which were worth around $15 billion per year; discounted electricity; or the lower taxes on manufacturers located in high-tech industrial zones. Foreign companies investing in special enterprise zones paid income taxes at very low rates, and some technology companies were exempt from income tax altogether. Auto manufacturers that exported received priority in obtaining loans and foreign currency. More than half the national government's subsidy payments during that period went toward promoting innovation and exports of high-tech products, mainly by helping firms that already exported develop new products for sale abroad. The goal was to create Chinese multinational companies that could compete worldwide.[16]

As China's auto industry grew, so did its tire industry. Prior to 1990, China's tire manufacturers were small and sold their products almost exclusively in the domestic market. Nearly sixty plants making tires for cars and light trucks opened between 1990 and 2014. The world's largest manufacturers arrived, but under strict terms: many were required to enter joint ventures with Chinese companies, and some plants were allowed to manufacture only for export. With help from a dozen different subsidies, ranging from cheap loans from state-owned banks to tax exemptions for imported equipment to grants from local governments, China was an irresistible factory location for tire makers of all nationalities. Its output of light vehicle tires soared from 84 million in 2004 to 399 million in 2014, with more than half shipped abroad.[17]

A similar story could be told about aluminum. An exhaustive 2019 study of the world's seventeen leading producers of primary aluminum—the high-quality stuff made by smelting bauxite ore rather than the lower-grade metal captured by melting recycled beer cans—found that every single firm had received government subsidies, but Chinese firms were more highly subsidized than those in Canada, Bahrain, Saudi Arabia, and Qatar. China's subsidies accounted for more than 60 percent of the $12.7 billion of subsidies the industry received worldwide over the five years 2013 through 2017. In 1995, China had been a minor player in a widely dispersed industry. By 2017, it was responsible for more than half the world's output of primary aluminum, thanks to energy subsidies, tax breaks, and extremely cheap credit from state-owned banks. At the same time, the Chinese government applied a 15 percent tax on exports of primary aluminum, ensuring a supply of cheap metal for manufacturers of aluminum products in China.[18]

Much the same pattern played out in many other industries, from papermaking, in which the tree-scarce country had no obvious comparative advantage, to manufacture of leading-edge video displays. It used subsidies to entice foreign companies to enter China, trade barriers to force them to serve its vast and fast-growing domestic market with domestic production rather than imports, and restrictions on foreign investment to press them to share technology with Chinese partners. By 2006, 40 percent of China's exports came from foreign-owned firms and another 20 percent from foreign-Chinese joint ventures: global companies were using their investments in China to sell around the world. Many of them found that the Chinese legal system offered scant protection for their patents and designs. If Chinese companies, whether state-owned or private, wished to copy a foreign product or technology, they could do so with little fear of the consequences.[19]

Over the seven years from 2001 to 2008, China's exports of manufactured goods increased a stunning 464 percent. Almost overnight, China became a major supplier of electronic equipment, auto parts, and steel to the global market. It also became a huge and highly lucrative market for international business. No other country could boast shoe factories with a hundred thousand workers and electronics factories with three hundred thousand, with dormitories on-site to ensure that labor was available to fill rush orders. One after another, foreign auto manufacturers set up shop in China through joint ventures with enterprises owned by provincial or local governments. In 2001, before China entered the WTO, its auto plants produced around seven hundred thousand passenger vehicles. In 2009, output reached nine million, making China the world's largest auto producer. By that year, Japanese automakers, which had no Chinese factories in 2000, counted on Chinese joint ventures for one-seventh of their global production.[20]

China's high-speed industrialization transformed the living conditions of hundreds of millions of people. In 1978, when reform began, 82 percent of Chinese lived in rural areas, often under very difficult circumstances. The rural population peaked around 1991, then began to fall as new factories drew migrants from distant villages. Cities were home to half the population by 2010. Life expectancy at birth, sixty-six years at the start of reform, reached seventy-five years three decades later, and the infant mortality rate fell by three-quarters. Sewerage service and piped drinking water spread through both rural and urban areas. One household in five hundred had a telephone in 1978; by 2010, mobile phones were ubiquitous. Income per person, adjusted for purchasing power, was fifteen times higher, and so many people had money to spend that China became the largest automobile market in the world. Never had so many people moved from poverty to prosperity so quickly.

12

Capturing Value

IN AN OFFICE PARK in Silicon Valley, a team of engineers designed a smartphone. Working with them, linked by computer, instant messaging, and video, was a team of colleagues at research centers in Europe and Asia. When the design was complete, the researchers' employer, based in the United States, transferred ownership to its subsidiary in Ireland for a nominal fee. The Irish entity licensed the design to a Taiwanese-owned manufacturer in China, which ordered displays from Japan, processor chips from South Korea, cameras from Germany, and headphones from the United States. The Chinese plant then assembled the components as directed and returned the finished products to the Silicon Valley company that designed them, which marketed them under its own brand name in many countries.

Now, consider the question: Where were the phones made?

Until the late 1980s, the "where" question was an easy one to answer. Most manufactured goods were made by the firm whose employees designed them, in the firm's own factories, mainly with components produced in-house or close by. Although Silicon Valley's high-tech manufacturers began outsourcing the decidedly low-tech jobs of soldering circuit boards and assembling computers in the 1980s, the work was almost always handed out to small firms located nearby; even when a firm like Seagate Technology decided that manufacturing computer hard drives in a low-wage country would be cheaper, it did the work in its own factory in Singapore. Similarly, when shoppers were choosing among Nikon, Kodak, and Leica, they were also choosing among cameras that were designed and manufactured almost entirely in Japan, the United States, and Germany. The flow of trade was simple to calculate: a Leica shipped to a French distributor from the German factory was registered as a French merchandise import and a German merchandise export.

What distinguished the Third Globalization, more than anything else, was a change in that equation. During the two earlier periods when the economic barriers among countries seemed to be dissolving, the forty years or so before World War One and the four decades after World War Two, trade and investment had been measured as the work of nations. The annual merchandise trade deficit or surplus and the extent to which one country's citizens owned assets in other countries were often taken as measures of economic success. Firms were thought of as citizens much as individuals were citizens, and when a firm did well, its home country was assumed to benefit.

Starting in the second half of the 1980s, international economic relations took on a very different character. Manufacturers and retailers spread their supply chains far and wide. Thanks to containerships and airfreight, the company that designed the smartphone could specify antennas, GPS receivers, and plastic cases made wherever the price was best or the quality highest and have them transported to the assembly plant at very little cost. A merchandise export and import were registered each time one of those components crossed a national boundary and then again when the assembly plant shipped the completed phone abroad, meaning that trade in communications equipment mushroomed. Equally confounding, inputs without physical form—the designs of the entire telephone and of the individual semiconductors inside it, the various pieces of software that let the phone send text messages and take photographs—were responsible for a large part of the phone's value. While the finished smartphone counted as a merchandise export, a lot of what made it valuable was not merchandise. Indeed, the series of transactions that went into its making was less a supply chain than a value chain.

The difference between a supply chain and a value chain was more than simply nomenclature. Supply chains mainly involved two sorts of business relationships: investment, in which a firm built or bought assets—factories, plantations, entire companies—to have control over critical inputs; and trade, in which it purchased goods or services from other firms in arm's-length transactions, international or domestic. A company's international trade was directly related to its investment in other countries; a US apparel company might export cotton fabric to an affiliated sewing plant in Central America, then send the finished cotton blouses back to the United States for sale. The stereotypical multinational company during the years of the Second Globalization, from the late 1940s to the late 1980s, operated its own factories, mines, or power plants in the countries where it wanted to do business. Perhaps it purchased some supplies from local vendors, but the production technology and the key inputs came from its own facilities back home.

Value chains, in contrast, are likely to entail more complex links among firms: licensing arrangements, joint ventures, research collaborations, long-term strategic partnerships, investments in which one firm holds a small ownership interest in another. There is no need for a manufacturer to own its own factory or an airline to own its own jets; many firms in both industries focus on only certain aspects of their business—designing and marketing a novel product, creating a unique experience for air travelers—and leave everything else to be handled by other firms under contract. Whether a company holds or avoids ownership stakes in other firms in its value chain is a matter of its business strategy: a 2019 study found that some leading international apparel and footwear firms had as many as twenty-five relationships with other entities per billion dollars of sales, while others had almost none. Very few of these relationships centered around producing goods; as the authors explained, when production involves relatively low-value tasks such as assembly, the firm that has organized the value chain is likely to purchase the product from an outside entity rather than investing in the producer or forming a joint venture.[1]

The great economic benefit of value chains is specialization. A tractor manufacturer can devote its efforts to designing, assembling, and marketing tractors and advising farmers on their use. Making tractor engines requires different technical skills and production knowledge than assembling tractors, so the tractor manufacturer might be better off purchasing engines from experts rather than trying to design and build them itself. The engine manufacturer, in turn, might find it sensible to rely on metalworking firms whose expertise lies in camshafts—and there is no reason why the camshaft factory would want to make its own steel. Each firm in the chain can hold down costs by making a particular type of product in large quantities for the global market rather than producing a range of tractor parts at smaller scale.

Much of the value in manufacturers' value chains, though, did not come from stamping metal or assembling components on a factory floor. Each firm in the tractor supply chain employed engineers and hired external engineering consultants to create its products, to identify the best type of steel for the camshafts and the camshaft design that was best for the engine. In the first years of the twenty-first century, as factories became increasingly automated, half the value added in producing manufactured goods came from services. Most of these services were outsourced—purchased from information-technology consultants, logistics contractors, advertising firms, and the like—but by 2015, four out of ten workers employed by manufacturing firms in the wealthy economies were engaged in services, not physical production work.

In a world in which commerce was organized around value chains, traditional thinking about trade no longer made sense. A country that put up tariffs to protect its domestic steel mills was also raising steel costs for domestic camshaft manufacturers. Engine manufacturers would turn away and purchase those critical inputs in countries where steel, and therefore camshaft production, cost less. The engine makers had no choice, for their own customers, tractor manufacturers, could not match competitors' prices if they had to pay extra for engines made with expensive camshafts forged from high-cost steel. Trade barriers affecting any link in this value chain might cause part or all of the chain to shift as each party sought to keep itself competitive in a global market.

These changes played havoc with public understanding of the international economy in the twenty-first century. They redefined what it meant to be an international company; as Samuel Palmisano, then the chief executive of computer giant IBM, acknowledged in 2006, "state borders define less and less the boundaries of corporate thinking or practice." They uprooted the long-standing assumption that trade had to do with where things were made or grown; services, it turned out, could be shipped across borders as readily as goods, and workers who audited purchase orders or processed insurance claims were as vulnerable to their work being transferred abroad as knitters in a sock factory or assemblers in a motorcycle plant. And the spread of value chains meant that the conventional statistics about exports, imports, trade surpluses, and trade deficits revealed very little about how economies were performing, or about how different countries' economies related to one another, or about workers' living standards and their communities' prosperity.[2]

———

When David Ricardo laid out his theory of comparative advantage in 1817, he used English exports of cloth to Portugal and Portuguese wine exports to England to illustrate why trade made both countries better off. English cloth was presumed to be the product of English capital and English labor, just as Portuguese capital and Portuguese labor created wine. For Ricardo, as for the mercantilists whose ideas he rejected, trade was something a *country* engaged in. The fact that most imports and exports arose from transactions between private parties in the two countries was not relevant to his analysis. Economists continued to view trade through that lens for most of the next two centuries. Even when twentieth-century petroleum companies took control of every stage of their businesses, from wells to tanker ships to gasoline stations oceans away from where the oil was pumped, there was no question about where their black gold was lifted from the ground and where it was refined.

With the arrival of international value chains, though, trade became a subject that concerned firms more than countries. During the 2010s, the two hungry assembly lines at Honda Motor Company's plant in Swindon, in England, consumed the contents of ten thousand containers during every shift, with three-quarters of the components coming from parts plants strewn across Europe—plants which, in many cases, relied on other parts imported from some other place. One Swindon model exported to the United States, a version of the Honda Civic, was said to contain 20 percent British content, 20 percent Japanese, and 20 percent North American, along with a transmission made in India. To call it a Japanese car would have been a serious misstatement.[3]

It was businesses, mainly very large businesses, that organized value chains, in which smaller firms were mere links. It was these firms, most of them based in Northern Europe, North America, Japan, Korea, or China, that made the decisions about where to produce each component and each final product, where to buy each service, what to import into this country and to export from that one, and when to do business with an outside firm rather than investing directly to build a factory, buy a distributor, or a merge with a customer. Very often, firms' choices about where to add value to their products had little relationship to the inherent advantages and disadvantages of particular countries or cities. Thanks to container shipping and airfreight, proximity to ports, a major attraction for manufacturers in the 1950s, mattered little. Few twenty-first-century industries found it essential to have wheat fields, mines, or natural gas pipelines nearby, and education levels rose so quickly in so many countries that skilled workers could be found even in poor economies. When companies in the headquarters countries decided how to lay out their value chains, government support was often decisive in determining who made what where.

Only a very small percentage of companies were truly global. The top 1 percent of firms controlled 82 percent of US foreign trade in 2007—fifteen times the share of the 1 percent of firms immediately beneath them. These large-scale traders typically dealt in dozens of different products, importing directly from eighteen countries—often from firms that themselves had imported inputs to their goods—and exporting to thirty-one. Their global scale helped them be more productive than other firms, which made it easier for them to expand even more. The role of the biggest firms in other countries' trade was similar. A study of Canadian manufacturers added a tantalizing detail: firms that had been part of global value chains but then ceased to import, ceased to export, or both saw their productivity drop immediately. For a successful business that hoped to grow and increase its profits, there was no alternative to globalization.[4]

Ricardo and generations of economists who followed him held that countries had comparative advantages that should cause them to export some products and import others. But as value chains spread, global corporations became powerful enough to create comparative advantage where none was obvious. When, for example, Intel Corporation announced in 1996 that it would assemble and test microprocessors in Costa Rica, its decision was based on favorable tax and tariff laws, a "probusiness environment" that was not welcoming to labor unions, and a desire to place its factories in diverse locations. Nothing about the Central American country was uniquely suited to making semiconductors. Intel soon accounted for one-fifth of Costa Rica's exports, and its presence created a technically sophisticated labor force. By 2014, when Intel moved microprocessor assembly to Asia, there were enough Costa Rican engineers to staff the Intel engineering and design center that took its place. In effect, Intel's large investment in microprocessor assembly gave the country a comparative advantage in electronics manufacturing it had not previously possessed.[5]

The amount exported from any of the countries in a firm's value chain reveals little about those countries' economies, because those exports contain content, whether parts or ideas, that originates elsewhere. The numbers that matter economically concern not exports, but value added. Value added is a simple enough concept: if a firm buys $8 worth of inputs and turns them into a product that it sells for $11, it has added $3 in value, which shows up in some combination of profits, employee compensation, and tax payments. But when applied to the globalized economy, value added gets harder to trace. The fact that the firm has created value does not reveal where that value was created nor how that value creation has affected workers or particular communities.

————

The smartphone discussed at the start of this chapter was the iPhone 3G sold by Apple Inc. In 2009, this item cost an estimated $178.96 to manufacture. Of that amount, only $6.50—3.6 percent of the manufacturing cost—went to the Chinese factory that assembled the product. The remaining $172.46 went largely to various Japanese, German, Korean, and American firms that supplied the phone's components. Unfortunately, the search for the sources of value ends there, for published information does not reveal whether the German firm that produced the phone's camera module or the Japanese company that made the touchscreen used foreign suppliers of its own.[6]

Consider how the iPhone 3G's complicated supply arrangements registered in merchandise trade statistics. China exported approximately $2 billion of the phones to the United States in 2009. Apple, on the other hand, exported no goods directly from the United States to China, and other US-made components shipped to the iPhone manufacturing plant were worth only $100 million or so. Thus, if either country had published official statistics covering trade in iPhone 3Gs, they would have shown China to have a $1.9 billion trade surplus with the United States. Yet in reality, the US-China relationship in iPhones tilted in the other direction. The total value that was added in China to all the iPhone 3Gs shipped to the United States in 2009, at $6.50 per phone, came to about $73 million, or less than the value of the US-made components shipped to China. Almost ten times as much of the phone's value originated in Japan as in China, but when those iPhones were shipped from China to the United States, they did not affect the official US trade deficit with Japan at all.[7]

There's more. In 2009, iPhone 3Gs retailed in the United States for $500. The total cost of all the physical content, from the semiconductors to the camera to the antennas to the assembly work, plus the software needed to run the phone, came to barely one-third of the selling price. The other two-thirds—$321 per phone—was collected by Apple, the factoryless manufacturer. Some of it paid for the salaries of the engineers and designers who developed the product. Another large chunk went for advertising. Retailers, including Apple's company-owned stores as well as independent shops, took a cut, and a small bit covered the cost of transporting the finished phones from China to the United States. The rest, probably about $95 per phone, was Apple's profit. That profit included compensation for the value of the company's designs and brand as well as a return on shareholders' investment in Apple's business. In sum, the iPhone's $500 selling price had very little to do with the cost of physically manufacturing the product and a great deal to do with the value of the intellectual property used to design, package, and market it.[8]

This brief exercise in arithmetic reveals several important ways in which global value chains changed the calculus of trade. The bilateral merchandise trade balance in iPhones was meaningless; although the phone registered as an export from China, any American who bought an iPhone 3G in 2009 purchased far more from Japan and Germany than from China. Attempting to calculate the balance of trade in services related to the iPhone was equally futile. Apple's design team may well have included engineers in other countries whose services were imported to Apple's California research center via the internet, but if they were all Apple employees, there might have been no cross-border transactions that would register in the official trade statistics. The company had no reason to care what percentage of the total cost of developing the iPhone was added by its engineers in India or Ireland, and government data collectors likely will never know.

There is one other fact worth noting. As the iPhone 3G became more popular in the United States, the US merchandise trade deficit in iPhones grew steadily larger, even though the majority of the money from each sale flowed into Apple's coffers. Apple's activities generated no US exports and provided no jobs for production workers in US electronics factories, but they did create employment for engineering, marketing, finance, and sales workers whose jobs, on the surface, had nothing to do with international trade. An unknown number of these individuals were employed by firms other than Apple. Value added in 2009, as measured by Apple, had no relationship to the value added by any country's economy.

———

"The World Is Flat," Thomas Friedman's best-selling book about globalization argued in 2004. In some ways, the world did become flat in the early years of the twentieth century: thanks to the internet, it became cost-effective for call-center workers in Manila and Mumbai to handle phone calls from bank customers in Manchester and Memphis, and anyone with a brilliant idea, a tempting offer, or a cute kitten was able to inform the entire world immediately at negligible expense. But when it came to the stuff of globalization, the goods and services that people produce and consume, the world did not flatten out nearly so much as widely believed. On close examination, the flow of trade moving through twentieth-century value chains turned out to be quite lumpy.

There is no question that long-distance value chains burgeoned. The initial reason was generally labor costs. Big industrial complexes were hard to manage and vulnerable to labor disruption, as a work stoppage at a single location could cripple an entire company. As transport and communications costs fell, companies sought out sites for smaller, more specialized plants, which often were located in places where unions were weaker and labor costs lower. Outsourcing—buying components from other firms rather than making them internally—could bring cost savings as well, but it also allowed a manufacturer to focus on its strengths and call on specialists to meet its other needs. This is why Apple purchased the iPhone 3G's semiconductors and antennas from other companies rather than making them itself. Outsourcing also made it possible for smaller companies to compete in a globalized economy by enabling them to ramp up quickly: instead of trying to raise the capital to build their own factories, they could contract with other manufacturers to do the actual work of physical production.

Most manufacturers, though, never made the leap from a domestic value chain to a global one. In the early 2000s, about 90 percent of manufactured goods moved from the factory directly to domestic customers, not foreign buyers. In other words, a typical factory producing goods for export drew mainly on domestic suppliers, relying on foreign sources mainly for advanced components. The American economist Teresa C. Fort found that the US factories that organized international value chains to provide their inputs were the most efficient, productive factories. Only they possessed the computer-aided design and manufacturing systems and the advanced communications technology to coordinate shipments across a complex cross-border production network. The same was true elsewhere. Indeed, maximizing domestic value added may be counterproductive: if a domestic good or service costs more than a foreign alternative or has lower quality, a firm that tries to add more value in its home country can make itself less competitive abroad.

As the economist Richard Baldwin has pointed out, most of the "factory economies" that provided cheap labor were linked to a single "headquarter economy," where the far better paid work of developing products and organizing production networks took place.[9] It was these networks that instigated the massive increase in global merchandise trade. Often, the value chain began with raw materials. The United States shipped millions of bales of cotton to feed Asia's textile mills, and bulk ships brought iron ore from Brazil and Australia to China and South Korea to be turned into iron, from iron into steel, and from steel into basic industrial goods such as fan housings and pistons. Those sorts of intermediate goods, not finished products for consumers, were what filled most of the shipping containers clogging the world's ports: the Chinese housings might have ended up in fans assembled in Japan, and the Korean pistons could have been shipped to a factory making automobile engines in the United States. All told, intermediate goods represented about 55 percent of the total value of manufactured imports around the world in the early 2000s. In some industries—electronics, transport equipment, chemicals—global value chains were critical, in other industries considerably less so.[10]

But for all the talk of globalization, manufacturing in the early twenty-first century was not as global as the term suggests. Back in 1986, when global supply chains were just taking shape, four countries—the United States, Japan, Germany, and the Soviet Union—were responsible for 58 percent of all factory production. A quarter-century later, China had emerged as the largest manufacturing nation and the Soviet Union had disintegrated, but it was still the case that four countries—now, China, the United States, Japan, and Germany—churned out 55 percent of the world's factory output. More than half the world's trade in intermediate goods moved within the European Union or between it and its immediate neighbors. A handful of other countries, notably Korea and India, had become manufacturing powerhouses, and there were a few other countries that industrialized quickly: Vietnam's exports rose twenty times over between 1990 and 2010, adjusted for inflation, and Indonesia's increased fourfold, as both became important suppliers of clothing and footwear. In many other countries, however, manufacturing failed to prosper. Most developing countries had little role in global value chains. With power cuts common and truck transport slow, they could not produce even simple household items—plastic buckets, flashlights—for less than it cost to import them from China. They could not develop the way Korea, Taiwan, and China did, using their abundant labor to make clothing and shoes as the first step on the ladder of industrialization.[11]

Some of them turned to exports of agricultural products—Mexican avocados, Kenyan flowers, Indonesian mangos. World trade in agricultural products grew five and a half times between 1985 and 2017, and in many developing countries industrial agriculture, built to provide large quantities of products cultivated to rich-country standards for export to rich-country supermarkets, sprang up alongside traditional farming. But industrial agriculture could not provide the large numbers of jobs once offered by factories, much less employ all the peasant farmers displaced as traditional farming was squeezed out. Often, the host countries added little value to the growing process beyond sun and cheap labor. And even when it came to a labor-intensive activity such as picking vegetables, a sizeable share of the growth in exports was captured by wealthy countries (with the help of immigrant workers). In 2010, the eight leading exporters of vegetables included the United States, the Netherlands, Spain, Canada, and France.

In many industries, trade patterns developed more along regional than global lines during the Third Globalization. In Europe, for example, Germany remained the number one location for assembling cars, but a large and growing share of the parts used in German-made cars came from lower-wage countries to the east. Japanese and Korean auto manufacturers relied heavily on China for the simplest parts, and NAFTA helped fuse US, Canadian, and Mexican auto plants into a regional network within which parts, assembled engines, and finished vehicles routinely moved across borders. Owing to their geographic locations, their high transport costs, or their unwelcoming economic policies, some countries with significant industrial sectors, notably Brazil and South Africa, were less attractive to manufacturers setting up international production networks and saw their manufacturing atrophy.

PART IV

Global Fears

13

Giants Afloat

THE INCORPORATION of Asian countries into global value chains generated a boom in maritime trade. Between 1994 and 2003, the number of containers moving between Asia and North America rose an average of nearly 9 percent per year. Demand to move goods between Asia and Europe, the most heavily trafficked shipping route, grew even faster as the Southeast Asian countries rebounded from an economic crisis in 1997 and as India, the world's second-most populous country, abandoned its long-standing policy of economic isolation. In just three years, between 2001 and 2004, India's exports more than doubled.

But to the maritime industry, it was China's emergence as the world's workshop that mattered most. Chinese factories were closely tied into global production networks that placed heavy demands on freight transportation. More factory production meant more imports of commodities, whether ore arriving in bulk ships, chemicals in tankers, or plastics aboard containerships. Although its domestic market was enormous, about one-fourth of China's manufacturing output was exported by sea over long distances to customers in Europe and the Americas. And much of what China exported eventually returned in the form of recycled materials like waste paper and used electronics, which were shipped to China for reprocessing because China-bound containerships were often half empty, encouraging carriers to offer rock-bottom rates to attract low-value cargo. As a maritime consultant observed, "The importance of shipping to China can hardly be overstated."

International trade involved substantially more transportation than ever in the past.[1]

———

The Asian export boom of the 1990s had presented Maersk Line, the largest container-shipping company, with golden opportunities. Maersk had ridden the tide of globalization like few other firms, capturing the largest share of trade between Europe and Asia and across the Pacific. In 1999, it had lengthened its lead by acquiring the South African line Safmarine and Malcom McLean's old company, Sea-Land, adding 120 vessels to its fleet and becoming a major operator of the port terminals where giant cranes moved containers on and off the ships. By 2003, Maersk owned 280 box ships, ran terminals in thirty ports, and even owned two factories that made shipping containers. Its fleet was operating near capacity, and profits were good.[2]

The ship line's managers projected smooth sailing ahead for the shipping industry as a whole. But in the early months of 2003, their worry was that Maersk might not be able to take part. Without new ships, Maersk would be left watching as its competitors expanded. If that were to occur, management feared, Maersk would lose market share, ending up with higher costs per container than its competitors and therefore with lower earnings per box. On the other hand, if Maersk could lay hands on new vessels, its planners estimated, it would be able to boost its traffic by more than one-fourth by 2008, moving an additional eight thousand forty-foot containers across the Pacific and seven thousand more through the Suez Canal each week. In Maersk's white-and-blue headquarters on the waterfront in Copenhagen, addressing the capacity shortfall was seen as a critical problem.[3]

On June 18, 2003, the ship line's boss created a secret committee to draft a proposal for building new ships. "You should particularly consider in your work that it is in our company interest to be ahead of competition with our tonnage and include features which decisively bring advantages for our liner business versus competition—preferably innovative features which could be patented," the fifteen members were instructed in a confidential memorandum. The committee was meant to hurry: its final proposal was to be ready for the partners—the top executives of A. P. Møller-Maersk, the ship line's parent company—in less than three months.

The committee came up with two solutions, one for each of the ship line's main markets. For the China–United States route, it proposed a small, fast vessel designed to race from the port of Yantian through the Panama Canal to Newark in less than three weeks. At a speed of nearly thirty knots,* these ships would move China's exports to the US Northeast faster than the usual alternatives, which involved either a slow all-water voyage through the Panama Canal or a faster ocean shipment to California or British Columbia coupled with a week-long train ride across North America. Cargo owners were typically very price sensitive when it came to shipping, but the committee thought a small subset of customers, fashion and toy companies, might pay a premium to get their Chinese-made goods to market a few days sooner. Maersk commissioned seven of the fast ships for delivery starting in 2006. They were a commercial disaster. Their high-speed engines guzzled fuel, and when oil prices rose, the vessels became too costly to operate. By 2010, all seven vessels, some straight from the shipyard, were tied together in a Scottish loch, forming a raft used as a set for a children's adventure television show.[4]

The committee's other idea, a concept known as Euromax, would prove more durable. The Euromax was envisioned as a revolutionary vessel. The size of new containerships had increased gradually over the years, but the Euromax was to represent a quantum leap in capacity. It should be a quarter-mile in length, the committee thought, longer than four American football fields. It should hold eighteen to twenty-two containers abreast on its deck, twice as many as the biggest ships in service at the time. Boxes should be stacked nine or ten high in its holds. When fully loaded, its keel should lie fourteen meters—forty-six feet—beneath the water line. And the committee proposed the unique design features Maersk's management had requested. The ship would be driven

*Approximately 55 kilometers or 34 miles per hour.

by a single huge propeller instead of the two smaller ones that normally powered large containerships. The propeller would be turned by a monstrous engine, weighing 2,300 tons, with the exhaust recycled back into the engine for reuse. These innovations would allow the fully loaded ship to steam at a brisk speed of 25.2 to 27.1 knots while burning less fuel per container and emitting fewer pollutants than other ships.

Such a vessel, the committee understood, would have limitations. Its size would make it more complicated to load and unload than smaller ships; a quarter of each forty-seven-day loop would be spent in ports, discharging and taking on boxes, rather than steaming. It needed too much water to call at such major ports as New York, Hamburg, and Nagoya. It was inflexible, useful only on the Asia–Europe loop; it would not fit through the Panama Canal, and it was too large for Maersk's routes across the Pacific. If it were to require repairs, only a handful of shipyards around the world had dry docks capacious enough to do the work. But the Euromax would give Maersk the capacity it so badly needed, allowing it to gain market share and recapture its status as the most profitable ship line.

Maersk's shipyard at Odense, two hours by train west of Copenhagen, analyzed ten different design options for the new ship. It picked one for further testing at the Maritime Institute of the Netherlands. A venerable research center in the tranquil university town of Wageningen, sixty miles from the sea, MARIN specialized in crafting scale models of ships in design, detailed enough to capture the precise shape of the bow and the curvature of the propeller blades, and sailing them back and forth in long tanks filled with salt water. An assemblage of instruments and sensors, mounted on a gantry that traveled the length of a tank above the model, allowed MARIN's engineers to measure performance in different wind and wave conditions and to predict whether heavy or light loadings would cause stability problems or create unwanted stresses. MARIN had never encountered a ship design like the Euromax, and it warned Maersk that "given the limited statistical data . . . for this type of ship, the accuracy may be less good compared to other cases." But its tests confirmed what Maersk most wanted to know: the Euromax would be very fuel-efficient if Maersk were willing to sail it a bit more slowly than the committee proposed.

All signals were go. Maersk's planners calculated that eight such vessels, sailing at a top speed of twenty-four knots, would support weekly service from southern China to Hong Kong and Malaysia, through the Suez Canal to Spain, on to northern Europe, and then back to China. All told, they estimated, an average of 44,001 forty-foot containers would be moved on and off each time a ship traveled the loop. The crew, as few as thirteen seafarers, would be no more than required aboard a smaller vessel. Counting construction and operating expenses, a single container slot aboard the new ships would cost 18 percent less than on the biggest ships then in Maersk's fleet.

Maersk projected the vessels would sail 90 percent full on the westbound leg, 56 percent full from Europe to Asia—but even if the world economy turned sour or international trade slowed, they would be highly profitable, paying for themselves in just eight and a half years. "Major slot cost advantages—difficult to match for competition," Maersk's top executives, known as managing partners, were told in November 2003. It was not hard to convince them. The partners agreed to spend an unprecedented $1.24 billion for eight ships, to be delivered from 2006 through 2008. One reason for their haste was that the European Union was cracking down on shipbuilding subsidies: it would allow the Danish government to pick up 6 percent of the cost only for vessels delivered by March 2007.

Maersk dropped hints in the press that big vessels were coming, but it kept the details under wraps by building the Euromax at the company-owned shipyard in Odense. While the first ships were under construction, in 2005, the company announced another blockbuster merger, purchasing the third-largest ship line, P&O Nedlloyd—itself the result of a union between British and Dutch lines—for $2.8 billion. Combining the companies gave Maersk around one-sixth of the container-shipping market worldwide, making it far and away the largest player. Maersk hinted that it hoped its commanding market share and its highly efficient new ships would drive smaller ship lines to join forces or close up shop, making it easier to avoid overbuilding and control the rate wars that periodically roiled the industry. In case competitors did not get the message, a Maersk executive issued a veiled warning: "We just see the need for industry consolidation."[5]

———

The capacity of a containership is measured in twenty-foot equivalent units (TEU), with a standard truck-sized container, forty feet long, registering as 2 TEU. When *Emma Maersk*, the first of the Euromax vessels, entered service in August 2006, her capacity was announced as 11,000 TEU, equal to the amount that could be transported by 5,500 trucks. This was an impressive figure, one-fifth more than any other containership could carry. But Maersk Line was calculating capacity in its own unique way. It soon told a leading shipping publication that *Emma* could carry 12,504 TEU. The publication guessed that the real size was 13,400. Eventually, Maersk revealed that the ship's true capacity, as measured by the standards employed by the rest of the shipping industry, was around 15,500 TEU. In other words, *Emma* was half again as large as any vessel in service or on order at the time she was launched. The entire maritime industry was stunned by her size. As one admiring headline put it, "Emma Maersk may be as big as a container ship can get."[6]

That turned out not to be the case.

Emma's size and her fuel efficiency threatened to give Maersk Line an intolerable cost advantage on the longest, most profitable routes. Other ship lines, whose leaders had no intention of playing second fiddle to the Danes, felt obliged to order large ships of their own, and then still larger ones, and bought up struggling competitors to obtain yet more. "Almost every week there are reports of new docks, new facilities, and even entire yards springing out in Asia," the shipping magazine *Fairplay* reported in September 2005.

In a single month alone, five Asian shipyards unveiled expansion plans. By the end of 2007, sixteen months after *Emma*'s launch, shipowners had ordered 118 container vessels with the capacity to carry 10,000 TEU or more. Two years earlier, except for the Euromax vessels, there had been none. The seeming advantages of scale transfixed everyone, and low interest rates and generous subsidies from governments eager to keep shipyards working made it possible to build ships at extremely attractive prices. What's more, while larger vessels placed greater demands on landside infrastructure and on ocean harbors, requiring bigger cranes, additional terminal gates, more highway connections, and expensive dredging to create wider and deeper channels from open ocean all the way to the dock, ship lines considered none of these costs when ordering new vessels. There was, in effect, no reason not to buy new ships. The world's merchant fleet was reshaped almost overnight. By 2010, it would be able to move half again as many boxes as in 2006, at much lower cost per box.[7]

In Copenhagen, Maersk executives began to have second thoughts about the shipping arms race they had triggered. A well-known Hamburg ship manager, which typically built vessels only when ship lines made rock-solid commitments to charter them, made known that it was ordering 13,000-TEU ships from Korean yards without charter contracts in place, and that it was planning ships even larger than *Emma Maersk*. "This is in my view very bad news," the head of Maersk Line wrote a colleague in April 2007. "I think we should use every opportunity to voice our view that this is indeed bad for industry to have such speculative overcapacity coming to market."

But the benefits promised by the Euromax's planners proved elusive. Maersk's 2005 purchase of P&O Nedlloyd went badly, its market share shrinking as customers fumed about delayed shipments and incompatible computer systems. Higher oil prices turned Maersk's one-year contracts with manufacturers and retailers to carry containers between Asia and North America into money losers. While most of its major competitors were profitable in 2006, Maersk Line lost $45 on every container it carried. To cut costs, Maersk slowed down its vessels to burn less oil. As a result, the new Euromax ships, fresh from the shipyard, were not sailing at the speeds for which they had been designed—and because slow steaming meant that ships took an extra week to sail an Asia–Europe–Asia circuit, Maersk could no longer provide the once-a-week sailings it had promised its customers in every port. "Do customers really want (i.e., willing to pay) for the on time services?" an internal memo asked plaintively. Other ship lines slowed their vessels as well, but Maersk's reputation for offering more reliable service than its competitors was tarnished.[8]

No one cared more about that reputation than Arnold Maersk Mc-Kinney Møller. At the age of ninety-three, Møller no longer oversaw the day-to-day affairs of the A. P. Møller-Maersk holding company or the ship line it owned. But as the son and grandson of the ship captains who had founded the business in 1904, he controlled most of the holding company's shares and was not shy about expressing his views. He was said to have opposed the purchase of P&O Nedlloyd in 2005. By the spring of 2007 he was complaining that the ship line was losing its way. Maersk Line, he complained, had become bureaucratic. It had too many initiatives underway, and no one knew the priorities. Møller admired Mediterranean Shipping Company, a family-owned firm in Geneva that had become the second-largest container carrier. Many at Maersk looked down upon it as a low-brow competitor, but Møller praised its lean, decisive management. Maersk Line, he said, "needs to set a few priorities and deal with the clear fact that our 'administration/overhead/running the business' costs no doubt are much higher than any of our competitors."

Maersk Line's managers, projecting 9 percent growth in container traffic in 2008 and 11 percent the following year, wanted to order more large containerships so the company could maintain its market share. Møller objected; he wanted profits instead. By the middle of 2007, three top executives responsible for the P&O Nedlloyd fiasco were gone. Maersk Line, for the moment, would focus on increasing returns for shareholders, not on increasing capacity.

Management changes could not alter the fact that the Euromax had fundamentally changed the shipping industry in a dangerous way. Since the onset of international container shipping in 1966, business had fluctuated with the growth of the world economy, and over time many ship lines exited the business because their investors couldn't stomach the ups and downs. But with the launch of *Emma Maersk* and the giant vessels that followed her, volatility took on a whole new meaning. Each new vessel easing down a slipway brought more capacity into the market than two or three of the older ships it replaced. It came with a very large mortgage that had to be serviced regardless of the ship's success in generating revenue. If international trade continued to grow strongly, as it had for two decades, Maersk and its leading competitors would be able to cope. But if the growth of trade were to taper off, the consequences for the shipping industry were likely to be deadly.

14

Risks Unmeasured

ON SEPTEMBER 29, 2002, every port along the Pacific coast of the United States fell quiet. From San Diego to Seattle and north to Alaska, the Pacific Maritime Association, representing ship lines and ocean terminals, locked out 10,500 members of the International Longshore and Warehouse Union from their jobs on the docks. The association claimed the union caused the dispute by loading and unloading ships at a glacial pace. The union blamed the employers for trying to introduce technology that would eliminate waterfront jobs. Within a day, more than a hundred containerships were stranded at the dock or anchored offshore, laden with merchandise for the upcoming Christmas holiday season.

Panic ensued. "I've got onions everywhere," lamented an Oregon produce handler whose exports were stuck on the docks. Honda Motor Company suspended production at three North American assembly plants for lack of imported components, and Injex Industries, a maker of plastic parts for the interiors of Toyota cars, laid off workers at its plant near Los Angeles. John Paul Richard, an apparel manufacturer, reported 120,000 pieces of women's clothing marooned outside Los Angeles harbor, and 3,400 metric tons of New Zealand lumber could not be unloaded from a vessel tied up at Sacramento. By October 10, when President George W. Bush ordered the docks reopened, some 220 oceangoing ships filled with import cargo were bobbing idly on the waves, and railroad trains with no freight to move sat motionless on tracks across the western states. Untangling the mess and getting the cargo where it was meant to be was a matter of weeks, not days.[1]

Tallied at the national level, the economic damage from the lockout was minor both for Asian countries and the United States. For many companies, on the other hand, the costs stung. The Gap, an apparel retailer, warned investors of lower earnings after 25 percent of the clothes intended for holiday promotions were caught in transit. Linksys, an electronics company, had to delay the introduction of a new switch to connect computer networks because of undelivered parts. Even Walmart Stores, the largest single importer into the United States, suffered losses. Dozens of US retailers resorted to airfreight to get Chinese-made toys on to their shelves in time for the Christmas selling season. They paid a high price—many times the cost of shipping by sea—for misjudging the risks of long-distance supply chains.[2]

———

Any business faces risks, and supply chains inherently pose risks aplenty: fire might strike the plant of a key supplier; a problematic lock on a river might block shipments of an essential raw material; a gasoline shortage might make it difficult for production workers to reach their jobs. Once, manufacturers managed this risk by controlling their supply chains directly. The exemplar, Ford Motor Company, owned forests, mines, and a rubber plantation; transported raw materials to its factories on a company-owned railroad; and built blast furnaces, a foundry, a steel rolling mill, a glass factory, a tire plant, and even a textile plant at its vast River Rouge complex near Detroit, where sand, iron ore, and raw rubber were transformed into auto parts and assembled into Model A cars. Controlling almost every part of its production process—vertical integration, economists call it—allowed Ford to ensure that its assembly plants had the parts they needed to keep churning out cars. By 1929, more than a hundred thousand workers were employed at the Rouge.[3]

Vertical integration, of course, created risks of its own. Huge manufacturing complexes like the Rouge, which covered 1.7 square miles of land, were difficult to manage. With so much production in one place, a strike, a flood, or a blizzard could cripple the entire company. Even if a manufacturer replaced one huge factory complex with several smaller ones, vertical integration had major downsides. Sourcing every part in-house might be more expensive than buying from outside suppliers. A vertically integrated firm making thousands of diverse products might be slower to advance new ideas than a supplier focusing on a particular niche such as fan motors or ski bindings. Perhaps most important for companies whose shares traded on stock markets, vertical integration fell into disfavor in the 1980s among investors who insisted companies should avoid tying up capital in buildings, research labs, land, and machinery. The path to greater profit, they insisted, was to become "asset-light."

For many companies, becoming asset-light involved "outsourcing." The idea that a firm would contract out important work to other firms was not new; in fashion capitals like New York and Paris, famous garment makers had long relied on contractors to help fill orders at peak times, and electronics companies in Japan and the United States had been outsourcing production of circuit boards to Hong Kong and South Korea since the 1960s. Producing semiconductors required highly specialized factories and equipment, and makers of computers and other electronic gear generally purchased chips rather than running their own semiconductor fabs; a shortage of memory chips from Japan delayed the launch of the first Apple computer with a color screen in 1988. By then, many televisions sold with big-name labels were assembled in South Korea by little-known companies such as Samsung and Lucky Goldstar. The main risk of outsourcing, as the electronics giants saw it, was that contractors would learn the secrets of their businesses and steal away their customers.[4]

As freight transportation became more reliable and less burdensome while tariffs on imports faded away, differences in production costs came to dominate companies' decisions about where to make their goods. Two factors in particular loomed large by the final years of the twentieth century. One was wages: the gap between the pay of factory workers in China, Mexico, or Turkey and those in Europe, Japan, or North America yawned so wide that even if the low-wage workers accomplished far less in an hour of work, producing abroad rather than at home made financial sense. The other draw was economies of scale.

Where an automaker's parts division would likely make headlights only for the parent company's cars, a headlight specialist could sell to many automakers, producing at enormous volume and, by spreading its administrative and engineering costs more widely, lowering the cost of making each unit.

These basic financial considerations—finding the least costly way to make and deliver the goods—drove decisions about organizing value chains. Once, foreign investment had been intimately related to exporting and importing, but that was no longer the case; with outsourcing, there was no need for the company at the top of the chain, the one that put its brand on the finished product and sold it to retailers, wholesalers, or end users, to undertake large investments in the countries where it wanted its components or its finished goods produced. Often, it had only a purchasing staff on the ground to visit potential suppliers and sign deals. It could rely entirely on separately owned factories to make the goods it needed and on freight forwarders to negotiate transportation with ship lines, trucking companies, and railroads. Everything from quality standards to confidentiality agreements to the relationships among the various companies in the value chain could be set by contract.

Executives in Europe, North America, Japan, Korea, and Taiwan were transfixed by the savings to be had by shifting production abroad. A study of ten large international manufacturers, wholesalers, and retailers found "a single-minded focus of top management on per-piece cost as the main driver of sourcing decisions" in case after case. "There was a tacit pressure to make the global sourcing decisions look appealing," the study found. "One way to do so was to focus only on purchase and transportation costs." Half the firms studied gave no consideration to the possibility that poor quality, long lead times, late deliveries, empty shelves, and dependence on a single source of critical products could hurt their bottom lines. Hardly any attention was paid to the risks arising from the sheer number of firms that might be involved in any given value chain, each needing to complete its tasks on schedule for the entire chain to function smoothly. Cheap was what mattered.[5]

Whether its inputs were sourced from high-wage countries or low-wage countries, the company at the top often had little insight into its suppliers' suppliers, several links down the chain. Such blindness proved costly for the German automaker BMW, which was forced to recall thousands of cars in 2005. The cause was a contaminated coating sold by the US chemical company DuPont to the US auto-parts manufacturer Federal-Mogul, which applied it to tiny metal sockets that were sold for a few cents apiece to Robert Bosch, then the world's largest auto-parts supplier. Bosch installed the sockets in pumps it assembled in Germany and sold to BMW, which used them to regulate the flow of fuel into diesel engines. BMW had no direct relationship with DuPont, but car buyers neither knew nor cared who was at fault. In addition to forcing a three-day shutdown of one of BMW's German auto assembly plants, the problem in a coating factory three links down its value chain led BMW to recall the affected cars, bruising the automaker's reputation.[6]

Two years later, in 2007, an earthquake struck a manufacturing complex in Kashiwazaki, in central Japan, that specialized in piston rings and other steel parts. In earlier years, most automakers had purchased such components from auto-parts companies that they themselves controlled. Since then, many of them had outsourced the work to Riken, an independent company. In order to minimize costs and gain economies of scale, Riken deliberately placed several factories close together. But when the earthquake knocked out water and power to Riken's complex and damaged two of its plants, that strategy backfired. Auto and truck assembly lines across Japan ground to a halt within hours. As the *Wall Street Journal* observed, "For want of a piston ring costing $1.50, nearly 70% of Japan's auto production has been temporarily paralyzed." To get their plants up and running, the automakers were forced to place rush orders for critical parts from the United States, eating into the savings they had enjoyed from embracing lean manufacturing.[7]

––––––––

International businesses were slow to grasp the ways in which their new business model had created new risks. The possibility of interruption had rarely been a factor in sourcing decisions in the 1980s and 1990s, when events such as the chip shortage that delayed Apple's color computer screen were put down to bad luck. After terrorist attacks on the United States in September 2001 led flights to be grounded and trucks carrying car parts from Canada to be inspected more intensely, the ensuing shutdowns of US auto assembly plants were brief. But disruptions with longer-lasting effects, such as the 2002 labor dispute in Pacific coast ports and the 2011 earthquake in Japan, revealed the extent of myopia about supply-chain risk.[8]

Business interruption was far from the only type of risk arising from globalization. Powerful global brands, it turned out, could be a source of vulnerability as well as profit. While corporations that owned such brands often imagined that they were engaging in arms-length transactions with foreign suppliers, consumers held them responsible for labor and environmental conditions throughout their supply chains, many links and many miles distant from the head office. Outsourcing production of athletic shoes to a factory in Indonesia or buying cocoa grown in Ghana through a trading company in Switzerland did not absolve footwear and confectionary companies of responsibility for working conditions and environmental impacts at their suppliers. Even companies that did not deal directly with consumers, such as ship lines and plastics manufacturers, found that their business customers harbored similar expectations. In the internet age, a company's brand could easily be tarnished by allegations of unethical conduct at firms that top executives may never have heard of, and such reputational damage was hard to undo.[9]

And then there was the all-but-forgotten risk of barriers to trade. Global value chains were forged at a time when market forces were in favor. Country after country had lowered import tariffs, eased restrictions on foreign investors, and entered pacts such as NAFTA, which removed barriers to trade within North America, and the Maastricht Treaty, in which the European Community agreed to create a single market that would allow people, goods, and money to move freely across the continent. Many developing countries, which had kept imports and foreign investors at bay, decided to welcome them instead.

But the assumption that international commerce would become steadily less restrained proved incorrect. In 1995, the member countries of the WTO had made only two attempts to restrict imports that were allegedly damaging domestic industries. As protectionist pressures surged in the wealthy economies, there would be nearly four hundred such efforts over the following quarter-century, each one threatening to disrupt firms' value chains by making it infeasible to import one product or another. Some developing countries had second thoughts about freer trade and investment as well. Foreign retailers were all but barred from India, one of the world's fastest-growing economies, to protect domestic shopkeepers. Foreign investors in China were often forced to work with state-owned firms, to use domestic inputs instead of imports, and to share their technology. Seamless trade relationships were no sure thing.[10]

As the evidence of supply-chain risk mounted, investors began demanding that corporate boards pay more attention to sourcing arrangements. Their argument was that the value of their shares might suffer if an obscure supplier in some distant country was discovered to be emitting toxic chemicals or employing under-age children, even if the firm in which they held stock had no direct responsibility for the problem. Large companies established codes of conduct for their suppliers and engaged inspectors to monitor adherence to those standards, even if the companies' constant pressure to keep prices low meant that those promises often were not fulfilled. Annual financial reports, once dominated by tables explicating sales and profits, were expanded to disclose not only reliance on a single supplier or a single country, but also firms' efforts to reduce greenhouse-gas emissions throughout their supply chains and to ensure that no children labored in their suppliers' factories.

———

Addressing supply-chain risk entailed costs. The Great Tohoku Earthquake drove the point home. On March 11, 2011, the most powerful earthquake ever recorded in Japan shook the Tohoku region, a four-hour drive north of Tokyo. It generated a tsunami that sent waves forty meters high crashing into coastal towns, inundating homes six miles inland from the seafront. More than twenty thousand people lost their lives in the catastrophe. Entire cities were rendered uninhabitable, and meltdowns at three nuclear power plants that had been hit by the tsunami led to rolling electricity blackouts across much of Japan, forcing shutdowns of hundreds of auto-industry plants and leading to worldwide shortages of everything from rubber components to pigments for automotive paints. Chrysler and Ford told their US dealers not to order vehicles in certain colors that their paint suppliers could no longer produce. The earthquake cut the size of Japan's economy by 1.2 percentage points, by one estimate, and industrial production in the disaster zone did not recover to the pre-earthquake level for more than a year. Across the Pacific, US manufacturing output dropped noticeably for six months as Japanese companies, lacking parts from Japan, cut back production at their US factories, depriving other firms of orders.[11]

The Tohoku region was the manufacturing base of Renesas Electronics, a company formed when three of Japan's leading electronics companies combined their semiconductor businesses a few years earlier. Renesas was the largest source of semiconductors and microcontrollers for the auto industry. When its plants shut down, auto assembly lines on three continents—once supplied by several different chipmakers— ground to a halt. Losses in the auto industry alone ran into the billions of dollars. After it finally resumed production, Renesas invested in flexibility, reorganizing its plants to ensure that one could quickly start making a particular microcontroller if another was forced offline, while Toyota Motor Corporation, one of its leading customers, compiled a database of parts stored at 650,000 locations so it could lay hands on components needed to keep assembly plants running even if a key parts plant shut down.[12]

Retailers also began paying more attention to making their supply chains flexible. Amazon reorganized its shipping and warehouse networks so that when another dock labor dispute threatened in 2014, it could quickly reroute its imports from China through ports in the eastern United States. As its US sales grew rapidly in 2015, Amazon deliberately began to route two-thirds of its imported items through ports on both the Atlantic and Pacific coasts, reducing its vulnerability to disruption anywhere in its transportation system. Walmart, Amazon's leading competitor and the largest importer of containers into the United States by a considerable margin, built an import distribution center near Houston that was designed to face both west and south: it could receive goods from China—the source of 87 percent of Walmart's imports—via rail from California ports, but also via containers imported aboard vessels passing through the Panama Canal and unloading at the nearby Port of Houston.[13]

Perhaps the most widespread method of making global value chains more reliable was also the costliest: boosting inventories. Inventories are goods that have been produced but have not been sold, whether they reside in the hold of a ship, on a warehouse shelf, on a factory floor, or on a car dealer's lot. Economists treat them as waste, because they tie up money and can lose value as they age. Reducing inventories was one of the main motivations for just-in-time manufacturing, a concept developed by Toyota Motor Corporation after World War Two. By the 1980s, the idea that industrial inputs should be made only as needed and then put to immediate use, rather than ending up in storerooms, had spread worldwide as "lean manufacturing." US economic data tracked the strenuous efforts of all sorts of businesses to keep fewer goods in stock, as the ratio of businesses' inventories to their monthly sales fell steadily from the 1980s into the early 2000s.

But inventories are not entirely waste. They are buffers. As international trade became less reliable in the twenty-first century, manufacturers, wholesalers, and retailers all began to worry that their value chains might not deliver as intended. They insulated themselves against that risk by keeping more goods on hand. Inventory levels began to creep higher.

Enlarging inventories, producing the same goods at multiple locations, establishing redundant transportation routes, and monitoring suppliers more carefully all added to the cost of doing business around the world. The risk that governments would yield to political pressure by slapping new restrictions on imports and foreign investment seemed very real. Once the potential cost of mitigating these risks was entered into firms' calculations about where to produce their goods, global value chains no longer seemed quite such a bargain.

15

The Crisis in Global Finance

BETWEEN 1948 AND 2008, through two distinct waves of globalization, world trade grew three times as fast as the world economy. Foreign goods, rare in shops in the 1940s, became commonplace in the early 2000s, as merchandise exports exceeded one-quarter of the world's economic output. The flood of forty-foot boxes filled with furniture and plastic resin and automobile headlamps reached proportions that once were inconceivable: six decades earlier, who could have imagined that nearly ten thousand trucks, most carrying containers filled with auto parts, would cross between Windsor, Ontario, and Detroit, Michigan, on the average day? The public had long since comprehended that large portions of many cherished "domestic" products were made abroad, and learning that the cable company's friendly customer service agent was speaking from Poland or the Philippines was no longer a surprise. The cross-border flow of money into ownership of businesses—what economists call foreign direct investment—topped $3 trillion in 2007, as large manufacturers snapped up foreign competitors, banks planted branches on street corners in countries with which executives had little acquaintance, and retailers such as Walmart, Carrefour, and Tesco convinced themselves that their sheer size would allow them to open profitable stores almost anywhere in the world. Banks' loans to foreigners, around $1 trillion at the time of the LDC debt crisis three decades earlier, reached a breathtaking $30 trillion.

The Second Globalization, between the late 1940s and the late 1980s, mainly involved closer links among the wealthy economies. Many of the poorer ones, whose roles were to provide the rich countries with raw materials and purchase their exports, saw little benefit. In much of Africa, Asia, and Latin America, incomes per person in 1985 were little higher than they had been in 1955, and save for a small economic elite, improvements in living standards were tenuous. Foreign trade and foreign investment were associated with exploitation, not prosperity.

The Third Globalization, on the other hand, brought real economic gains to some of the poorest places on earth. Countries that only a few years earlier seemed hopelessly poor and backward—Bangladesh, China, Indonesia, Vietnam—emerged as important trading nations starting in the late 1980s. By the end of the century, manufactured goods accounted for more than 80 percent of developing countries' exports, as many countries broke their dependence on volatile exports of minerals and agricultural products.

While complaints about unsafe factory working conditions and grotesque environmental damage were fully justified, there was no denying that cash wages brought rapid improvements in health, education, and material well-being. Consumers, even in remote mountain villages, could choose from an almost unfathomable array of imported goods, delivered at prices that domestic suppliers could not match. Stronger international competition forced sheltered industries to modernize and brought new technologies to market faster: many Kenyan farmers had access to electronic banking through their Chinese-made mobile phones before they had access to reliable electricity. By the World Bank's measure, more than one-third of the world's population was living in extreme poverty as the Third Globalization began. Two decades later, that share had fallen by more than half. As economists Giovanni Federico and Antonio Tena Junguito summed up the situation, "By 2007, the world was more open than a century earlier and its inhabitants gained from trade substantially more than their ancestors did."[1]

And then, starting in the second half of 2008, international trade collapsed. That collapse was a cause, but also a consequence, of what might rightly be called the first truly global recession.

———

The recession, which began in the United States toward the end of 2007, was rooted in falling US home prices, the result of years of overbuilding and deceitful lending against "subprime" mortgages to homebuyers who lacked the means to pay. Many borrowers qualified for loans thanks only to artificially low initial interest rates; when the rates rose steeply after three or four years, they could no longer afford the monthly payments. Some lenders even offered credit to borrowers who could not document their purported income and wealth—and, unsurprisingly, rarely had the income they claimed to have. The banks that extended these loans packaged the mortgages into securities that offered attractive returns to investors. But when masses of borrowers failed to make their loan payments, the securities holding those subprime mortgages lost value. In June 2007, defaults on subprime mortgages rocked two funds managed by Bear Stearns, a Wall Street investment bank. News of their problems set off a race for the exits as investors, unsure where the risks lay and how great they were, tried to move their money into the safest investments they could find. Governments seemed to be the only good credit risks around.[2]

Globalization transmitted the US subprime lending crisis around the world. Banks and industrial companies that routinely borrowed money for a few days or a couple months scrambled to raise cash when creditors suddenly declined to renew their borrowings. Many foreign banks, particularly in Western Europe, had speculated in US residential mortgages. As the financial markets seized up, major financial institutions in the United States and Europe were forced to their knees. Credit, which even the most dubious borrowers could obtain easily in 2007, was all but shut off by 2009: lenders were too weak to lend, while retailers, manufacturers, and property developers, many of which had binged on low-interest-rate debt a couple of years earlier, were too stressed to borrow. In the United States, where nearly two million construction jobs disappeared in a two-year period, one in ten workers was unemployed by October 2009. In Spain, where the housing bubble was even more inflated than across the Atlantic, unemployment would soon touch one adult in five. Falling home prices left tens of millions of borrowers owing more than their houses were worth, and they responded by slashing their spending.

The United States purchased far more imported goods than any other country, and as US imports cratered in 2009, manufacturers everywhere trimmed production and laid off workers, who cut back their own spending in turn. Germany and France, Chile and Venezuela, Malaysia and South Africa all staggered into recession; Korea and the Philippines came close. International trade often retreats when the world's economic growth slows, but the subprime crisis and the European debt crisis that followed brought unprecedented devastation. Every single one of the 104 nations that reported data to the World Trade Organization saw both imports and exports fall during the second half of 2008 and the first half of 2009. What's more, in each of those countries, trade fell faster and farther than industrial production. No forecaster had envisioned such a scenario. Countries with strong banks, healthy housing markets, and no connection to shady dealings in US mortgage lending saw their exports plummet even more than those at the heart of the crisis. Worldwide, international trade fell a stunning 17 percent between the second quarter of 2008 and the second quarter of 2009. As economists Richard Baldwin and Daria Taglioni commented, only slightly tongue in cheek, "As it turns out, most of world trade is composed of postponeables." With incomes falling and insecurity rising, every purchase that could be postponed was put on hold. The world's total economic output fell in 2009 for the first time since the World Bank began calculating such a statistic in 1961.[3]

What lay behind the Great Trade Collapse? Thanks to the spread of international value chains, the growth of trade had outpaced the growth of the world economy for years on end. Now, the process was abruptly thrown into reverse. When a US factory put off plans to buy a German machine, its action reduced not only German exports, but also German imports of components from other countries, which in turn relied on parts or raw materials from still other places. For every cancelled order, five or six or a dozen planned international transactions were called off. The age-old distinction between exports and imports no longer applied: exports had become so intimately connected to imports that when one fell sharply, so did the other. Consider Japan: between April and September of 2009, its export volume was 36 percent lower than during the previous year, and its import volume contracted a startling 40 percent. Japan had neither a mortgage crisis nor a weak banking system, but it suffered a much deeper recession than any other large economy owing to the disruption of its companies' value chains.[4]

The efficiency of the globalized economy was now its enemy. With just-in-time logistics systems, the time lag between a buyer's change of heart and cutbacks all along the value chain had become very short. If European consumers cut back on their purchases of desk lamps, retailers' data systems could spot the trend within days. The retailers would try to reduce their inventories, sending emails directing lamp factories in China to delay shipments. Those factories would give the same notice to their suppliers of electrical cord and enamel, which would in turn scale back their purchases of copper wire and titanium dioxide. In the just-in-time economy, no one wanted to fill warehouse shelves with goods that would not sell quickly. But what began as a relatively small adjustment by a diversified retailer required large adjustments by companies that specialized in making nothing but lamp switches and globes. Factories halfway around the world urgently ratcheted back production and threw unneeded workers out on the street.

The world's transportation system felt the effects immediately. Air cargo shipments slumped. Container traffic on US railroads, largely imports, took the steepest fall ever. And 2009 became the worst year in the history of the container shipping industry. The number of boxes shipped across the oceans fell by one-fourth. Freight rates sank so low many ships could not earn enough revenue to cover their fuel costs. More than five hundred containerships were taken out of service and anchored. Maersk Line lost more than $2 billion in a single year, and all its competitors sank deeply into the red.

———

In decades past, downturns in exports and imports had been brief, and the rising line showing the growth rate of international trade had always veered back to its long-term trend. The 2009 trade slump, economists judged, would end similarly. The main cause was thought to be weak demand from anxious consumers and businesses, so it seemed likely that as governments in Europe, North America, and Asia acted in unison to revive their economies, employers and consumers would regain confidence, hiring back workers and reviving demand for imports. The first part of the prediction came true: although the threat that governments in Greece, Portugal, Spain, and Italy would default on their borrowings from European banks prolonged the economic weakness in Europe, tax cuts, emergency spending programs, and interest rates close to zero eventually did restore economic growth. The second part of the forecast, though, fell very wide of the mark. Imports did not return to their previous growth trend. After plummeting in 2009, merchandise trade, measured against the size of the world economy, rose in 2010 and 2011, but then receded. By 2017, trade was less important to the world economy than it had been a dozen years earlier.

Purely as a matter of arithmetic, the headlong growth of goods trade would have been difficult to maintain. From the 1990s until 2008, manufacturers by the hundreds had closed factories in high-wage countries and shifted production to low-wage countries, either exporting goods from their own plants or buying from plants owned by other firms. A series of major trade agreements created a free-trade area within North America and an even larger one within Europe, and brought China, Taiwan, Vietnam, and Saudi Arabia into the WTO, strongly encouraging manufacturers to organize their production across international borders. On top of that, many pairs of countries—Turkey and Morocco in 2006, Japan and Indonesia in 2008, the United States and Peru in 2009—agreed to lower barriers to each other's exports of goods, and often of services as well. Each deal drove globalization still farther.

But by the end of the Great Recession, the exodus of manufacturing from Europe, Japan, and the United States and Canada was waning. The impulse from free-trade arrangements weakened as time passed. US imports from Mexico rose four and a half times between January 1994, when NAFTA gave Mexican goods free access to the US market, and October 2008; in the decade thereafter, they did not even double. Similarly, trade within the European Union rose roughly 6 percent per year between 2002, when twelve countries adopted the euro as their currency, and 2008, but barely 2 percent a year after 2008. By then, most factory work that could be done more economically in China, India, Mexico, or some other developing country had already shifted. The manufacturing that remained in the high-wage countries was mainly at the high end, too automated, too secret, or too sensitive to government procurement rules to transfer to countries that had weak legal systems and few protections for patents and other intellectual property. The geographic relocation of so much manufacturing to low-wage countries had given trade a forceful push, but that phase of globalization was over.[5]

The sluggish growth of trade was reflected in the value chains through which the world economy had globalized over the previous two decades. One way to measure the importance of value chains is to consider what portion of the value of a country's exports was produced in a different country. For the world as a whole, this measure nearly tripled between the early 1990s, when it was first calculated, and 2008. In that year, trade within value chains accounted for nearly one-fifth of the world's total economic output, far outdistancing trade in products created entirely in a single country. But the share of foreign value added in exports dropped suddenly in 2009, rose a bit the next year, and then began a slow decline. For the first time in many years, manufacturers were relying less on foreign inputs and more on domestic sources of value.[6]

———

Government policies around the world drove the push for more domestic value added. None was more aggressive than China's. Long before hundreds of thousands of Chinese workers were assembling the iPhone 3G from imported components, Chinese economists worried that their country's fast-rising exports contained little value created within the country. At the turn of the twenty-first century, as China was negotiating to enter the WTO, imported parts and raw materials accounted for almost half the value of its manufactured exports; China added little to their value save labor. In Japan, in sharp contrast, 91 percent of the value of exports was added domestically. In high technology, China had even less to offer: of the $59 billion of electronic and optical products it exported in 2000, Chinese workers and suppliers were responsible for only $16 billion. The rest originated elsewhere, notably Japan, the United States, South Korea, and Taiwan. The bulk of China's foreign commerce involved what was known as processing trade, in which manufacturers brought in foreign-made goods, assembled or packaged them using low-wage labor, and then exported the resulting products. Although goods made in China flooded foreign markets, they did so under foreign brand names. The better-paid jobs and most of the profits remained abroad.

To capture more of this wealth for China, the government used both carrots and sticks: in order to sell in the fast-growing domestic market—a very tempting carrot—foreign companies had to place more sophisticated manufacturing operations in China or share technological secrets with Chinese partners. A dozen years later, nearly two-thirds of the value of Chinese manufactured exports was created within China. As China began exporting Haier refrigerators and Lenovo computers rather than components without brand names, the processing trade fell sharply starting around 2008—at the cost of angering other countries that feared production of airplanes and electric vehicles would follow the low-wage assembly work that had already shifted to Asia. When Apple unveiled its iPhone X in 2018, Chinese content amounted to 10.4 percent of the selling price, compared with just 1.3 percent for the iPhone 3G nine years earlier. China's exports fell from over one-third of the economy's total output in 2007 to barely one-sixth by 2019, a sign that more of the stages in value chains were occurring within China and fewer components were being moved back and forth across borders.[7]

China's economy was so large that its efforts to force foreign companies to add value in the country made waves round the world. After deciding that "new-energy vehicles" deserved government support as one of several "strategic emerging industries," China's national and provincial governments spent an estimated $59 billion subsidizing battery-powered vehicles between 2009 and 2017, an amount equal to 42 percent of the country's sales of electric vehicles during that period. Some of the subsidies went to Chinese automakers, and some, such as a sales-tax exemption on electric vehicles, went directly to consumers. Alongside the subsidies and tax breaks, the national government used a 25 percent tariff on auto imports to induce foreign companies to make electric vehicles in China, but allowed them to do so only if they shared their technology with Chinese joint venture partners. While European countries, the United States, Japan, and South Korea subsidized development of electric vehicles as well, their efforts were dwarfed by China's.[8]

A similar combination of inducements and controls was applied to many other industries. They not only helped make China into the world's largest exporter, but also enabled it to export the same types of products as the United States, the European Union, and Japan. China's economic policies were enormously effective in building a modern economy. Between 1991 and 2013, as the country plunged headlong into globalization, its economy grew at least 7.5 percent in every single year. In the final year of that period, China's economic output was six times as large as at the start.

For China, the subsidies became a trap. As the subsidized growth of Chinese industry created global overcapacity in many products, profits sagged, and the government had to keep paying subsidies to keep factories alive and workers employed. The amounts are difficult to verify, but they appear to have been considerable. One estimate puts state subsidies to Chinese companies in 2017 at 430 billion renminbi (roughly $64 billion). Another, for 2018, finds 154 billion renminbi ($22 billion) of subsidies shown in the financial reports of companies traded on the stock market; no corresponding figure was available for the much larger number of firms whose shares were not traded publicly. Many of the beneficiaries of these subsidies, such as automakers, competed with foreign companies in China or foreign markets, and the subsidies were openly designed to give them an edge.[9]

———

Other countries complained bitterly about how China's subsidies affected the flow of trade in the first decades of the twenty-first century. None of them were blameless. A venerable truism among economists holds that international trade patterns reveal comparative advantage: each country is assumed to export those goods and services it can produce most efficiently and import the rest. That assumption is valid, however, only if trade patterns are dictated by market forces. In a world in which goods and services flow at little cost and with few restraints, though, subsidies may matter more than comparative advantage in determining what gets made where and who profits from making it. In the Third Globalization and then the Fourth, with freight transportation very cheap and communications almost costless, subsidies came to shape the international economy as never before. Studies by the IMF and the World Bank found that most developing countries offered partial corporate tax holidays, temporarily reduced rates, and other inducements to manufacturers dangling the promise of new jobs. In many cases, those incentives did reel in foreign companies: new export tax incentives persuaded foreign automakers to use South Africa as an export base, increasing the country's auto exports from $500 million in 1996, when tax incentives were introduced, to nearly $2.5 billion a decade later.[10]

Wealthy countries were no less involved. In 2017, Denmark spent an astonishing 1.5 percent of its entire national income on subsidies for industry, for such purposes as helping firms reduce use of fossil fuels. Across the European Union, that year's collective bill for subsidies to industry, not counting railroads or agriculture, came to €116 billion (roughly US$130 billion). In Canada's largest provinces, businesses received subsidies of C$700 to C$1,200 (approximately US$630 to $1,050) per citizen each year between 2005 and 2015, largely through tax breaks that lowered the costs of farmers or manufacturers facing international competition. In the United States, state and local governments funneled an estimated $70 billion a year to attract businesses that promised employment. In 2012, Alabama gifted Airbus $158 million to open a plant in Mobile, Alabama, three years after South Carolina offered its US-based competitor, Boeing, $900 million to assemble jets near Charleston— and just before the state of Washington granted Boeing an $8.7 billion package in return for making its 777 aircraft near Seattle. German automakers Volkswagen, Daimler, and BMW all received large incentives to build assembly plants in the southeastern United States, from which they exported vehicles that might otherwise have been produced in Europe or Mexico. Amid the subsidy frenzy, the Taiwanese manufacturer Foxconn was awarded over $4 billion in 2017 to build a massive factory in Wisconsin to make panels for television screens. The project was heralded as a means to shift electronics production from China to the United States—although it foundered, in part, on doubts that Americans would be eager to work on Foxconn's notoriously rigid assembly lines.[11]

Cash subsidies to factory owners were not the only lure. India set requirements that solar cells and modules be made domestically. Indonesia insisted on local content in smartphones. Russia directed state-owned enterprises to buy domestic goods and services unless they cost significantly more than imports. In the United States, although it was an article of faith that government should not "pick winners and losers," federally funded transit cars had to be assembled domestically (although many components could be imported), and one flatware manufacturer convinced Congress in 2019 that military dining halls should purchase only US-made forks and spoons. The WTO spotted a jump in the number of "technical barriers" to trade, such as product standards crafted to make life hard for importers; it counted 27 in force in 2007, 449 just nine years later.

These sorts of inducements and regulations increasingly shaped businesses' decisions about where to invest and how to organize value chains. When the European Central Bank surveyed forty-four Europe-based multinational companies in 2016, it found an increasing trend for industrial firms to produce in the markets where their goods were sold—a trend that would inevitably make imports and exports less important. "Sourcing and production in local markets are substituting earlier trade flows," the bank reported. Worldwide, exports ceased to grow faster than the world economy, ending a trend that had been in place since the 1960s.[12]

The sluggish growth of trade was not the only sign that globalization had gone awry. Investors that had charged aggressively into foreign markets now backed away. Worldwide, foreign direct investment peaked in

2008, and was lower in 2018 than it had been eighteen years earlier. The number of cross-border mergers and acquisitions nose-dived, especially in finance: banks lost their enthusiasm for planting their flags around the world, and tougher regulations made it less profitable for them to do so. Cross-border lending contracted after early 2008, then steadied at a much lower level. The international bond market stopped growing. International retailers began to retreat from their foreign beachheads, after learning at high cost that merchandising techniques honed for one country might have little appeal in another. In a variety of ways, globalization seemed to have passed its prime.

16

Backlash

FAR FROM THE bustling industrial cities of coastal China, the social and economic effects of the Third Globalization were severe. Entire factory towns emptied out as production shifted to Mexico, Asia, and Eastern Europe, leaving unemployment and desolation behind: Great Britain lost nearly half its manufacturing jobs in the quarter-century after 1990, Japan one-third, the United States one-quarter. While some of the job loss was due to automation, the creation of global supply chains turned a steady but gradual decline in factory employment in the wealthy economies into an agonizing collapse. A study of Norway found a strong correlation between imports from China and manufacturing job loss. In Spain, whose imports from China soared from $4 billion in 1999 to $25 billion in 2007, competition from China was blamed for the loss of 340,000 manufacturing jobs. In the United States, manufacturing provided about 17 percent of all employment in 1990 but only 9 percent in the 2010s; by one estimate, one-fifth of that decline was due to increased import competition from China. US factories made 222 million automobile tires in 2004 but only 126 million in 2014, as companies that had once made tires in Ohio, Kentucky, and Texas imported them from China instead. While tire manufacturing flourished in Dalian and Qingdao, the US tire industry imploded.[1]

On average, the Third Globalization helped improve living conditions around the world. The number of people mired in extreme poverty plummeted, life expectancy and literacy improved almost everywhere, two billion people gained access to electric power, and mobile phones became ubiquitous in all but the very poorest countries. Asia's growth, in particular, brought incomes closer to those in Europe and North America: between 1980 and 2016, average income per person rose 66 percent in the European Union and 84 percent in the United States and Canada, but 230 percent in Asia—and an astounding 1,237 percent in China. Averages, though, can be deceiving. Most parts of Africa and Latin America were on the wrong side of the yawning income gap. Adjusting for differences in the cost of living, the income of the average adult in Latin America was nine times that of the average adult in China in 1980. China was intensely engaged in globalization during the ensuing decades, while most of Latin America was not, and by 2016 average incomes per adult in China and in Latin America were nearly the same.[2]

These averages, though, obscure the greater inequality of incomes within many countries. In almost every country, a disproportionate share of income growth during the Third Globalization went to a small percentage of the population. In part, this was due to the boom in financial markets after worldwide inflation began to recede in 1982: the prices of stocks and bonds rose much faster than wages, and those who had the wealth to participate in the financial market boom reaped the benefits. Technological change created new opportunities for many workers but hurt many others as routine jobs in offices and on factory floors were displaced by automation. Slow economic growth across the wealthy economies encouraged manufacturers to invest in countries where demand for their products would grow faster, leaving pockets of high unemployment behind; workers displaced from manufacturing often had no alternative to taking jobs in other fields that required less skill and offered less pay.[3]

———

Globalization had a significant role in widening the income divide, bringing fatter paychecks for people who managed international firms or whose skills gave them some particular advantage in the international economy but undermining the bargaining power of many more. Increased trade pushed down the prices of imports in many countries, putting intense pressure on domestic manufacturers; this depressed the wages not only in manufacturing, but in other industries where displaced factory workers might seek jobs. The ability of labor unions to demand that workers share in higher profits diminished almost everywhere, as companies could credibly threaten to move work to a different country if labor costs were too high. "The economic gains from globalization have accrued mostly to the top two deciles of the Canadian population," a study for a Canadian think tank concluded.[4]

Less wealthy countries were not immune from globalization's pains. By 2010, nearly 70 percent of China's imports from developing countries were commodities, while its exports to developing countries were manufactured goods—the old mercantilist trade pattern once more. Imports of Chinese goods devastated industry as seriously in the suburbs of São Paulo as in Ohio and Alsace. Countries in Africa and East Asia that hoped to use manufacturing to build flourishing economies, as Japan, Hong Kong, and South Korea had done, now found that their low-wage workers could not compete making even the simplest products. Instead, their traders set up shop in Shenzhen and Guangdong, snapping up deals on umbrellas, electrical adapters, and plastic handbags and shipping them home by the container-load. The more China exported, the less their own labor-intensive industries could create jobs that involved making things rather than trading them.[5]

Factories in many countries were no longer hiring, but other industries were not growing fast enough to make up the difference. Economists' disputes about how much to blame technology rather than globalization were of no interest to people whose incomes declined either way. Older workers, protected by union contracts, might manage to hang on to steady paychecks and the right to retire by age sixty, but younger job seekers often found only options such as "mini-jobs," a form of low-wage part-time employment permitted in Germany starting in 2003, and "zero-hours contracts," a British innovation involving employment contracts with no guaranteed hours of work. Temporary employment accounted for one in nine jobs in the wealthy economies—one in four in Spain. Stagnant wages and insecurity, it seemed, were the price of globalization. Even the massive increase in foreign investment, touted as a way to provide jobs, also proved to damp wage growth: according to a Bank of Japan study, the desire to attract foreign investment into Japanese industries that relied heavily on exports caused firms to clamp down tightly on wages.[6]

The globalization of finance contributed to greater inequality by making it far easier for those in higher-income groups to shift their incomes and assets to tax havens. In 2007, by one estimate, 8 percent of the world's wealth, almost all of it owned by a relative handful of individuals, was held in countries where it was hardly taxed. Tax havens, along with the ability of the wealthy to tap investment opportunities that might be imprudent for a family with little savings, made it easier for the wealthy to grow wealthier. According to an estimate based on European, American, and Chinese data, the top 1 percent of the population held 26 percent of wealth in 1985 but 33 percent in 2015. That increase came at the expense of middle-class households, whose share of wealth declined to a similar extent. The bottom half of the population was unaffected, because it had so little wealth to begin with.[7]

Corporations, whose shares are largely owned by wealthy individuals, directly or indirectly, played the tax-avoidance game as well. Indeed, the most consequential subsidies related to globalization took the form of profit shifting. Almost all businesses face income taxes, but companies operating on a global scale have a unique ability to decide where they should pay. They can sell their products from one subsidiary to another to book profits in countries with low tax rates, or they can organize their borrowing through subsidiaries in high-tax countries where the ability to deduct interest payments from income is most valuable. In addition, a growing number of "tax haven" countries offered foreign companies unique tax preferences, often in return for opening a local office or factory. As of 2018, the Organisation for Economic Co-operation and Development (OECD) had identified no fewer than twenty-one thousand secret corporate tax deals around the world.

In 2013 alone, by one estimate, governments, mainly in the wealthy countries, lost $123 billion of tax revenue to such corporate tax dodges. "Profit shifting has proved to be an effective way for US firms to cut their taxes and boost the after-tax returns on their foreign operations," economists Thomas Wright and Gabriel Zucman reported. The same was true for firms based in other countries. Shareholders benefit from higher share prices and dividends, leaving taxpayers at large to bear the cost through some combination of higher taxes, reduced government services, and interest on the government borrowing needed to make up for revenue shortfalls. By making it more profitable for companies to invest abroad than at home, corporate tax avoidance both widened the income gap and encouraged firms to import rather than manufacturing domestically, building international value chains that otherwise might not have been desirable.[8]

––––––

Given the intense and long-standing controversies over globalization—the improbable 19 percent vote tally for US presidential candidate Ross Perot, running against NAFTA, in 1992; the anarchic protests of tens of thousands at a WTO meeting in Seattle in 1999; the violent police response to throngs of protesters during a summit of world leaders in Genoa in 2001—one might have expected the decline in international trade and investment following the financial crisis to be a welcome event, at least in the wealthy economies. Instead, it was barely noticed. The financial crisis focused attention on the increasingly inequitable distribution of income and wealth, not on globalization. When the Occupy Wall Street movement unexpectedly set up camp a few blocks from the New York Stock Exchange in September 2011, its message assailed corporate greed and "big finance," not imports and the loss of US factory jobs.[9]

The forces of globalization were unavoidable, but their effects on workers and families had more to do with individual countries' social policies and tax systems than with international trade and finance. Countries whose governments provided extra social benefits to households whose incomes fell and spent more on worker education and training saw a more even distribution of income gains than countries where workers were left to fend for themselves. Countries such as the United States, which provided dramatic income-tax reductions to high-income groups and all but eliminated inheritance taxes, predictably saw the distribution of income and wealth become much more uneven, as did countries such as Russia, which allowed a few well-connected individuals to take over state-owned assets during the privatization wave of the 1990s. Globalization was less the cause of greater inequality than the scapegoat for national governments' inability, or unwillingness, to address the reality of a globalized economy.

That reality meant that trade policy, the main tool governments have long used to control the flow of commerce, no longer worked the way it used to. The spread of international value chains was a direct, if unanticipated, result of many years of trade policies that lowered tariffs, eliminated import quotas, and put limits on other measures, such as government procurement regulations, that might interfere with companies' efforts to organize the flow of goods as they deemed best. But as value chains developed, they rendered many of the traditional trade policy tools useless, or even counterproductive, confounding the bureaucrats, diplomats, and politicians whose careers revolved around making and enforcing rules for trade and making it harder for governments to offer a politically acceptable response to the negative side effects of globalization.

Historically, every country's trade policy has involved finding a balance between the short-term imperative of preserving jobs in the face of foreign competition and the long-term goals of encouraging economic growth and protecting national security. At one time or another, most governments have managed trade to promote specific industries or capture economic activity that might otherwise have ended up in another country—an idea the mercantilists would have embraced wholeheartedly. On the opposing side, a nearly unanimous chorus of economists declares that barriers to imports hurt domestic consumers. The annual cost to the economy of "saving" a job by import protection in the late twentieth century was often higher than the wages those protected workers earned, with consumers paying the bill in the form of higher prices. The more pernicious effects of protection were tougher to pin down, but they were real. Protection arguably depressed long-term growth prospects by keeping zombie companies alive, encouraging investment in industries that were uncompetitive, and relieving the pressure on farms and factories to innovate and become more efficient. And if protection led other countries to retaliate by throwing up their own roadblocks to imports, places that produced the affected exports could be badly hurt, with consumers cutting back their spending as local exporters saw their sales plummet.[10]

The argument that the costs of protection outweigh the benefits, though, has traditionally been hard to carry in the face of protectionist lobbying by labor unions, industrialists, and local leaders in places where factories are limping or farmers are under stress. Once a high tariff, a quota on an imported good, or some other policy favoring a particular company or industry is in place, gaining enough support to remove it is challenging. It was this dilemma that led to the first modern trade agreement, signed in 1860, in which Great Britain and France agreed to reduce duties on each other's exports. The United States tried something similar in 1934, when Congress authorized reciprocal trade agreements as a tactic for reducing very high US tariffs. Such pacts were carefully tailored to meet the needs of politically powerful industries; the first, the US-Cuba agreement of 1934, satisfied US exporters by requiring Cuba to lower tariffs on tableware and lightbulbs, in return for which the United States reduced tariffs on Cuban floor tiles, sugar, and cucumbers. While official US tariff rates remained high, twenty-one countries accounting for over 60 percent of US trade struck such special deals by 1940.[11]

These two-country arrangements were arduous to negotiate, and they sacrificed some of the economic gains that international trade was supposed to create: if the United States was importing floor tiles from Cuba rather than Portugal simply because the Cubans had negotiated a lower tariff rate, then the pact was not rewarding efficiency. This is one reason two-country negotiations lost favor after World War Two, replaced by bargaining among multiple countries at the GATT and within the European Economic Community. But that, too, had its limits. By the time China joined the World Trade Organization in 2001, more than 140 countries were involved. Fitting them around a conference table proved difficult, and getting them all to approve a new international trade agreement proved impossible, especially when, as they always had, negotiators sought deals that would increase their country's exports while controlling imports of politically sensitive products. A fad for regional arrangements, such as the 2014 pact to expand economic ties between Chile, Colombia, Mexico, and Peru and a 2016 treaty to free goods trade between the European Union and six countries in southern Africa, emerged because larger trade agreements were beyond reach.

The Third Globalization upended the political calculus underlying trade negotiations. Exporters that participate in global value chains are frequently importers as well, bringing raw materials or partially finished products into their country before processing and sending them back out. A kilo of iron ore, to take a simple example, might cross borders half a dozen times as it is melted into steel billets that are rolled into wire that is forged into bolts that are threaded and hardened before being used in a mounting that eventually becomes part of a knitting machine. An import quota that raises the price of steel wire in order to aid the wire mill increases the price at every link farther along the chain; all the more so if, say, the country where the bolts are made imposes import tariffs based on the elevated price of the wire. The net result may be to render the knitting machine uncompetitive in the international market, thereby harming not only the wire mill the policy was meant to assist, but also any other domestic factories that are involved in making the machine.

Complicating matters further, technological change has meant that services accounted for a steadily greater share of the value of manufactured goods during the Third Globalization. Thanks to the internet, it became simple to trade many of those services internationally, such that national trade policies meant to protect a domestic manufacturing industry could end up hurting domestic service industries. If some of the value of a Japanese-made pickup truck sold in the United States is attributable to engineers, designers, and computer experts in California, then US tariffs on those trucks, while perhaps protecting the jobs of some US factory workers, would threaten the jobs of those other US workers who helped create the vehicle. In fact, if the tariff were to be based on the import price, the United States would be taxing the contribution of those US workers to the finished product. The effects of trade restrictions on the service sector generally attract little attention, but they are often large: by one estimate, 30 percent of tariffs collected in 2009 were paid on the value of services that were incorporated into manufactured goods. One study of European shoe manufacturing showed that more than half the value of Chinese-made shoes sold to European consumers took the form of services provided in Europe, making the point that potential trade restrictions on Chinese shoes would harm European shoe designers, production engineers, shipping-line employees, and home-office executives, with that harm perhaps outweighing any benefit to workers in European shoe factories.[12]

Whether or not trade policies were to blame, the belief that globalization was undermining stable, well-paid employment and shredding social safety nets festered. Originating on the political left, which had objected that globalization favored multinational corporations from rich countries over impoverished people in poor ones, it was embraced after the financial crisis more effectively by the political right as part of a demand for stronger national control over immigration, finance, and trade. Pressure from the extreme right led to the 2016 referendum in which the British, rallying behind the slogan "Let's take back control," favored leaving the European Union; a poll conducted shortly thereafter found that British adults, especially those over age forty-five, strongly associated globalization with greater inequality and lower wages. As refugees fleeing civil war in Syria and poverty in Africa poured into Europe, Marine Le Pen, running for president of France in 2017, foresaw "a totally new dividing line: not the right against the left, but the patriots against the globalists." While Le Pen's candidacy failed, such a mainstream politician as British prime minister Theresa May heard her message. As May acknowledged in January 2017 at the World Economic Forum, the famed assembly of the global elite in the Swiss village of Davos, "Talk of greater globalization can make people fearful."[13]

PART V
The Fourth Globalization

17

Red Tide

THE BAYONNE BRIDGE is an architectural marvel. Opened in November 1931, it spans the Kill Van Kull, a grimy tidal waterway lined by oil tanks and ship repair yards that separates Bayonne, in New Jersey, from the New York City borough of Staten Island. While it lacks the majesty of the George Washington Bridge, a few miles to the north, the Bayonne Bridge has a grandeur of its own. Its 1,657-foot steel arch was for decades the longest in the world, supporting a roadway 151 feet above mean high water. The vessels that began the container revolution in 1956 sailed beneath it on their way from Newark to Houston, and generations of tankers and containerships passed below the arch on their way down the Kill Van Kull to and from the largest port on the Atlantic coast of North America.

When the launch of *Emma Maersk* in 2006 led to a frenzy of orders for ships that would dwarf those already at sea, the graceful bridge became an obstacle. Vessels carrying as much cargo as eight thousand full-size trucks were on order, ready to enter service as early as 2010. After the widening of the Panama Canal was completed in 2015, enabling larger ships to pass through, the new vessels would dramatically reduce the cost of moving cargo by sea between East Asia and New York. The Bayonne Bridge, built for a different age, threatened to block those big ships from calling at the port's busiest container terminals, in New Jersey. As the US Army Corps of Engineers, the agency charged with maintaining US harbors, assessed the situation in 2009: "The Bayonne Bridge impedes the carriers' ability to realize economies of scale associated with the use of economically efficiently loaded vessels." Ships might sail only to Baltimore or Norfolk and skip New York's port, or could deliver boxes to Pacific coast ports for movement east by rail, the Corps warned. Either way, it determined, America's largest urban area would lose port-related businesses, jobs, and tax revenue, and the country would pay more, on average, for its foreign trade.[1]

Building a new bridge or tunneling beneath the Kill Van Kull would have been impossibly expensive, but there was another solution. Backed by a chorus of local politicians and trade union leaders, the call went out to raise the Bayonne Bridge. In 2013, the Port Authority of New York and New Jersey began to remove the highway crossing the arch. In its place, it constructed a new road, sixty-four feet higher. The rebuilt bridge, a miracle of engineering, opened to traffic in 2017, allowing megaships to reach the New Jersey docks. The project was a boon for shippers using the port, for the ocean carriers that served it, and for the owners of the terminals where the big vessels would henceforth be able to call. It was less beneficial for the region's commuters: most of the $1.7 billion cost of accommodating larger vessels was borne not by shipping interests or cargo owners, but by automobile drivers who faced higher tolls at the Port Authority's tunnels and bridges.

These vast outlays, both public and private, were predicated on the firm conviction that globalization would flourish as it had for decades. That conviction proved disastrously wrong. Instead of expanding, international commerce seized up. Economic crisis shook Europe and the United States, lessening the need to move goods from Asia's factories to customers across the seas. Demand for airfreight evaporated, and containerships sailed the globe half empty. Once the crisis passed, it became clear that supply chains had become slower and less reliable. Strikes, storms, and earthquakes had disrupted production at distant factories. By 2012, it would take several days longer to send a container of shoes from Shanghai to Seattle than it had in the 1990s, and the goods were less likely to arrive on time. Retailers, wholesalers, and manufacturers reacted by building warehouses in more places and stocking them with more goods—fixes that limited risk but raised costs, destroying much of the rationale for creating global value chains in the first place.

From the dawn of the container age until 2009, there had never been an annual decline in container traffic. Every dip in the growth rate, precipitated by a slowdown in the world economy, had been followed by a boom. As the world emerged from economic crisis in 2010, the smart money bet on a repeat. Maersk Line forecast that demand for container shipping would grow 7 percent per year. Worried once again that it lacked the ships to handle the expected flood of cargo, it decided to leapfrog the competition. In 2011, with its ships carrying far more containers than ever before but losing about $75 on each one, Maersk began construction of a generation of ships one-fifth again as large as *Emma Maersk*. These vessels, to be delivered starting in 2013, were called the Triple-Es to highlight their key features: economies of scale, energy efficiency, and environmental improvement. Each would be able to carry over eighteen thousand TEU, equivalent to the load aboard nine thousand trucks, while reducing greenhouse-gas emissions per container-mile by half. By building thirty Triple-Es in Korean shipyards, Maersk projected, it could undercut its competitors' costs per container by one-fourth.[2]

Again, Maersk's aggressiveness took other ship lines by surprise. Again, they were confronted with an unwelcome choice. They could do nothing and face a future in which they would have much higher costs than their largest competitor, or they could stretch their finances to order new ships they might not be able to fill. But this was no choice at all. French carrier CMA CGM ordered three ships larger than *Emma Maersk*, a move that placed such stress on the secretive family-owned ship line that it needed to seek outside investment. In 2012, the founder of Mediterranean Shipping Company, the third-largest line, said his company would not purchase eighteen-thousand-TEU vessels—and it promptly ordered even larger ships. Other lines followed suit, building dozens of ships far larger than *Emma*. Whether there was really a need for a ship that could deliver loads for eleven thousand full-size trucks was almost a second thought. "The development of the world container fleet over the last decade is completely disconnected from developments in global trade and actual demand," the OECD's International Transport Forum observed in 2015.[3]

Most of the major ship lines were state run or family controlled, and their powerful leaders had no intention of playing second fiddle to the Danes. Reckless expansion drove freight rates so low that ship lines' revenue did not cover their operating costs, much less the mortgages on their ships, flooding the oceans with red ink. "Contrary to all logic, instead of reducing the existing capacity on the market, the large shipping companies have rushed to add new capacity," economist Michele Acciaro observed in 2015. Acciaro diagnosed a contagious disease: "naval gigantism."[4]

Gigantism spread well beyond the ship lines. Giant ships bred giant terminals: with their customers merging at every opportunity, the companies that loaded and unloaded containerships sought out merger partners of their own to share the expense of lengthening wharves, installing cranes the size of fifteen-story buildings, and building computer-controlled storage yards. Quays needed to be reinforced, because larger ships force more water up against them while docking and because servicing larger ships requires heavier cranes than many quays had been built to support. Container storage areas were too small to accommodate vessels that discharged and then took on thousands of containers at a time, and new terminal gates were required to control the thousands of additional trucks moving in and out.[5]

Governments everywhere invested in gigantic infrastructure—deeper harbors, larger canals, higher bridges—so the new vessels could call. Highways were widened, rail yards expanded, new train tracks laid, all to accommodate even more cargo. In Durban, the state-owned company controlling South Africa's largest port agreed in 2018 to lay out $500 million to deepen berths for larger vessels. Egypt's government spent $8 billion to widen and deepen the Suez Canal, to dissuade ship traffic between South Asia and the North Atlantic from diverting to the newly widened Panama Canal. In Hamburg, after years of inaction, the city-owned port authority won a decade-long battle with environmentalists to deepen the Elbe River to allow containerships to carry another 1,800 TEU per call, at a cost of $700 million—a decision agreed only after the four-hundred-meter-long *CSCL Indian Ocean* spent six days aground in the Elbe in February 2016. A study for Sweden's largest port declared in 2015 that "Gothenburg will have to improve maritime access if it would like to remain competitive vis-à-vis other North European ports," meaning that it would need to spend in excess of $400 million of state funds to deepen a channel and berths to 16.5 meters. Genoa's port authority agreed to spend €1 billion to build a breakwater capacious enough for megaships to enter the port, plus additional hundreds of millions of euros to remove the existing breakwater. The Port of Miami, having completed the $205 million "Deep Dredge" project to excavate a fifty-foot channel in 2015, announced three years later that it needed to go deeper, as harbor pilots were complaining that big ships were struggling to enter the port.[6]

And then there was the question of where those big ships should call. After 1983, when Prime Minister Margaret Thatcher pushed through the sale of the state-owned British Transport Docks Board to a private operator, for-profit companies increasingly had taken charge of the terminals at which ships loaded and unloaded cargo. Responsibility for maintaining harbors and protecting navigation, however, remained firmly with public authorities. It had always been thus: governments could collect taxes on commerce if traders moved goods through their ports, so keeping navigation safe could be a worthwhile investment. If few ships came to call, though, the investment would go for naught.

Those costs were spare change compared to the truly massive freight transportation projects developed by governments across Asia. The emirate of Dubai, once a quiet trading village along a tidal creek, grew rich overnight when oil prices spiked in 1973 and again in 1979. Determined to diversify the economy, the state-owned ports company dredged the Persian Gulf to create the Port of Jebel Ali, building one artificial island after another to turn an unpromising sandbar into one of the largest ports in the world.

Aside from Hong Kong, an autonomous territory, no Chinese port ranked among the world's ten largest in 1997. Two decades later, after massive investments by state-owned companies, seven of the top ten were in China. To overcome shallow waters near shore, the government turned a handful of islets off Shanghai into the world's largest container terminal and erected a twenty-mile bridge, with an attached fuel pipeline, to connect the port to the mainland. Various terminal operators shared some of the $18 billion cost, but the bulk of the money came from various government entities, part of a national strategy to facilitate exports as China transformed itself into the world's largest manufacturer. China's "Belt and Road Initiative," adopted in 2013, channeled hundreds of billions of dollars into land and maritime transportation projects designed to offer new paths for importing raw materials vital to Chinese industry and exporting its finished goods, strengthening the country's strategic position in the process. One highly publicized Belt and Road project involved moving freight 7,500 miles by train between China and Great Britain; in addition to significant infrastructure costs, the China–Europe railroad required massive operating subsidies from Chinese provinces, because the $3,000 shippers paid to move each forty-foot container was only one-third the cost of running the trains.[7]

The ship lines, importers, and exporters who stood to profit from such infrastructure investments usually did not pay the bill. Ships typically were charged fees when they visited ports, and some governments taxed incoming cargo. But during the Third Globalization, those fees and taxes were rarely calibrated to cover the cost of dredging harbors, raising bridges, building artificial islands, and installing high-speed cranes. Nor did the ship lines face long-term commitments: while government agencies looked forward to thirty years of payments on bonds sold to finance port improvements, the ship lines that demanded those improvements were free to shift vessels and cargo to other ports, thereby erasing the promised benefits of the costly public-sector investments. Under the incessant pressure to deepen harbors and lengthen wharves, ports on every continent created far more capacity than needed to handle the flow of cargo, imperiling the finances of regional and local governments and giving the ship lines even greater bargaining power to demand better port facilities, lower costs, or both.

As in the earlier days of the container shipping industry, expansion-minded carriers were abetted by governments determined to preserve shipyards at all cost. South Korea's government judged shipbuilding to be a vital industry, not least because shipyards accounted for more than a fifth of the country's total demand for steel. Its big shipyards were more advanced than the Chinese yards, and they rode the wave of orders for big containerships following the launch of *Emma Maersk*. When international trade collapsed at the end of 2008 and new orders stopped, the state responded generously. Between 2008 and 2013, South Korea's state-owned lenders provided shipbuilders $45 billion of loans and loan guarantees. When some of the borrowers could not repay, the government converted those debts into majority ownership of two major yards. The bailouts allowed South Korea to hang on to a third of the world shipbuilding market and more than half the market for containerships, but profitability was something else again. After another meltdown in 2015, the state-owned Korea Development Bank converted yet more of Daewoo Shipbuilding's loans into shares, giving the government a 79 percent stake in a very troubled company.

More state aid flowed to shipbuilders and their customers after the glut of container shipping brought the bankruptcy of South Korea's Hanjin Shipping Co. in August 2016. Two months later, the Korean government kept alive the country's only surviving containership operator, Hyundai Merchant Marine, by purchasing some of Hyundai's containerships at market value and leasing them back to the company at bargain rates. When that bailout proved insufficient, the government lent the carrier $2.8 billion in 2018 to acquire twenty containerships for which it had no need. Those ships, of course, would be built in Korean yards—adding yet more subsidized shipping capacity to a global fleet that already had capacity to excess.[8]

South Korea was not alone. In November 2016, the government of Taiwan shoveled $1.9 billion of low-cost loans to two containership lines, Evergreen Marine and Yang Ming Marine Transport, which were staggering under the cost of acquiring megaships. Shipping, a government minister told the *Wall Street Journal*, "is key to our economic development." With new megaships going for close to $200 million apiece, smaller ship lines lacking such subsidies could not afford to stay in the game. In December 2014, the Chilean carrier CSAV joined with Germany's Hapag-Lloyd. In 2015, China's government ordered the two large state-owned container lines to merge. The three Japanese lines, hard-pressed to finance new ships, placed their container businesses in a joint venture in 2016; as the president of the largest of the companies, NYK Line, acknowledged, "The purpose of becoming one at this time is so none of us become zero." When the joint venture failed to stanch the bleeding, the three lines merged in 2018. Hapag-Lloyd and United Arab Shipping joined forces, and Maersk swallowed up Germany's Hamburg-Süd. In August 2016, Hanjin, the seventh-largest container line, collapsed in bankruptcy. And in 2018, Overseas Orient, owned by the Singaporean government, was sold to the Chinese.[9]

Maersk, now easily the leader with 18 percent of global capacity, had nearly achieved its goal of squeezing out the weak. Four alliances of containership lines dominated the global market, serving every continent and handling the affairs of the largest international corporations. Smaller carriers survived only by cozying up to the giants. In the span of a few years, a highly competitive industry had become an oligopoly.[10]

Maersk conceived the megaship as the vehicle that would lift globalization to its highest stage. It would be so efficient, carrying so many containers at so little expense, that freight transportation costs, already low, would become vanishingly small. Organizing long-distance value chains would be even cheaper and easier for customers, creating yet more demand for space aboard Maersk's ships. Greenhouse-gas emissions from shipping would diminish. Global commerce would thrive. And while revenue per container was certain to fall, costs would fall even more, leaving a comfortable profit as the industry consolidated to a handful of firms following Maersk, the industry leader.

Maersk Line had carefully studied the traffic on its routes and the demands of its customers, and its optimistic forecasts indicated that new eighteen-thousand-TEU ships would best meet its needs. The largest ships already in its fleet, fifteen-thousand-TEU vessels the size of *Emma Maersk*, would be shifted—"cascaded," in industry-speak—to less busy routes, giving Maersk additional capacity there as well. Maersk would be well positioned to handle an upturn in business, but the efficiency of the global logistical system within which Maersk functioned was not the ship line's concern. Terminal operators, including Maersk Line's sister company, APM Terminals, were not consulted; if some ports or terminals did not wish to make the investments necessary to handle the bigger ships, other ports and terminals would beg for the business. Nor did Maersk worry about whether its giant vessels would affect the movement of boxes to and from the ports. It simply assumed that railroads, truckers, and barge lines would deal with the traffic. The competitors that ordered their own megaships in Maersk's wake took the same attitude, and their vessels, as large as twenty-three thousand TEU, were even bigger than Maersk's. At sea, there seemed no question that bigger was better. And if it was cheaper, customers would go along with it.

The ship lines' calculations were predicated on the assumption that their new ships would sail nearly full. But instead of growing at 6 or 7 percent a year, container traffic grew only 3 or 4 percent, and in some years less. Sailing half full because of the dearth of cargo, the giant new vessels brought none of the efficiency gains or environmental benefits their creators had promised.

The cost of shipping a container fell, but shippers paid for that benefit in the form of slower, less reliable transportation. As ship lines trimmed excess capacity by anchoring vessels and cancelling services, a box might have to sit longer in the container yard before it could be loaded aboard ship. The process of discharging and reloading the vessel took much longer as well, and not only because there were more boxes to move off and on. The Triple-Es and the even larger vessels that followed them were barely longer than ships of the *Emma Maersk* generation, but were three meters wider. This meant that there was no room to line up additional cranes along the side of the ship, but that each crane would need to reach farther across the ship, adding seconds to the average time required to move each box. More boxes multiplied by more handling time per box could add hours, or even days, to each port call. Delays were legion. By 2018, 30 percent of the ships leaving China were behind schedule.

Once, containerships would have been able to make up those delays in route. But that was no longer possible. The megaships were uniformly designed to steam more slowly than the ships they replaced in order to save fuel. Instead of twenty-four or twenty-five knots, they traveled at nineteen or twenty, adding several days to the long voyage between Asia and Europe. And where earlier ships were able to speed up if required to get back on schedule, the megaships could not. If a ship was late departing Shanghai, it was likely to arrive late in Malaysia, Sri Lanka, and Spain. Moving goods through value chains on tight schedules became significantly more complicated.

The land side of the shipping business was scrambled as well. Megaships brought feast or famine: fewer vessels called, but each one moved more boxes off and on, alternatively leaving equipment and infrastructure unused and overwhelmed. Mountains of boxes stuffed with imports and exports filled storage patios. The higher the stacks grew, the longer it took the stacker cranes to locate a particular container, remove it from the stack, and place it aboard the transporter that would take it to the wharf for loading aboard ship or to the rail yard or truck terminal for delivery to a customer. Freight railroads, which faced physical limits on the length of their trains and the number they could run, could not readily add capacity simply because ships had become larger; where once they might have transported a shipload of imports to inland destinations within a day, now it could take two or three. And often enough, the partners in one of the four alliances that dominated ocean shipping did not use the same terminal in a particular port, requiring purposeless truck trips just to move a box from an inbound ship at one terminal to an outbound ship at another.

An honest balance sheet would show that the megaship made transport less reliable, undermining the global value chains it was meant to strengthen. For the company that started the race, A. P. Møller-Maersk, the megaship proved to be an albatross. The financial burden was more than the conglomerate could bear. Under pressure, it sold its 49 percent ownership of Denmark's largest retail chain in 2014. A year later, out went its one-fifth interest in Denmark's largest bank. In 2016, the company's controlling family fired the CEO and announced that A. P. Møller-Maersk would divest energy-related businesses that provided one-fourth of its revenue. Despite this desperate maneuvering, and despite its fleet of megaships promising economies of scale, the company's share price was lower in June 2018 than it had been when *Emma Maersk* was ordered back in December 2003. Maersk Line's market share had grown, but its container shipping business had performed no better than those of the competitors it sought to push aside. As its chief executive sighed, "There's no point in being the largest carrier if we don't translate that into above-average margins." In plain English, the megaship was a disaster for all concerned.[11]

That went for the shipbuilders as well. In February 2019, the state-run Korean Development Bank, which controlled Daewoo Shipbuilding, agreed that Daewoo and Hyundai Heavy Industry, the two largest Korean shipbuilders, should merge, a plan that alarmed competition authorities in several countries. A few months later, the Chinese government responded by ordering two state-owned shipbuilders, China State Shipbuilding and China Shipbuilding Industry Corporation, to join up. The mergers were designed to leave the two surviving entities, one Korean and the other Chinese, in control of 56 percent of the world's shipbuilding market. Whether that would finally translate into profits for shipbuilders that had rarely managed to earn them was anyone's guess.

18

Food Miles

ON MAY 31, 2019, the *Bavaria*, a sixteen-year-old containership previously known as the *APL Panama*, registered in Liberia and run by a Singaporean company on behalf of the Danish ship line Maersk, left Subic Bay in the Philippines bound for Taiwan, carrying sixty-nine containers of household garbage and obsolete electronics that originated in Canada. A private company had exported the refuse to the Philippines, ostensibly for recycling but in fact for cheap disposal. After impounding the containers for more than five years, the Filipino government saw fit to send them back where they had come from. Following a change of ships in Taiwan, the repatriated waste reached Vancouver on June 29, where it was burned to generate electricity.

The voluminous trade in trash, from plastic soft-drink bottles to hazardous medical waste, did not exist in the precontainer era: shipping recycled newspapers five thousand miles was not worth the cost. Its prominence in the 2010s was just one manifestation of a world in which distance and borders mattered less than before. Demand to export beef, soybeans, and palm oil brought the loss of forests and marshlands, contributing to the extinction of entire plant and animal species. Freer trade tempted manufacturers to flee countries with tight environmental controls for places where rules against dumping toxic chemicals and polluting the water were less likely to be enforced. Particulates from Indonesian coal burned in Pakistani power plants blew across Asia's borders. The explosive growth of long-distance trade made almost every economy more transport intensive, increasing the use of petroleum-based fuels and thereby contributing to the ceaseless rise in the concentration of greenhouse gases that were changing the earth's climate.

Blaming globalization for environmental degradation is morally fraught. Increased foreign trade, foreign investment, and foreign lending raised the incomes of billions of people: while globalization left many behind and drove others to migrate in search of work and safety, it lifted many more out of poverty. Apartment towers and multistory shopping malls, each requiring the production and transportation of concrete, glass, steel beams, and copper pipes, sprouted in former swamps and rice paddies around the world. Roughly 3.5 billion people had electricity in their homes in the late 1980s; by 2017, that figure reached 6.5 billion—a task accomplished by hastily constructing hundreds of power plants, many of them importing the dirtiest of all fuels, coal. Television sets and airplane trips came within reach of a rapidly expanding middle class, and global consumption of beef, once a luxury in many parts of the world, increased by half between 1990 and 2017. These achievements cannot be dismissed out of hand.[1]

Yet the fact that more people enjoyed greater material wealth than ever before was undeniably associated with a greater burden on the environment. It was true, as an OECD report acknowledged memorably, that "Globalisation is often an ally of the chainsaw." Countries whose primitive economies were transformed overnight lacked the scientific expertise and bureaucratic infrastructure to oversee the factories, waste disposal sites, and industrial-scale plantations springing up within their borders. In China's rush to expand manufacturing, factories were permitted to dump contaminated water into sewers or nearby rivers with little oversight, to the point that many rivers were unfit to drink from. Air quality, measured in terms of exposure to small particulates, grew dangerously poor—and then a crash program to reduce particulate emissions changed atmospheric chemistry in a way that raised ozone levels in Chinese cities. According to one study, China's production of goods for export contributed more than one-third of sulfur dioxide emissions, a quarter of the nitrogen oxides, and a fifth of the carbon monoxide emitted by Chinese sources in 2006. China's emissions of greenhouse gases tripled between 1978 and the early 2000s, owing to hundreds of new coal-burning power plants and smoke-belching factories. Particulates emitted by Chinese industry fouled the air in Korea and Japan. So much pollution was blown across the Pacific that up to a quarter of sulfate concentrations in the western United States were attributed to manufacturing of Chinese exports.[2]

Weak environmental laws and sporadic enforcement—state-owned companies with close ties to high government officials often had the worst environmental records—meant that firms often did not face the true economic costs of their activities, and these costs were not reflected in decisions about producing and transporting their products. Mounting public pressure to force businesses to recognize the environmental costs of their activities eventually helped reshape globalization.

————

The risk that a more integrated world might injure the environment was evident long before "globalization" was applied to the economy. In 1947, the United Nations Educational, Scientific, and Cultural Organization, UNESCO, a new branch of the two-year-old United Nations, decided to convene international meetings on conservation and natural resources. The first one occurred a year later, when delegates from thirty-three countries, representing private organizations as well as governments, met in Fontainebleau, south of Paris, to establish the International Union for the Protection of Nature. At the time, no country had an environment ministry. California had just created the first modern air pollution control program, in Los Angeles. London's "killer smog," which would be blamed for four thousand deaths and eventually lead Parliament to approve the Clean Air Act, was still four years in the future, and the US Congress would not pass its first environmental law, the Air Pollution Control Act, until 1955. The conference in Fontainebleau, however, did not discuss pollution control at all. Rather, the concern was that trade and economic development would threaten flora and fauna, particularly in European colonies in Africa. Creating nature reserves and protecting big game were the main topics of interest.[3]

Through the 1950s and 1960s, a series of influential books—Rachel Carson's *Silent Spring*, documenting the effects of the insecticide DDT on fish, birds, and humans; *The Population Bomb*, a 1968 best seller in which the Stanford University biologist Paul Ehrlich warned that over-population was bringing unavoidable starvation; *The Limits to Growth*, a 1972 sensation that used novel computer models to forecast "a rather sudden and uncontrollable decline in both population and industrial capacity" due to overconsumption—brought environmental issues front and center. As scientists documented the health risks from air and water pollution and toxic chemicals, demands for a cleaner environment grew louder in the wealthy economies, where environmental concerns became more prominent as incomes rose and living conditions improved. Between 1970 and 1972, Canada, the United States, Japan, and many countries in Western Europe created national environmental agencies to address pollution problems head on. Their urgency was not shared in developing countries, where the rich world's newfound concern about overconsumption seemed to imply that poorer countries should not aspire to the living standards of the richer ones.[4]

New environmental regulations focused first on the most visible polluters, factories and power plants that dumped untreated effluent into rivers and vented noxious gases into the air. The principle that polluters, or at least corporate polluters, should pay the full cost of whatever harm they imposed on the public seemed straightforward. But in a world of increasingly free trade, differences in countries' environmental regulations could have major economic implications. Why pay to install a costly new emissions-control system at a smoke-belching foundry when it would be cheaper to import metal castings from a country without such rules? Why abandon a familiar process for making a chemical, potentially entailing the loss of jobs and profits, when the work could be shifted to a country where widespread poverty and rampant unemployment meant that controlling pollution was not a burning issue?

In 1974, two US scientists discovered that chlorofluorocarbons, chemicals widely used in spray cans and air conditioners, were destroying ozone gas in the stratosphere, where it shields the earth from ultraviolet radiation. Panic ensued, as headlines screamed warnings that ultraviolet rays would cause more skin cancer in humans and mutations in plants and animals. "It's like AIDS from the sky," an anxious engineer from Chile, one of the countries most exposed to higher radiation levels, told *Newsweek*. Several countries soon banned the chemicals, but this was a problem that could not be solved at the national level. International negotiations advanced with unusual speed. In the Montreal Protocol, signed in 1987, countries agreed not only to phase out the production and use of more than one hundred chemicals, but also to ban imports containing the chemicals from countries that refused to sign the pact. This was the first case in which the movement toward freer trade, enshrined in the GATT, was trumped by anxieties about the environment—and the first in which developing countries were both induced and required to comply. Manufacturers of refrigerators and air conditioners were forced to develop new ways to keep food cool; they could not evade the new rules by exporting from countries with weak regulations to countries with strong ones.[5]

Acid rain posed a different sort of cross-border challenge. Through the late 1970s, researchers reported that sulfur dioxide created by burning coal in power plants and smelters, carried northeast on the prevailing winds and then falling to earth in rainfall, was killing off maple and birch forests and eliminating fish in thousands of lakes in Canada and the northeastern United States. Although emissions from both countries were to blame, the damage in Canada was far larger and the issue far more emotional; on his first foreign trip as US president, Ronald Reagan visited Ottawa in March 1981 to be greeted by protesters holding placards demanding "Stop Acid Rain." A fix was politically complicated: electricity users in Ohio and Indiana faced higher bills if their power plants had to install scrubbers to make Canada's air cleaner, and the powerful US coal industry rejected any responsibility. It took a decade for Canada to work out a domestic emissions-control scheme, for the United States to create a novel program to curb sulfur emissions from power plants, and for the two countries to sign a bilateral air quality agreement—and longer for acid concentrations to decline enough for fish to repopulate barren lakes.

As international trade expanded, environmental concerns increasingly ran against trade policy head on. Denmark required in 1990 not only that beer bottles be recyclable, but that a large share of them actually be refilled—a stopper for foreign brewers who would have had to ship empty bottles back to distant breweries. A 1991 German law mandated that retailers accept used packaging from customers and return it to manufacturers for recycling; the ecological purpose was sensible enough, but the burden of compliance stood to be much higher for importers selling only small quantities in Germany than for firms emphasizing the German market. Most emotional was a US ban on imports of tuna from countries that did not take measures to reduce the incidental harm to Pacific dolphins, including Mexico, Venezuela, Vanuatu, Panama, and Ecuador. Just as talks to create a North American free-trade area got underway in early 1991, Mexico asked the GATT to determine whether the US Marine Mammal Act, which authorized the ban, improperly interfered with trade. The Mexican petition unexpectedly introduced a sensitive environmental debate into a trade negotiation.[6]

Mexico, heavily encumbered by its foreign debts, had joined the GATT only four years earlier. It was cautiously opening parts of its economy to foreign investment as it sought to escape its lingering debt crisis; it wanted a North American free-trade agreement to move its economy beyond labor-intensive tasks, such as stitching blue jeans and assembling wire harnesses for cars, and toward more sophisticated manufacturing. US and Canadian companies saw Mexico as an attractive market for exports and a closer source of imports than distant Asia, and the US government hoped NAFTA might help stabilize an increasingly shaky neighbor. The pact, signed in late 1992, met strenuous opposition in the United States, not only from labor unions and some farming interests, but also from environmental groups complaining about uncontrolled air pollution and chemical dumping on the Mexican side of the border. To placate critics, the three countries reached a side agreement to NAFTA creating an environmental commission, the first time any international trade agreement included a commitment to improving the environment.

Ironically, NAFTA ended up benefiting Mexico's environment. Many of Mexico's most pressing environmental problems—the lack of sewage treatment, the dust clouds constantly stirred up by traffic on unpaved city streets—predated NAFTA by years, if not decades. The environmental commission offered funds to pave streets and build sewage plants in some places, and foreign companies considering investments in Mexico demanded improvements in others. Imports allowed under NAFTA, as well as new plants within Mexico, drove older, smoke-belching factories and cement plants out of business. Motor vehicles as modern as those assembled in Canada and the United States supplanted the antiquated and highly polluting fleets for which Mexico was known. Perhaps most importantly, domestic environmental groups finally gained political influence in parts of the country, demanding action against deforestation, creation of new nature reserves, and tougher environmental laws.[7]

———

Climate change posed a very different challenge to globalization than more traditional forms of pollution. Unlike the environmental issues raised by European recycling policies and NAFTA negotiations, the rising concentrations of greenhouse gases in the atmosphere, due principally to the burning of fossil fuels, were inherently a global problem. In most countries, international trade was by no means the main source; by one estimate, emissions from producing and transporting imports and exports accounted for less than one-fourth of production-related emissions in the early 2000s, and an even smaller share of total emissions. By the calculations of Joseph Shapiro, an American economist, international trade added about 5 percent to the world's emissions of greenhouse gases, increasing global emissions of carbon dioxide by 1.7 gigatons a year.[8]

In 1997, thirty-seven countries, mainly in Europe, signed the Kyoto Protocol, an agreement to reduce their greenhouse-gas emissions. While many of those countries seemed to be living up to their promises in the early twenty-first century, their downward-sloping trend lines were an illusion. There were genuine improvements—heating systems became more fuel efficient and wind and solar power took market share from coal—but global value chains served to disguise the fact that many countries were restraining their emissions of carbon dioxide, methane, and other gases by stepping up imports from countries that had done little to reduce emissions. Moreover, when tariff rates are adjusted for the greenhouse-gas emissions involved in producing specific goods, many countries charge less on dirtier imports, such as basic metal products, than on cleaner ones, effectively encouraging dirty industries to move offshore. Closing smelters and steel plants and buying exports from poor countries instead flattered rich countries' statistics, but it did not bring down the quantity of greenhouse gases entering the atmosphere. Overall emissions from exports grew 4.3 percent per year from 1990 to 2008, three times as fast as the world's population. Trade allowed the wealthy economies to push their emissions out of sight.[9]

Economists, almost unanimously, favor using taxes to deter greenhouse-gas emissions: economic theory teaches that a tax on emissions would give factories and power plants financial reason to emit less. Taxing individual drivers and farmers is politically treacherous, but the European Union, a handful of US states, and several Canadian provinces attempted to force power plants and factories to pay for each ton of carbon dioxide coming out of their smokestacks. In a globalized economy, though, taxing emissions is not so simple. A tax high enough to induce a plant to install more fuel-efficient equipment would raise prices for customers, who might choose instead to import from countries where greenhouse-gas emissions are not taxed. Transporting cement over long distances is costly relative to the value of the product, so taxing a cement plant's emissions has little effect on trade. But electricity is a major cost in making aluminum, and a tax that makes electricity dearer might well tip the balance in favor of imported ingots and billets.[10]

Trade in manufactured goods is only one source of emissions related to globalization. By the 2010s, more than one-fifth of the calories produced by farmers were traded each year, much of it in the form of oils pressed from soybeans, corn, cotton, and other crops. While the largest share of agricultural exports occurred within the European Union,

Chile shipped large volumes of cherries (166,304 tons in the 2018-19 season) and plums (76,784 tons) to China, and Mexico discovered burgeoning markets for avocadoes in Canada and Japan. Alaskan fish distributors flew freshly caught Dungeness crabs to China, where the meat was extracted from the shells and packed for US customers, and Boeing 747s laden with fish caught off Namibia made nonstop runs to Zaragoza, Spain, where fish processor Caladero filleted them for sale in Spanish supermarkets.[11]

The large-scale cutting of forests to create palm-oil plantations and cattle ranches was a major source of greenhouse gases, and moving food so many miles added to emissions. Worries about climate change meshed with decades-old critiques that large firms and long-distance freight shipments were destroying self-sufficient local economies. A 1994 report by the Sustainable Agriculture, Food, and Environment (SAFE) Alliance, a British group, gave consumers a way to measure the true cost of imported food by introducing the concept of "food miles." Its claim was that long-distance shipments of food wasted both energy and food, benefiting big supermarket chains but increasing pollution. Minimizing the number of miles food traveled by purchasing from local farms, it contended, was better for the environment than purchasing imports.[12]

"Food miles" struck a chord with the spreading antiglobalization movement. The assertion that food imports were artificially cheap because consumers did not have to pay the full cost of the environmental harm they caused, including greenhouse-gas emissions, was accurate. Yet the underlying claim that buying locally produced food was better for the environment was not necessarily true. Because British farmers typically bought factory-made food concentrates for their livestock rather than feeding them entirely on grass, a ton of lamb raised in Britain embodied four times the greenhouse-gas emissions of lamb imported from New Zealand, while milk powder shipped from New Zealand resulted in less than half the emissions of the British domestic product. Similarly, a British government study found that importing organic wheat by sea from the United States led to much less air pollution and lower greenhouse-gas emissions than growing the same wheat in Great Britain. Reducing food miles would not necessarily reduce greenhouse-gas emissions, the study pointed out, because small, local food producers might be less energy efficient than larger ones and might make the distribution system less energy efficient as well. So far as the environment was concerned, buying global sometimes turned out to be better.[13]

———

As wine drinkers know well, the dearest French wines bear the label "Mis en bouteille au château." That etiquette, promising that the wine was bottled on the estate where all the grapes used to make it were grown and fermented, supposedly ensures the purest, highest-quality libation. Oenophiles may dispute the importance of the label. But one thing is not in dispute: transporting estate-bottled wine means roughly 40 percent more greenhouse-gas emissions than if the wine is moved in a stainless-steel tank and bottled near where it will be consumed.[14]

Reducing emissions from freight transportation became a priority in the second decade of the twenty-first century. Transportation of all sorts accounted for around one-tenth of all greenhouse-gas emissions in 2007 and a large share of other types of air pollution. Truck engines were the main source, but international ocean shipping was responsible for about 3 percent of global emissions and freight carried aboard international flights for another percent or 2. Freight transportation emitted significantly less than power generation and manufacturing, but with an important difference. Whereas power plants and highly polluting factories are fixed in place, difficult to disguise, and clearly subject to the jurisdiction of a particular government, ships and planes are often owned by residents of one country, registered in another, and following routes between countries unconnected to the owner or the place of registry. They were not easily regulated: In 2012, when the European Union required airlines to purchase greenhouse-gas emissions permits for all flights taking off from or landing within its borders, other countries objected loudly that this violated international agreements, and the requirement was applied only to flights entirely within the European Union.

Airfreight flourished in the Third Globalization. The best measure, the number of ton-kilometers, was five times as high in 2017 as it had been in 1987, mainly because airfreight had become much cheaper. Adjusted for general price inflation, the average cost of airfreight declined more than 2 percent annually during the late 1990s and early 2000s. Measured by volume, only a tiny fraction of world trade moved by air in 2017; measured by value, though, planes carried more than one-third of exports and imports, from US semiconductors headed to Shanghai to Kenyan roses destined for Amsterdam. But while newer jets burned less fuel per ton-kilometer than older ones, the rate of improvement declined over time, and old fuel guzzlers remained in use for decades—often with the seats removed to turn them into freighters. The aviation industry's rapid growth made reducing emissions of greenhouse gases and other pollutants all but impossible.[15]

The shipping industry faced a similar conundrum. Most oceangoing vessels burn a thick low-grade oil left over after crude petroleum is refined into gasoline, jet fuel, and other high-value products. Because it is stored in the engine's fuel tanks, or bunkers, ship fuel is often called "bunker fuel." Bunker fuel tends to be a dirty and noxious product, but it has the virtue of being cheap. With oceangoing vessels spending most of their time in international waters where no country's pollution-control laws applied, shipowners had no incentive to use cleaner, costlier fuels. Reducing fuel use, however, was in the interest of both ship lines and their customers, as fuel was generally the largest cost involved in operating a ship. Around 2007, when shipowners embraced slow steaming to save fuel, shippers did not object. At the same time, carriers began acquiring new vessels that burned less fuel per ton-mile than older ones—at least when the ships were full. Shippers, especially those doing business directly with consumers, were under pressure to make their supply chains greener, and they could rightly boast that their average greenhouse-gas emissions from transporting each container or each ton of wheat were coming down. Whether total emissions from ocean shipping were declining, though, was a matter of some dispute, as the total volume of international freight continued to increase.[16]

The world's shipping industry is loosely overseen by the International Maritime Organization, a branch of the United Nations. Operating by consensus, the IMO does not move quickly, but as individual countries adopted environmental rules that would affect international shipping, it felt rising pressure to act. In 2005, new IMO rules limited ships' nitrogen oxide emissions and set a limit on allowable sulfur content in vessel fuels to control emissions of sulfur dioxide, the chemical responsible for acid rain. Six years later, the IMO mandated energy-efficient designs for new ships, and in 2018 it announced a strategy to cut greenhouse-gas emissions to half the 2008 level by 2050. None of these initiatives had immediate consequences, but all of them promised to raise the cost of shipping over time. Meeting the IMO's requirement that an estimated 110,000 ships burn only low-sulfur fuel starting in 2020 required refineries to retool, adding a projected $60 billion per year to the cost of transporting freight.[17]

By the second decade of the twenty-first century, environmental stress was casting a shadow over globalization. Although individual countries' environmental policies were erratic, the movement toward tighter environmental controls was unmistakable. Higher-income countries acted to phase out coal-fired power plants, subsidize battery-powered cars, and reduce the amount of waste sent to incinerators or landfill. Developing countries that had only recently turned a blind eye to environmental concerns found their newly prosperous citizens no longer willing to accept dirty air and dirty water as unavoidable costs of economic growth. China, Indonesia, Malaysia, Thailand, and Vietnam all cracked down on imports of rich-country garbage, and even poorer countries like Kenya and Tanzania prohibited the ubiquitous plastic bags that clogged waterways and hung from tree branches. Higher taxes on fuels and on greenhouse-gas emissions threatened to make the cost of moving freight an important consideration instead of an afterthought.[18]

Perhaps most consequential of all, investors as well as consumers were demanding to know what firms were doing to minimize their environmental impact. As businesses gave environmental costs greater weight when deciding what to produce and how to transport it, global value chains began to seem riskier and potentially more expensive than corporate bean counters had ever imagined.

19

Broken Chains

THE VERY NAME of Monessen hints of globalization: "Mon" is a nod to the Monongahela River, busy with coal barges winding their way past the town to the steel mills of Pittsburgh, twenty miles farther north, while "essen" alludes to the eponymous steelmaking center in the German Ruhr. Apparently, the Pittsburgh financier who laid out the town in 1897 thought a bit of global flair would draw in residents. Yet beyond immigrants—Monessen had Finnish, Swedish, and German Lutheran churches—there was little global about the place. The main local industry for most of the twentieth century, a steel plant that once employed six thousand workers, had sought import restrictions to keep foreign competitors at bay almost continuously from 1962 until it finally closed in 1986. By then, Monessen already was labeled a "Decaying Company Town," and matters did not improve with time. It was a place where the world economy was a threat, never an opportunity.[1]

When presidential candidate Donald Trump chose Monessen for a campaign speech in June 2016, the population had fallen two-thirds from its 1940 peak. The largest remaining factory, a plant that distilled coal into coke for purifying liquid steel in blast furnaces, emitted a sulfurous smell pungent enough to extinguish hopes that workers in Pittsburgh's vibrant medical and high-tech industries might make homes or open businesses nearby. Speaking words that might have been written with Monessen in mind, Trump attacked globalization head on. "Globalization . . . has left millions of our workers with nothing but poverty and heartache," he declaimed. Although he fell shy of capturing Monessen's vote, his message resonated through the tired coal and steel towns of western Pennsylvania. In the election in November 2016, Westmoreland County, with Monessen in its southwest corner, went for Trump nearly two to one.[2]

Yet the anger and anguish pertained to a stage of globalization that already was ebbing. Well before the introspection triggered by Trump's surprise election victory, the British vote for Brexit, and the rise of nationalist politicians across Europe, Latin America, and Asia, the world economy had taken on a very different look.

———

The defining feature of the period since the late 1980s had been the intricate value chains that grew to bind the world economy together. As they forged these chains, international companies moved much of their goods production out of Europe, North America, and Japan to countries with lower wages and business-friendly labor laws, mainly in Eastern Europe, Mexico, China, and Southeast Asia. In the process, namebrand companies often outsourced work that had always been the essence of manufacturing, hiring low-profile firms to stamp, mold, and assemble their products while their own employees focused on finance, design, and marketing. In Serang, Indonesia, a little-known Taiwanese company employed fifteen thousand workers to make athletic shoes for an iconic German company to sell in Canada. In Waterford, Ireland, a US-owned factory molded and assembled precision medical devices sold under famous European brand names. Near Guatemala City, five thousand people worked in plants owned by a South Korean firm, sewing clothing bearing the labels of US retailers. Although foreign trade, foreign investment, foreign lending, and cross-border migration were not at all new, never before was the process of manufacturing so intimately shared among countries.[3]

Trade had flourished in the 1990s and 2000s as these value chains had become longer and more complicated. In automaking, where the production process is among the most complex, there could be eight or more tiers in the value chain for a particular vehicle, with suppliers on lower tiers furnishing raw materials and simple components to manufacturers of more sophisticated products in the tiers above them; inputs might cross borders multiple times as crude oil was transformed into a plastic resin that was molded into a button that was installed in an audio control panel that was built into a steering wheel that was attached to a steering column that was incorporated into a steering system that became part of a car, with each step in the process occurring in a separate location. When the US Federal Aviation Administration looked into defective parts in the wings of some Boeing 737 jets in 2019, it traced the problem to a metal plating company that was at least four links removed from Boeing's assembly plants.[4] The containerships that became the icons of globalization mainly carried not products ready to sell in retail stores, but materials and components on their way to become something else. Similarly, industrial inputs filled the trucks shuttled by train through the Eurotunnel between France and Britain and the jet planes linking semiconductor plants in Japan with testing and packaging facilities in Southeast Asia and from there with smartphone factories in China.[5]

The deep economic crisis that began in late 2007, starting with the collapse of the US housing market and prolonged by the threat that the debts of Greece, Portugal, and Spain would bring down Europe's biggest banks, put the brakes on the Third Globalization. As always happens in a recession, the volume of world trade declined. The conventional wisdom—the wisdom that inspired so much investment in megaships and container terminals—was that after the slump ended, exports and imports would again grow faster than the world's output, as they had for many years. The conventional wisdom missed the mark. After bouncing back in 2010 and 2011, exports went flat. Instead of growing at twice the rate of the world economy, as it had in the late 1990s and early 2000s, goods trade underperformed the world economy, growing at an anemic 0.8 percent per year. By the World Bank's reckoning, total merchandise trade—the sum of exports and imports of commodities and manufactured goods—peaked at 51 percent of the world's output in 2008. A decade on, it accounted for five percentage points less. Put another way, almost all the growth of the world economy in the years after the finan-

cial crisis was due to businesses producing goods and services for domestic clients. Almost none of it was due to increased foreign trade.

Global corporate giants, hard-pressed by the crisis, started to shrink,
eliminating operations that were marginally profitable and withdrawing
from parts of the world where they had no advantage. The annual flow
of foreign direct investment, money going to build factories and buy
companies and property outside the investor's home country, fell by
two-thirds from its precrisis peak. International bank lending waned,
and so did issuance of bonds in foreign markets, although interest rates
were very low. By 2016, even the flow of money sent home by migrants
was flatlining, squeezing the economies of many poor countries that
relied on remittances by their citizens abroad to help relatives pay school
fees, build homes, and start businesses.

The waning of the Third Globalization was partly a matter of simple
arithmetic. Over the previous two decades, hundreds of thousands of
factories in wealthy countries—more than seventy thousand in the
United States alone—had closed as production was shifted to places
where wages were lower or demand was growing faster. As Japanese
electronics companies sent assembly work to Malaysia and European
clothing chains ordered more apparel from Bangladesh, massive amounts
of foreign investment built new manufacturing facilities abroad, and the
total amount of foreign trade increased. But there was a finite number of
rich-country factories whose work could profitably be relocated. Once
the great exodus of manufacturing from high-wage countries petered out,
production shifting no longer provided a boost to trade.

At the same time, many manufacturers and retailers concluded that
complicated long-distance supply chains were less profitable than they
had imagined. As freight transportation became slower and less reliable,
and as more sole-source factories experienced unplanned outages, executives and their shareholders became more attuned to the vulnerabilities created by corporate strategies. Minimizing production costs was
no longer the sole priority; making sure the goods were available when
needed ranked just as highly.

Lowering the risk of business interruptions is neither cheap nor
simple. Increasing inventories ties up money in merchandise that grows

stale; to unload last year's fashions, department stores have to mark the clothes down, and last year's cars lose value sitting on the dealer's lot. Producing critical components at multiple locations rather than in one big factory creates flexibility, but consumes precious investment dollars and may raise the cost of making each item, placing the manufacturer at a competitive disadvantage when no crisis is at hand. Dividing exports among several ship lines and sending them through different ports improves resilience but can inflate the freight bill. Trading a long-distance value chain for a local one creates risks of its own: should that one place suffer an earthquake or a catastrophic fire, the firm could be crippled.

Meanwhile, the desire for more reliable value chains ran headlong into customers' changing expectations. Customers, whether families or businesses, increasingly demanded next-day delivery or even same-day delivery. For sellers in many industries, particularly retailing, quick turnaround was no longer a high-priced option but a basic requirement just to stay in the game. Firms credited their sophisticated logistical systems, guided by artificial intelligence, with making fast delivery easy. But at the end of the day, goods were still goods, and the only way manufacturers, wholesalers, and retailers could deliver them almost immediately was to keep more goods in their distribution centers, ready to ship out at the click of a mouse. For the first time since the early days of just-in-time manufacturing, inventories began to rise.

———

The backlash against globalization only added to the sense of greater risk. For seven decades, ever since the Bretton Woods meeting of Allied governments in 1944, governments in many parts of the world had joined forces to make borders more porous. In the immediate postwar years, many imports into the wealthy economies faced tariffs that inflated their prices by one-fifth or more. In addition, most countries used an assortment of other policies that fenced out foreign goods, such as quotas on specific products, controls on the use of foreign currency to pay for imports, and requirements that certain goods purchased by the government be produced domestically. By the 2010s, repeated negotiations through the GATT had brought the average import duty down to around 3 percent in the wealthy countries, and many countries had free-trade agreements with one another that eliminated tariffs altogether. Businesses could confidently extend their supply chains without worrying that a tax collected at the border would wreak havoc with their plans.[6]

While the wealthy economies were relatively open to imports of manufactured goods, many of the developing countries kept tariffs high to protect their emerging manufacturing sectors. Average tariff rates in developing countries—9 percent in Vietnam, 10 percent in India, 11 percent in China, 17 percent in Ethiopia—were three or four times the rates in wealthy countries, and a smaller share of imports entered duty-free. In addition, many developing countries erected other obstacles: whatever the official tariff rates, it was exceedingly difficult to import cars into China and medicines into India. The belief that developing countries were enjoying unfair advantages contributed to a powerful reaction in Europe and North America, where manufacturing jobs were vanishing and wages stagnating. The critics who had been protesting globalization for two decades scored their first major victory in 2008, when the Doha Round, a trade negotiation involving 164 countries, broke down amid acrimony over rules for agricultural products and for services such as banking and telecommunications. With so many countries at the bargaining table, each pressed by domestic interests intent on keeping foreign competition at bay, another worldwide agreement seemed implausible. Any future agreements to eliminate obstacles to trade would need to be worked out among smaller groups of countries.

At that point in time, most leading politicians in the wealthy countries strongly supported greater trade and foreign investment. But the aftermath of the financial crisis destroyed that consensus. A generation of politicians favoring stronger borders rose to prominence. Nationalists from Greece to Sweden campaigned against the free movement of goods and labor within the European Union, which the Dutch anti-Islamist Geert Wilders labeled "the monster in Brussels." In Italy, Matteo

Salvini, who described the euro—the common currency adopted by nineteen European nations—as "a crime against humanity," became leader of the Northern League party and, eventually, deputy prime minister. In China, the country that arguably benefited the most from the Third Globalization, Premier Xi Jinping introduced measures that made life harder for foreign companies, demanding that they reveal their proprietary technology and produce more components in China, even as he praised open trade. Just before the 2012 presidential election in the United States, President Barack Obama's administration asked the WTO to rule that China was illegally blocking US auto imports while subsidizing exports of cars and auto parts, while his opponent, Mitt Romney, promised to put tariffs on imports from China to counteract its purported currency manipulation.[7]

This unwelcoming tone soured many corporate executives considering where and how to make their goods: if critical products made for export were suddenly to face import restrictions in key markets, the financial losses could be very large. Then, too, labor costs were rising rapidly in some popular locations for outsourcing. To the extent that rich-country firms had moved labor-intensive work to China and Eastern Europe to take advantage of cheap labor, their strategies no longer made sense. Around 2011, as the result of independent decisions by some of the world's largest companies, trade patterns began to shift as multinational companies reconsidered their value chains.

The effects showed up not only in export and import figures, but also in a set of obscure calculations that track the extent to which one country's manufacturers use inputs that were imported from another country. In 2011, these OECD data show, 42 percent of the value of South Korea's exports—things like Hyundai cars and Daewoo tanker ships—came from imported materials and components; six years later, the corresponding figure was only 30 percent. For China, imported content was 23 percent of the value of manufactured exports in 2011, but only 17 percent five years later. The United States, Great Britain, Germany, Italy, Japan, and Sweden all experienced the same trend. So did Taiwan, Indonesia, and Malaysia. There are only two likely explanations. One is that manufacturers in these countries cut back on exporting goods that used a lot of foreign inputs. The other is that they decided to obtain more of their inputs at home rather than sourcing them abroad. Either way, manufacturing became less global.

In economic terms, this was not necessarily positive. Research strongly supports the idea that participating extensively in global value chains helps countries raise productivity by disseminating the latest foreign knowledge. Attempting to capture every link in a value chain, on the other hand, may leave a country wastefully performing tasks that might be done elsewhere more efficiently. In Malaysia, which eagerly sought investment by foreign manufacturers, the central bank objected in 2017 that the country was admitting too many low-skilled migrants to work in factories, thereby reducing incentives for manufacturers to invest in advanced technology. "Reliance on low-wage, low-cost production methods is an untenable long-term strategy with risks of Malaysia being left behind," the bank warned. The government of China, the world's leading exporter, aggressively pushed manufacturers to create research centers and high-technology factories within the country and unveiled a ten-year plan, Made in China 2025, calling for self-sufficiency in electric vehicles, synthetic materials, robotics, and other leading-edge industries—despite ample evidence that squeezing out foreign firms and excluding foreign inputs are likely to retard a country's growth rather than accelerate it.[8]

———

All these trends were well established prior to 2016, the year in which British voters supported Brexit and Donald Trump was elected US president, albeit with a minority of the popular vote. Trump, like the other nationalist leaders of the time, was suspicious of globalization in many spheres: he was as critical of the North Atlantic Treaty Organization (NATO), a twenty-nine-nation military alliance, as of the WTO; clamped down on immigration; encouraged the breakup of the European Union; and flatly rejected the Trans-Pacific Partnership, a 2015 trade agreement among twelve Pacific Rim countries aimed at restraining the growing economic power of China. The eleven other countries went ahead with the partnership, leaving the United States with poorer access to their markets than had it signed on.

Once in office in 2017, Trump slapped tariffs—taxes on imports—on a wide range of foreign goods and promised even more; for good measure, he threatened to dissolve NAFTA and tightened scrutiny of foreigners investing in the United States. Other countries responded in kind, raising tariffs on US exports and putting new controls on foreign investment. China, then the United States' largest trading partner, clamped down on imports of pork, soybeans, and hundreds of other products from the United States; when the United States alleged that communications gear made by two Chinese firms would allow China to spy on other countries, China retaliated by fining a US-based automaker for price-fixing. The government's apparent desire to keep important value chains entirely within China had already set off alarms from Canberra to Berlin, drawing other countries into the flaring US-China conflict. The US accusation that China was manipulating its exchange rate to make its exports cheaper in the United States, counteracting the effects of the higher US tariffs, raised the stakes higher. With a trade war between the world's two great economic powers heating up, firms scrambled to move parts of their value chains out of China.

For the Trump administration, that was a welcome result. Trump's favored measure of international economic success was the US trade balance with individual countries; the fact that America's trade deficit in electronic products with China was due mainly to inputs created in other countries and that much of the profit went to the shareholders of US-based corporations did not impress him. "It does the American economy no long-term good to only keep the big box factories where we are now assembling 'American' products that are composed primarily of foreign components," one of his counselors declared in early 2017. "We need to manufacture those components in a robust domestic supply chain that will spur job and wage growth."[9]

Like China's policies, the US initiatives to capture more of the links in supply chains did not stimulate domestic manufacturing. Neither country had a surplus of unemployed workers eager to work in factories: the size of China's labor force peaked in 2017, according to the

World Bank, while the US labor force, cut off from an influx of undocu-
mented immigrants from Latin America, was barely growing. In both
countries, interest in factory work waned as higher living standards and
education levels raised workers' career expectations.

Instead of stimulating domestic manufacturing industries, nationalistic policies reinforced a different trend: in manufacturing of many
types of goods, globalization was giving way to regionalization. Step by
step, investment by investment, the world economy reorganized itself
around three hubs. Germany emerged as the center of a trade network
that encompassed dozens of countries from Russia to Ireland; its exports of specialized components accounted for most of the imports
consumed by manufacturers elsewhere in Europe. Asian and Pacific
countries that had once been in the US orbit now revolved around
China, which imported so much from them that its international trade
was nearly in balance; Japan, Asia's industrial powerhouse into the
1990s, had long since ceased to be the region's economic driver. Goods
production in the United States was linked tightly with Mexico and
Canada, because of geography as well as a free-trade agreement among
the three countries that made trading simple and inexpensive; its most
important trading relationships with other parts of the world involved
services rather than goods. Value chains remained strong, but they had
become far less likely to girdle the globe.[10]

20

The Next Wave

ONE TREND above all drove the Third Globalization: a rapidly improving material standard of living. In 1987, China's streets were crowded with bicycles, and its auto plants turned out all of 17,840 new cars; thirty years later, Beijing was famous for bumper-to-bumper traffic, and China produced more motor vehicles by far than any other country. The price of girls' clothing, by the estimates of US government number crunchers, was far lower in the 2010s than it had been in the 1980s; perhaps that explains why the average person in Great Britain purchased five times as many pieces of apparel in 2017 as three decades earlier. The median new home built in the United States in 2017 was 38 percent larger than in 1987, with 2,426 square feet of space to furnish with lounge chairs, rugs, and free weights; there was a one-in-three chance that it had more than one refrigerator. Without much exaggeration, the years of the Third Globalization could aptly be named the age of stuff.[1]

Stuff did not go out of fashion, but by the late 2010s globalization seemed to be in retreat as changes in technology, demography, and consumer tastes transformed economic geography once again. The international bodies whose rules undergirded the world economy, from the WTO to the IMO, were under attack, and state efforts to control the flow of digital information, such as the famed Great Firewall of China, raised the prospect that many national internets, each under tight government control, would supplant an almost unregulated global one. As fears of terror and illegal migration made stricter border security ubiquitous, quick cross-border shopping trips lost much of their allure. The explosive COVID-19 pandemic, which forced the closure of thousands of factories in China in January 2020, paralyzed South Korea in February, and all but halted business in Europe and North America by March, served as yet another reminder that value chains brought risks alongside opportunities. When governments all but shut down international airline service in their struggles to control the virus, they severed connections that the world had long since taken for granted.

In other ways, though, globalization was a more powerful force than ever: KFC, formerly Kentucky Fried Chicken, was far and away the largest restaurant chain in China; the leading football teams in England's Premier League, few of them either starring or owned by Englishmen, were widely watched across Africa; and Russian sunseekers visiting the Mall of Dubai could browse housewares at Galeries Lafayette, jewelry at Van Cleef & Arpels, and fragrances at Chanel, topped off with a macaroon from Ladurée, all without the bother of flying to Paris. Worldwide, 1.5 billion tourist arrivals were recorded in 2019, four times as many as in 1987, and, according to the company's figures, nearly one-fifth of the world's population checked Facebook on the average day. Companies in industries whose products are intangible—software, accommodation, real estate, computer services—accounted for a greater share of the largest multinational enterprises, while major industrial companies shrank under relentless competitive pressure. In the emerging Fourth Globalization, moving ideas, services, and people around the world mattered more than transporting boatloads of goods—and seemed likely to create very different sets of winners and losers.[2]

———

Manufacturing drove the Third Globalization. While fish, fruits, flowers, coal, and petroleum also moved through long value chains, factory output was much greater and more valuable. Yet over the years, manufacturing gradually lost economic importance. Its decline was a little-noticed success story: the intense trade in manufactured goods pushed down their prices relative to the prices of services, which were generally subject to less foreign competition. By the World Bank's estimates, manufacturing was responsible for more than 17 percent of the world's total output in 2002, but nearly two percentage points less in the 2010s. China, Mexico, Indonesia, and the European Union all showed the same trend. Manufacturing simply did not matter in the way it had before.[3]

This trend was visible as well in the way households and businesses spent their money. Data from many countries suggest that families increasingly purchased services and experiences rather than goods. In France, to take one example, services accounted for 43 percent of consumer spending at the dawn of the Third Globalization but 55 percent by 2018, leaving a smaller share for the sorts of goods, from coffeemakers to running shoes, that are delivered by ships in the service of value chains. The same pattern was evident in South Africa, a much poorer country, where services accounted for 43 percent of consumers' spending in 2017, up by eight percentage points since 1987: consumer spending tilted toward transport, education, healthcare, and telecommunications and away from physical goods.

There are several reasons "stuff" is losing ground. One is that the world is aging. The median age of the global population, 23.3 years in 1985, was 31 years and climbing in 2019. While there were plenty of young consumers in Africa and South Asia, there were not so many in wealthier economies; by 2018, half the people in Japan and Germany were over age 47, and in Russia, China, and the United States the median age approached 40. Older households have had years to accumulate home furnishings and wardrobes full of clothing, and they are often disinclined to acquire more; vacation trips, restaurant meals, and medical bills are likely to figure larger in their spending than furniture and fixtures. Restaurants and hospitals also buy tables and chairs, of course, but their needs will not make up for fewer purchases by households. The share of the global population under age 15, 38 percent in the late 1960s, shrank to a mere 25 percent half a century later. With fewer young households to replace aging ones, housing, and the furnishings that go with it, is in less demand. By the European Central Bank's count, the European Union had fewer dwellings in 2018 than two years earlier.[4]

Another factor suppressing demand for physical products is the transformation of goods into services. The multipiece stereo systems that graced every student's bedroom at the start of the Third Globalization, with racks of plastic cases filled with compact discs close by, gave way in the early 2000s to computers that featured internal disc drives for data storage and optical drives to play CDs; those vanished in turn in the 2010s as both data storage and content came to be provided over the internet, via servers that are used far more intensively than the average personal computer. Culture is arguably more global than ever before, but digital downloads and streaming services have made it possible to enjoy films, books, and music without physically possessing the sorts of goods once sold in book and record stores. Major auto manufacturers anticipate that personal transportation will become a service as well; they are investing in car-sharing services as a bet that consumers will prefer to pay for access to a vehicle when needed rather than purchasing one for exclusive use—a development that seems likely to lead to a decline in the total number of registered vehicles. No one envisioned that many women could share a single dress until an internet-based company turned apparel from a personal possession into a lending service that could be engaged as needed. In economic terms, sharing reduces the waste of assets sitting idle—and thereby reduces the demand for those assets. Instead of being ridden for just a few minutes each day, a bicycle may be in use constantly as different subscribers to a bike-sharing service take their turns.

A third force that will reshape the market for stuff is that technology is making it easier to manufacture on a smaller scale. The Third Globalization was an age of mass production, epitomized by the 2.2-square-mile plant in Zhengzhou, China, where Foxconn, a Taiwan-based contract manufacturer, put together as many as half a million Apple iPhones a day. As of 2016, Foxconn used components from more than two hundred suppliers to make those phones. It paid to ship screens and microphones and semiconductors from distant places to Zhengzhou only because large sums could be saved by assembling identical phones in great quantity—and because shipping in great quantity was inexpensive. As shorter production runs become economically feasible, the scale economies of gigantic factories matter less. Manufacturers can produce goods targeted to smaller markets or even make customized products at a competitive price, enabling shoppers to obtain features they want without buying features they don't want.[5]

Businesses, too, don't spend like they used to. Once, business investment meant purchases of hard assets such as buildings and machinery, creating demand for factory products like bulldozers and production equipment. By the 2010s, though, more than one-fifth of business investment in many countries went into research, software, and other nonphysical expenditures, two or three times the share of the late 1980s. The outsourcing of information technology—and particularly the storage of data in "cloud" computer banks managed by technology companies and accessible over the internet rather than in computers located in-house—has held down spending on computer equipment, one of the most globalized of products. Increasingly, updating industrial machinery has come to mean downloading software rather than replacing hardware, taking a further bite out of factories' sales.

The very meaning of "manufacturing" has changed over time in a way that is profoundly affecting globalization. Technology has enabled manufacturers to devote far less attention to molding, extruding, stamping, and assembling physical products and far more to services related to the goods they sell: clever engineering, creative marketing, and after-sales repair and maintenance offer better returns on investment and higher obstacles to potential competitors than running assembly lines. In addition to assembling wings and fuselages, aircraft manufacturers embed tens of millions of lines of code in each new commercial plane to adjust wing flaps, send out navigation signals, detect maintenance needs, and perform dozens of other tasks; it was flaws in software, not defects in hardware, that caused the two fatal crashes that led to the grounding of Boeing's 737 Max jet in March 2019. Software, McKinsey & Company estimated in 2018, will account for 30 percent of the value of a large car by 2030. Many of the programs installed on the vehicle are likely to have no identifiable national origin, but to be written by teams located in several countries. How the launch of a new vehicle affects any nation's workforce will be difficult to determine: shifting the source of a braking system from the United States to Mexico is likely to bring identifiable job losses in the former country and new jobs in the latter, but there may be no ready way to know whether a coder in Los Angeles has been displaced because some part of the software that manages the brakes has been written in Guadalajara.[6]

In many industries, the manufacturing process itself will likely become simpler, requiring far less labor. For environmental reasons, many governments have encouraged a shift from vehicles powered by gasoline or diesel engines to electric vehicles. EVs do not have engines, transmissions, or emissions-control equipment, so as they gain market share, there will be less need for workers to produce gears and piston rings—and less reason to farm production out to low-wage countries. Robots, initially used in factories to perform tasks too uncomfortable or dangerous for humans, have become sophisticated enough to mass-produce T-shirts, a development that could make it feasible for high-wage countries to be competitive in making some types of clothing. Automated factories are now making athletic shoes in the United States and Germany, taking jobs from factory workers in Indonesia. With additive manufacturing, in which a computer directs a printer to build an object by depositing layer upon layer of a plastic or metallic material at precise locations, manufacturers can make specialized parts in small quantities near where they are needed instead of shipping them from far away. By squeezing out labor costs, such technologies are eliminating one of the main rationales for far-flung value chains.[7]

All these developments were underway well before China announced its Made in China 2025 plan in 2015, the British voted to leave the European Union in 2016, and the United States distanced itself from multilateral trade agreements in 2017. They will continue even if the United States and China retreat from the brink of a trade war, whether or not the world continues to divide itself into regional trading blocs. Even with generous subsidies for manufacturers, shipbuilders, and ocean carriers, the perception that long value chains have become costlier, riskier, less reliable, and less essential was bringing an end to the globalization of the early twenty-first century well before the coronavirus arrived on the scene. Regardless of what actions governments take, goods trade is likely to grow more slowly than the world economy in the years ahead, and may soon start to decline.

———

Is globalization over? Not by any stretch. Rather, it has entered a new stage. While globalization is retreating with respect to factory production and foreign investment, it is advancing quickly when it comes to the flow of services and ideas. The vision of the Third Globalization was that engineers and designers working for large corporations in the advanced economies would create products to be manufactured in places where wages were lower, which those corporations could then sell around the world. In the Fourth Globalization, it is the research, engineering, and design work that is being globalized: the hundred largest companies accounted for more than one-third of all business research and development spending worldwide, often distributing it among technical centers in multiple countries in order to take advantage of local talent and to shape products to local tastes. The manufacturing, meanwhile, can be done almost anywhere. The diminished role of physical production is reflected in the tendency of industrial companies to structure their foreign involvements through licensing arrangements with local firms and contracts with suppliers of manufacturing services, rather than by investing their shareholders' money and hiring their own production employees abroad—one reason for the decline in foreign direct investment. Workers with the requisite technical training can look forward to opportunities in highly automated factories, even in places where wages are high.

Workers in many service industries, on the other hand, may face serious foreign competition for the first time in their careers. In some service industries, foreign competition is an old story. Already in 1981, American Airlines relocated a data processing operation to the Caribbean island of Barbados, where hundreds of women punched information from passengers' ticket stubs into computers that transmitted it via satellite to the United States. A few years later, US insurers began flying claims forms to Shannon, Ireland, for data processing, with the processed claims then beamed back across the Atlantic. Within a decade, optical scanning eliminated much of the need for data entry, and the Irish processing centers gave way to call centers in which an estimated ten thousand workers answered customer calls for European banks and American technology companies. These investments, similar to many investments in manufacturing value chains, were driven by government subsidies and differences in wage costs. Its operation in Barbados, American Airlines estimated, processed ticket stubs for only half of the cost of doing the work in Tulsa, Oklahoma.[8]

Over time, trade in services came to involve more sophisticated work. In 1989, US-based General Electric Company, then one of the largest multinational corporations, began outsourcing software coding to India. By 2017, the sales of India's technology outsourcing industry reached an estimated $150 billion a year. Passenger airlines, many of which had hired contractors to handle some of their aircraft maintenance, began shifting some of that work to places with lower labor costs; by 2006, US airlines sent more than one-third of their heavy maintenance to foreign repair stations. Ready access to the internet allowed portrait photographers in the United States and Europe to send digital photos to Pakistan for retouching and clerks in Poland to process expense accounts for banks in London. Cross-border trade in "other commercial services"—a category that excludes transportation, travel, and goods-related services—increased roughly 8 percent per year during the first two decades of the twenty-first century, reaching $3.1 trillion by 2018. More highly trained workers in high-wage countries felt the effects: despite a massive increase in the use of information technology, competition from India held wage gains for US computer systems designers and programmers below the rate of inflation.[9]

As globalization increasingly has to do with exchanging products that do not physically cross borders, services and information-industry workers will bear more of the brunt. Artificial intelligence, including rapid advances in computers' ability to translate speech and writing, will open new industries and new countries to foreign competition in services: the fact that few people outside Italy speak Italian will no longer protect the jobs of Italian mortgage processors if a computer assist enables foreigners unschooled in Italian to do the work more cheaply. A movie can be made anywhere—and the multinational corporations that sell video programming around the world have incentives to make and edit it wherever the cost is lowest.[10]

Governments will use regulations to soften the blow, but to limited effect: while it is easy to insist that only a locally licensed architect can design a building, it is all but impossible to ensure that she does not import her detailed drawings in digital form from draftsmen in another country. It is much tougher to inhibit the international exchange of financial data, medical charts, or theme-park rides than the physical movement of goods, and all but impossible to determine which individuals are being hurt by services produced abroad and delivered over the internet. If work can go anywhere, capturing it requires that governments focus on education policy rather than trade policy. A large supply of low-wage workers helped some countries industrialize during the Third Globalization, but it may be a highly trained workforce with flexible skills that will be the greatest source of economic strength during the Fourth. A social insurance system that supports and retrains service and information workers whose jobs suddenly vanish may become important to protect social stability.

That is not an idle concern. The supercharged industrialization of China and a few other countries, along with an ample flow of credit at very low interest rates, kept the world economy perking during the Third Globalization, powering it through the technology-industry slowdown in 2001 and the severe financial crisis of 2008–9. But during the 2010s, average income per person, spread across the world, rose less than 1.7 percent per year. This is easily the lowest rate since the 1940s, a rate so imperceptible that it would take more than 40 years for average incomes to double—and because the distribution of income became more skewed in most countries, many workers saw few income gains at all. The Fourth Globalization may well be less kind to workers in service and information industries than the Third, but gaping income disparities will not fade away.[11]

The interruption of international commerce owing to COVID-19 is unlikely to change these trends. When the virus fouled international trade in first part of 2020, it was heralded as laying bare the vulnerabilities of global value chains. That its effects were large is indisputable: by one estimate, fifty-one thousand companies around the world had a direct supplier in the affected provinces of China, where the pandemic began, and at least five million companies purchased from suppliers that themselves relied on suppliers in the region. But while the magnitude of value-chain disruption was unprecedented, the vulnerabilities inherent in depending on key components available from only one source had long since been revealed. Many companies had been trying for years to lengthen the odds of business interruption by diversifying their value chains, while others felt compelled by competition to accept the risks of sole sourcing. COVID-19 underscored the urgency of a shift that was already underway.[12]

Nor does the pandemic seem likely to pump up the flow of foreign direct investment, which peaked at 5.4 percent of the world's economic output in 2007 and slipped to less than one-third of that share by 2018. If anything, the disruption caused by the virus will stimulate even greater efforts to do business internationally without making long-term commitments in factories, office buildings, machinery, and land. By bringing international travel almost to a stop after airlines cancelled flights and governments directed arriving passengers to spend two weeks in quarantine, COVID-19 forced firms to manage their foreign interests without customary site visits and face-to-face meetings, and travel-weary executives may not be eager to return to the old ways even after the virus is a distant memory. Leisure travelers, on the other hand, found that international travel could involve more complicated adventures than they imagined when they boarded a cruise ship or booked a trek in the Andes. The much-publicized experience of tens of thousands of stranded travelers may slow the growth of international tourism, and foreign investment in hotels, airports, and shopping malls along with it.

———

And how will countries fare in the Fourth Globalization? Ever since the days of David Ricardo, two centuries ago, economists have taught that

countries should specialize in those activities they perform most efficiently and import the rest. But "comparative advantage," already suspect because of the role of subsidies in influencing the pattern of trade
in goods, is all but meaningless in the digital age, as it becomes steadily
more challenging to figure out how much of a product's value was added
in one place and how much in another. The balance of trade, then, has
become a useless measure for tracking winners and losers, an idea
whose time has come and gone. A country's success in the Fourth Globalization will depend not on whether the statisticians compute a surplus or a deficit, but on whether its citizens' living standards rise as they
navigate a fast-changing world economy—and whether it ensures that
the benefits of a globalized world are shared widely among its citizens.

If economic outlines of the Fourth Globalization already seem clear,
the political outlines remain indistinct. Perhaps the most serious question is what will happen to the arrangements that encouraged globalization and shaped international relations for the better part of a century.
These arrangements were far from perfect; COVID-19 highlighted the
weak frameworks for countries to cooperate in sharing information
about diseases and in monitoring the health of international travelers.
But the diplomatic achievements of previous decades, from the military
alliance of the North Atlantic Treaty Organization to the political alliance of the Organization for African Unity to the economic rules ad-
ministered by the World Trade Organization, should not be dismissed.
For all their many flaws, they reduced the frequency and breadth of
armed conflict around the world and brought a remarkable improvement in the living standards of billions of people.

Undermining international cooperation was a major goal of the political attacks on globalization in the 2010s. It is imaginable that these
assaults will supplant globalization with regionalization; the combined
efforts of the United States and China, some scholars suggest, "may be
moving the world back to the historic norm of political and economic
blocs." But that is no sure bet, for many of the new obstacles impede
regionalization just as much. In 2015, after fifteen years of seamless travel
on a new rail line to Copenhagen, Swedish commuters found themselves scrutinized daily by Danish border police on the lookout for

illegal immigrants. In 2017, the United States put trade sanctions on Canada and Mexico—its partners in a regional free-trade agreement— while sharp Chinese criticism of South Korea's new missile defense system stirred up a consumer boycott that drove Lotte Group, a Korean retailer that had invested $10 billion in China, to leave the country. Two years later, long-standing tensions over noneconomic matters kindled a trade war between Japan and South Korea, neighbors with a large and close trading relationship, and disrupted their military cooperation in a volatile corner of the world. Proximity does not always bring friendship, mutual understanding, or close relations.[13]

Emma Maersk did not set sail on uncharted seas. Her course was guided by an international framework of trade rules, investment policies, and financial regulations constructed over many decades—a framework that arguably allowed globalization to run out of control. In the 2010s, national leaders, often driven by their own domestic political imperatives, made quick work of disassembling important parts of this edifice with surprisingly little concern for what, if anything, would replace it. If, as this book suggests, a less intense form of globalization lies in store, that will require a framework as well. Building it is likely to prove far more difficult than demolishing the structures of the past.

ACKNOWLEDGMENTS

THIS BOOK draws on research undertaken over the years at many libraries and archives, and during numerous interviews. I am grateful for the opportunity to have presented some of my ideas at meetings organized by the American Historical Association, Business History Conference, Copenhagen Business School, German Historical Institute, National History Center, Organization of American Historians, and Swiss Federal Institute of Technology. At the risk of omitting some of the people whose ideas and comments informed my understanding and helped me develop the ideas I present, I would especially like to thank Michele Acciaro, Viktor Allgurén, Nikolai Birger, Kevin Cullinane, Charles Cushing, Guy Erb, Rod Franklin, Gary Gerstle, Michael Weigaard Heimann, Hans-Jörg Heims, Patrick Hooijmans, Gisela Hürlimann, Martin Jes Iversen, Max Johns, Walter Kemmsies, Geraldine Knatz, Christopher Koch, Thomas Koch, Uwe Köhler, Dalia Marin, Alan McKinnon, Paolo Montrone, Henning Morgen, René Taudal Poulsen, Otto Schacht, Scudder Smith, Henrik Sornn-Friese, Mira Wilkins, and Mary Yeager.

NOTES

Introduction

1. Paul James and Manfred B. Steger, "A Genealogy of 'Globalization': The Career of a Concept," *Globalizations* 11 (2014): 417–34. According to James and Steger, the term "globalization" first appeared in J. O. Decroly, *La fonction de globalisation et l'enseignement* (Brussels: Lamertin, 1929). The first English-language use cited in the *Oxford English Dictionary*, in 1930, also pertained to education. Theodore Levitt, "The Globalization of Markets," *Harvard Business Review*, May–June 1983, 92–102.

2. Jürgen Osterhammel and Niels P. Petersson, *A Short History of Globalization* (Princeton, NJ: Princeton University Press, 2005), 26; David Clingingsmith and Jeffrey G. Williamson, "Deindustrialization in 18th and 19th Century India," *Explorations in Economic History* 45 (2008): 209–34.

3. Ben Zimmer, "The Origins of the Globalist Slur," *Atlantic*, March 14, 2018, https://www .theatlantic.com/politics/archive/2018/03/the-origins-of-the-globalist-slur/555479/; *New York Times*, September 3, 1943.

4. Growth in manufactured goods trade calculated from General Agreement on Tariffs and Trade, *International Trade 1986–87* (Geneva, 1987), 10, 18. The term "multinational corporation" seems to have been first used by David Lilienthal, an investment banker, who defined them to be corporations that placed operations involving managerial responsibility outside their home country. See D. Eleanor Westney, "The Organizational Architecture of the Multinational Corporation," in *Orchestration of the Global Network Corporation*, ed. Laszlo Tihanyi et al. (Bingley, UK: Emerald Group, 2014), 7–10.

5. Philip Turner, "Capital Flows in the 1980s: A Survey of Major Trends," BIS Economic Paper no. 30, Bank for International Settlements, April 1991, 22; Simon Evenett, "The Cross-Border Mergers and Acquisitions Wave of the Late 1990s," in *Challenges to Globalization: Analyzing the Economics*, ed. Robert E. Baldwin and L. Alan Winters (Chicago: University of Chicago Press, 2004), 411–67.

6. James Goldsmith, *The Trap* (London: Carrol and Graf, 1994); Viviane Forrester, *L'horreur économique* (Paris: Fayard, 1996); Anthony Giddens, *Runaway World: How Globalisation is Reshaping Our Lives* (London: Profile Books, 1999); John Micklethwait and Adrian Wooldridge, *A Future Perfect* (New York: Crown, 2000).

7. John Tagliabue, "Eastern Europe Becomes a Center for Outsourcing," *New York Times*, April 19, 2007; William Greene, "Growth in Services Outsourcing to India: Propellant or Drain

on the U.S. Economy?" US International Trade Commission Office of Economics, working paper 2006–01-A (2007), 4–6, 11–12, 15, quote A-4.

8. Donald Trump speech, West Palm Beach, Florida, October 13, 2016; "Le Pen Says Will Defend France against Globalization," Reuters, April 23, 2017, https://www.reuters.com/article/us-france-election-le-pen-idUSKBN17P0TW.

9. Chiara Criscuolo and Jonathan Timmis, "The Relationship between Global Value Chains and Productivity," *OECD International Productivity Monitor* 32 (2017): 61–83.

10. Federico J. Díez, Jiayue Fan, and Carolina Villegas-Sánchez, "Global Declining Competition," International Monetary Fund working paper WP/19/92 (2019).

Chapter 1

1. For sources on Hasenclever's life and business, see Marc Levinson, "Peter Hasenclever (1716–1793)," in *Immigrant Entrepreneurship: German-American Business Biographies, 1720 to the Present*, vol. 1, ed. Marianne S. Wokeck (Washington, DC: German Historical Institute), last updated January 4, 2016, https://www.immigrantentrepreneurship.org/entry.php?rec=224.

2. Audrey W. Douglas, "Cotton Textiles in England: The East India Company's Attempt to Exploit Developments in Fashion, 1660–1721," *Journal of British Studies* 8 (1969): 28–43; David Hancock, *Citizens of the World* (Cambridge: Cambridge University Press, 1995), ch. 6. Estimates of the size of the African slave trade are taken from the Slave Voyages database, www.slavevoyages.org.

3. Ole J. Benedictow, "The Black Death: The Greatest Catastrophe Ever," *History Today* 55, no. 3 (2005): 42–49.

4. Kenneth Pomeranz, *The Great Divergence: Europe, China, and the Making of the Modern World Economy* (Princeton, NJ: Princeton University Press, 2000), 117, 157. The estimate of Hansa trade is from the International Maritime Museum, Hamburg.

5. Sheilagh Ogilvie, *The European Guilds: An Economic Analysis* (Princeton, NJ: Princeton University Press, 2019), 229; Giovanni Federico and Antonio Tena Junguito, "World Trade, 1800–1938: A New Data Set," EHES Working Papers in Economic History, no. 93 (2016); Hendrik Van den Bert, *International Economics: A Heterodox Approach* (Abingdon, UK: Routledge, 2015), 85; Angus Maddison, *The World Economy*, vol. 1, *A Millennial Perspective* (Paris: Organisation for Economic Co-operation and Development [OECD], 2006), 95. According to the United Nations Conference on Trade and Development (UNCTAD), *Review of Maritime Transport 2019* (New York: UN, 2019), global shipping capacity in 2018 was 1.9 billion metric tons.

6. Frederic Chapin Lane, *Venetian Ships and Shipbuilders of the Renaissance* (Baltimore: Johns Hopkins University Press, 1934; repr. Westport, CT: Greenwood, 1975), 13–24, 239.

7. Maddison, *World Economy*, 64, 84; Filipe Castro, Nuno Fonseca, and Audrey Wells, "Outfitting the Pepper Wreck," *Historical Archaeology* 44 (2010): 14–34.

8. Ronald Findlay and Kevin H. O'Rourke, *Power and Plenty* (Princeton, NJ: Princeton University Press, 2007), 307.

9. Dan Bogart, "The Transport Revolution in Industrializing Britain: A Survey," in *Cambridge Economic History of Britain 1700 to 1870*, ed. Roderick Floud and Jane Humphries, 3rd ed. (Cambridge: Cambridge University Press, 2014), 370; W.H.R. Curtler, *A Short History of English Agriculture* (Oxford: Clarendon, 1909), ch. 17.

10. Fernand Braudel, *The Mediterranean and the Mediterranean World in the Age of Philip II*, vol. 1, trans. Sian Reynolds (Berkeley, CA: University of California Press, 1995), 432; J.K.J. Thomson, "Industrial Structure in Pre-industrial Languedoc," in *Manufacture in Town and Country before the Factory*, ed. Maxine Berg, Pat Hudson, and Michael Sonenscher (Cambridge: Cambridge University Press, 1983), 75; Christopher Clark, "Social Structure and Manufacturing before the Factory: Rural New England, 1750–1830," in *The Workplace before the Factory: Artisans and Proletarians, 1500–1800*, ed. Thomas Max Safley and Leonard N. Rosenband (Ithaca, NY: Cornell University Press, 1993), 31.

11. N.S.B. Gras, "The Origin of the National Customs-Revenue of England," *Quarterly Journal of Economics* 27 (1912): 107–49; Eli F. Heckscher, *Mercantilism*, vol. 1, trans. Mendel Schapiro (London: George Allen and Unwin, 1935), 57, 77; Johannes Hasebroek, *Trade and Politics in Ancient Greece*, trans. L. M. Fraser and D. C. Macgregor (London: G. Bell and Sons, 1933), 161; Fritz Machlup, *A History of Thought on Economic Integration* (London: Palgrave Macmillan, 1977), 107; Findlay and O'Rourke, *Power and Plenty*, 287.

12. Quote Heckscher, *Mercantilism*, 85; Joseph H. Davis and Douglas Irwin, "Trade Disruptions and America's Early Industrialization," National Bureau of Economic Research (NBER) working paper 9944 (2003).

13. Hironori Asakura, *World History of the Customs and Tariffs* (World Customs Organization, 2003, e-book), 188–96.

14. "William III, 1698: An Act to prevent the Exportation of Wool out of the Kingdoms of Ireland and England into Forreigne parts and for the Incouragement of the Woollen Manufactures in the Kingdom of England," in *Statutes of the Realm*, vol. 7, *1695–1701*, ed. John Raithby (s.l.: Great Britain Record Commission, 1820), 524–28. Lord Cornbury to Charles Hedges, July 15, 1705, in "America and West Indies: July 1701, 11–20," in *Calendar of State Papers Colonial, America and West Indies*, vol. 22, *1704–1705*, ed. Cecil Headlam (London: Stationery Office, 1916), 567–84.

15. Markus Zbroschzyk, "Die preußische Peuplierungspolitik in den rheinischen Territorien Kleve, Geldern und Moers" (PhD dissertation, University of Bonn, 2014).

16. Zhuo Li, Laura Panza, and Yong Song, "The Evolution of Ottoman-European Market Linkages, 1469–1914," working paper, August 28, 2017, https://mpra.ub.uni-muenchen.de/80953/; Pomeranz, *Great Divergence*, 53; Joel Mokyr, *Lever of Riches: Technological Creativity and Economic Progress* (Oxford: Oxford University Press, 1992), 98.

Chapter 2

1. John P. Henderson, *The Life and Economics of David Ricardo* (New York: Springer, 1995), 81–82, 105–11, 120; David Weatherall, *David Ricardo: A Biography* (The Hague: Martinus Nijhoff, 1976), 5, 13.

2. David Ricardo, *The Works of David Ricardo, Esq., M.P.* (Union, NJ: The Lawbook Exchange, 2000), 385, 75.

3. Larry Neal and Jeffrey G. Williamson, "The Future of Capitalism," in *The Cambridge History of Capitalism*, ed. Neal and Williamson (Cambridge: Cambridge University Press, 2014), 532.

4. "An Act to repeal the Laws relative to Artificers going into Foreign Parts," 5 Geo. 4 c. 97. On Ricardo's role, see the comments of Joseph Hume on February 12, 1824, in *Hansard*, 10 Parl. Deb. (2nd ser.) (1824) col. 141. The best known of these laws repealed the Corn Laws in 1846.

5. Findlay and O'Rourke, *Power and Plenty*, 314, 325. On the timing of the first globalization, see Giovanni Federico and Antonio Tena-Junguito, "A Tale of Two Globalizations: Gains from Trade and Openness 1800–2010," *Review of World Economics* 153 (2017): 601–26, and Michel Fouquin and Jules Hugot, "Back to the Future: International Trade Costs and the Two Global-izations," Centre d'études prospectives et d'informations internationales, working paper no. 2016–13 (2016).

6. Sven Beckert, *Empire of Cotton: A Global History* (New York: Knopf, 2015), 199–241, 306–7, 334; Roderick Floud and Bernard Harris, "Health, Height, and Welfare: Britain 1700–1980," in *Health and Welfare During Industrialization*, ed. Richard H. Steckel and Floud (Chicago: University of Chicago Press, 1997), 91–126; Charles Dickens, *Oliver Twist*, ch. 50.

7. Pomeranz, *Great Divergence*, 33; Richard E. Baldwin and Philippe Martin, "Two Waves of Globalisation: Superficial Similarities, Fundamental Differences," NBER working paper 6904 (1999).

8. C. Knick Harley, "Ocean Freight Rates and Productivity, 1740–1913," *Journal of Economic History* 48 (1988): 857–58. Based on Harley's data, the average ship from America arriving in Liverpool carried approximately 1.4 million pounds (700 tons) of cotton in 1859, compared to 229,000 pounds (115 tons) in 1820. This discussion draws on data in Federico and Tena Junguito, "World Trade, 1800–1938." David S. Jacks and Krishna Pendakur, in "Global Trade and the Mari-time Transport Revolution," *Review of Economics and Statistics* 92 (2010): 745–55, emphasize that the causality between cheaper transport and increased trade runs in both directions.

9. Sailing ships still dominated trade in East Asia and across the Pacific in the 1870s; see Bert Becker, "Coastal Shipping in East Asia in the Late Nineteenth Century," *Journal of the Royal Asiatic Society Hong Kong Branch* 50 (2010): 245–302, and Max E. Fletcher, "The Suez Canal and World Shipping, 1869–1914," *Journal of Economic History* 18, no. 4 (1958): 556–73. On US trade, see Charles H. Fitch, "Report on Marine Engines and Steam Vessels in the United States Mer-chant Service" (1880), in *Report on Power and Machinery Employed in Manufactures*, by US De-partment of the Interior (Washington, DC: Department of the Interior, Census Office, 1888). Most vessels built in British shipyards were sailing ships up until 1876; see Mark Dunkley, *Ships and Boats, 1840–1950* (s.l.: Historic England, 2016). On freight rates, see Douglass C. North, "Ocean Freight Rates and Economic Development 1750–1913," *Journal of Economic History* 18 (1958): 537–55; Federico and Tena Junguito, "World Trade, 1800–1938."

10. Gelina Harlaftis, *Creating Global Shipping* (Cambridge: Cambridge University Press, 2019); Håken Lobell, "Foreign Exchange Rates, 1804–1914," Swedish Rjksbank, https://www .riksbank.se/globalassets/media/forskning/monetar-statistik/volym1/6.pdf, table A-6, accessed March 15, 2020.

11. Antoni Estevadeordal, Brian Frantz, and Alan M. Taylor, "The Rise and Fall of World Trade, 1870–1939," *Quarterly Journal of Economics* 188 (2003): 359–407; Findlay and O'Rourke, *Power and Plenty*, 404–5.

12. Dong-Woon Kim, "J. & P. Coats as a Multinational before 1914," *Business and Economic History* 26 (1997): 526–39; Alan Green and M. C. Urquhart, "Factor and Commodity Flows in the International Economy of 1870–1914: A Multi-Country View," *Journal of Economic History* 36 (1976): 217–52; Kevin H. O'Rourke and Jeffrey G. Williamson, "Introduction: The Spread of and Resistance to Global Capitalism," in Neal and Williamson, *Cambridge History of Capitalism*, 11; John H. Dunning, *Studies in International Investment* (London: George Allen and Unwin,

1970), 171; John H. Dunning, "Changes in the Level and Structure of International Production: The Last One Hundred Years," in *The Growth of International Business*, ed. Mark Casson (London: George Allen and Unwin, 1983), 84–139.

13. Campbell Gibson and Emily Lennon, "Nativity of the Population and Place of Birth of the Native Population, 1850 to 1990," US Census Bureau, Population Division, revised October 31, 2011, https://www.census.gov/population/www/documentation/twps0029/tab01.html; Stefan Zweig, *The World of Yesterday* (New York: Viking, 1943; repr. Lincoln: University of Nebraska Press, 1964), 194; Barry R. Chiswick and Timothy J. Hatton, "International Migration and the Integration of Labor Markets," in *Globalization in Historical Perspective*, ed. Michael D. Bordo, Alan M. Taylor, and Jeffrey G. Williamson (Chicago: University of Chicago Press, 2003), 81.

14. Adam McKeown, "Global Migration, 1846–1940," *Journal of World History* 15 (2004): 155–89.

15. Dunning, "Changes in the Level," 87–88; Hein A. M. Klemann, "The Central Commission for Navigation on the Rhine," in *The Rhine: A Transnational Economic History*, ed. Ralf Banken and Ben Wubs (Baden Baden: Nomos, 2017), 31–68; Leslie Hannah, "Logistics, Market Size, and Giant Plants in the Early Twentieth Century: A Global View," *Journal of Economic History* 68 (2008): 46–79; Sidney Pollard, "The Integration of European Business in the 'Long' Nineteenth Century," *Vierteljahrschrift für Sozial- und Wirtschaftsgeschichte* 84, no. 2 (1997): 156–70.

16. Manufactured goods accounted for 27% of US exports to Europe in 1906, but most of those were products with little manufacturing value added, such as refined copper and petroleum. See US Department of Commerce and Labor, *Exports of Manufactures from the United States and Their Distribution by Articles and Countries, 1800 to 1906* (Washington, DC: Government Printing Office, 1906), 32–33, and Douglas Irwin, "Explaining America's Surge in Manufactured Exports, 1880–1913," *Review of Economics and Statistics* 85 (2003): 364–76. On the Belgian Congo, see Maya Jasanoff, *The Dawn Watch* (New York: Penguin, 2017), 205–10.

17. Pomeranz, *Great Divergence*, 55; David Chilosi and Giovanni Federico, "Asian Globalizations: Market Integration, Trade, and Economic Growth, 1800–1938," London School of Economics Department of Economic History working paper 183 (2013). Trade data for Asia, Africa, and Latin America were compiled by John R. Hanson for *Trade in Transition: Exports from the Third World, 1840–1900* (New York: Academic, 1980), and were viewed on the Economic History Association's eh.net on August 9, 2018. Shares of world trade are from Federico and Tena Junguito, "World Trade, 1800–1938."

18. On British caloric input, see Michael Miller, *Europe and the Maritime World* (Cambridge: Cambridge University Press, 2012), 218. Low estimates of world trade relative to output come from Ronald Findlay and Kevin H. O'Rourke, "Commodity Market Integration, 1500–2000," in Bordo, Taylor, and Williamson, *Globalization in Historical Perspective*, 13–64. Federico and Tena Junguito, "World Trade, 1800–1938," and Giovanni Federico and Antonio Tena Junguito, "Federico-Tena World Trade Historical Database: World Share Primary Products Exports and Imports," e-cienciaDatos, V2, 2018, doi:10.21950/O53TLR, offer higher estimates.

19. US Department of Commerce and Labor, *Exports of Manufactures*, 5, 34. The value of materials used is for 1905.

Chapter 3

1. H.G.S. Noble, *The New York Stock Exchange in the Crisis of 1914* (Garden City, NY: Country Life, 1915), 12. Noble writes of the sounding of a "gong," but the exchange's gong had been replaced by a brass bell in 1903. William L. Silber, *When Washington Shut Down Wall Street* (Princeton, NJ: Princeton University Press, 2007).

2. Mira Wilkins, *The History of Foreign Investment in the United States, 1914–1945* (Cambridge, MA: Harvard University Press, 2004), 9, 22–37. Wilkins estimates total foreign investment in the US economy in 1914, including debt, to have been $7.1 billion. The total output of the US economy at the time was $34.5 billon.

3. J. A. Salter, *Allied Shipping Control: An Experiment in International Administration* (Oxford: Clarendon, 1921), 1.

4. Wilkins, *History of Foreign Investment*, 15–16. German trade data are from Giovanni Federico and Antonio Tena Junguito, "Federico-Tena World Trade Historical Database: Europe," e-cienciaDatos, V1, 2018, doi:10.21950/XBOWYN. For an official analysis of the blockade's effectiveness, see "Memorandum in Regard to the Present Position of the Blockade, January 1st, 1917," War Cabinet, Miscellaneous Records, UK National Archives CAB1/22.

5. Peninsular & Oriental, known as P&O, controlled 1.1 million tons of gross shipping in 1914, second only to Royal Mail Steamship Company. See Gordon Boyce, *Information, Mediation, and Institutional Development: The Rise of Large-Scale British Shipping, 1870–1919* (Manchester: Manchester University Press, 1995), 128. On China Navigation, see Miller, *Maritime World*, 88–93. Salter, *Allied Shipping Control*, 24–29, 352–53.

6. Salter, *Allied Shipping Control*, 80–81, 123, 355–59. Approximately 12.5 million tons of shipping owned by allied or neutral countries was destroyed over the course of the war, according to Salter; at the start of the war, those countries had controlled roughly 31 million gross tons of oceangoing vessels, yielding a loss rate of 40%. Estimates of Chinese and Persian trade are from Giovanni Federico and Antonio Tena Junguito, "Federico-Tena World Trade Historical Database: Asia," e-cienciaDatos, V2, 2018, doi:10.21950/05CZKM.

7. Miller, *Maritime World*, 243–44.

8. Margaret Macmillan, *Versailles 1919* (New York: Random House, 2001), 13.

9. Giovanni Federico and Antonio Tena Junguito, "Federico-Tena World Trade Historical Database: World Trade," e-cienciaDatos, V2, 2018, doi:10.21950/JKZFDP; Maurice Obstfeld and Alan M. Taylor, "Globalization in Capital Markets," in Bordo, Taylor, and Williamson, *Globalization in Historical Perspective*, 141.

10. The Safeguarding of Industries Act 1921 was codified as 11 & 12 Geo. 5, c. 47. US Department of Commerce and Labor, *Foreign Tariff Notes* 42 (Washington, DC: Government Printing Office, 1921), 188; Douglas A. Irwin, *Peddling Protectionism* (Princeton, NJ: Princeton University Press, 2011), 17; Edward S. Kaplan, "The Fordney-McCumber Tariff of 1922," *EH.Net Encyclopedia*, ed. Robert Whaples, March 16, 2008, https://eh.net/encyclopedia/the-fordney-mccumber-tariff-of-1922/. Michael Clemens and Jeffrey G. Williamson point out that many tariffs during this era were levied as a specific amount per item or per pound rather than as a percentage of import value, so tariff rates automatically rose as a percentage of value if prices fell; see "A Tariff-Growth Paradox: Protectionism's Impact the World Around, 1875–1997," NBER working paper 8459 (2001).

11. Saif I. Shah Mohammed and Jeffrey G. Williamson, "Freight Rates and Productivity Gains in British Tramp Shipping 1869–1950," *Explorations in Economic History* 41 (2004): 172–203; Fiona Scott Morton, "Entry and Predation: British Shipping Cartels, 1879–1929," *Journal of Economics and Management Strategy* 6 (1997): 679–724; Estevadeordal, Frantz, and Taylor, "Rise and Fall."

12. Mira Wilkins and Frank Ernest Hill, *American Business Abroad: Ford on Six Continents* (Detroit: Wayne State University Press, 1964); "Ford in Europe: A Historical Timeline," *Automotive News*, June 2, 2003; Petri Paju and Thomas Haigh, "IBM Rebuilds Europe: The Curious Case of the Transnational Typewriter," *Enterprise and Society* 17 (2016): 281; Wilkins and Hill, *American Business Abroad*, 132, 145; Don Nerbas, *Dominion of Capital: The Politics of Big Business and the Crisis of the Canadian Bourgeoisie, 1914–1947* (Toronto: University of Toronto Press, 2013), 170; Geoffrey Jones, *Multinationals and Global Capitalism* (Oxford: Oxford University Press, 2005), 81.

13. McKeown, "Global Migration, 1846–1940."

14. Òscar Jordà, Moritz Schularick, and Alan M. Taylor, "Microfinancial History and the New Business Cycle Facts," in *NBER Macroeconomics Annual 2016*, ed. Martin Eichenbaum and Jonathan A. Parker (Chicago: University of Chicago Press, 2017), 213–63; Harold James, *The End of Globalization: Lessons from the Great Depression* (Cambridge, MA: Harvard University Press, 2001).

15. In 1948, the US Department of Labor estimated average unemployment in 1930 to have been 4.34 million out of a civilian labor force of 49.82 million. These estimates yield an unemployment rate of 8.7%. For this and other estimates, see Stanley Lebergott, "Labor Force, Employment, and Unemployment, 1929–1939: Estimating Methods," *Monthly Labor Review*, July 1948, 50–53. On farm wages, see US Census Bureau, *Historical Statistics of the United States*, Bicentennial Ed. (Washington, DC: Government Printing Office, 1976), 468. Estimates of economic growth, expressed in constant dollars at purchasing power parity, are taken from J. P. Smits, P. J. Woltjer, and D. Ma, "A Dataset on Comparative Historical National Accounts, ca. 1870–1950: A Time-Series Perspective," Groningen Growth and Development Centre research memorandum GD-107 (2009).

16. There are various ways of calculating effective duty rates; see Irwin, *Peddling Protectionism*, 103–6.

17. Quoted in Irwin, 170–74. The volume of manufactured exports worldwide fell 15% in 1930; see Statistical Office of the United Nations, "International Trade Statistics, 1900–1960," draft paper (1962), UN Trade Statistics, https://unstats.un.org/unsd/trade/data/tables.asp#historical. The Smoot-Hawley tariff was enacted halfway through the year.

18. Peter S. Jacks, "From Boom to Bust: A Typology of Real Commodity Prices in the Long Run," NBER working paper 18874 (2016); Peter H. Lindert and Jeffrey G. Williamson, "Does Globalization Make the World More Unequal?" in Bordo, Taylor, and Williamson, *Globalization in Historical Perspective*, 264.

Chapter 4

1. Barry Eichengreen and Peter Temin, "Fetters of Gold and Paper," NBER working paper 16202 (2010); Barry Eichengreen, *Golden Fetters: The Gold Standard and the Great Depression, 1919–1939* (New York: Oxford University Press, 1992).

2. Barry Eichengreen, *Globalizing Capital* (Princeton, NJ: Princeton University Press, 2008), ch. 4; Lawrence H. Officer, "Exchange Rates between the United States Dollar and Forty-one Currencies," MeasuringWorth, 2018, http://www.measuringworth.com/exchangeglobal/; Robinson quoted in Wilkins, *History of Foreign Investment*, 566.

3. Chad P. Bown and Douglas A. Irwin, "The GATT's Starting Point: Tariff Levels circa 1947," NBER working paper 21782 (2015); *Reciprocal Trade Agreement between the United States of America and Nicaragua*, effective October 1, 1936, US Department of State Executive Agreement Series, No. 95. The language governing customs unions and free-trade agreements appears in GATT article XXIV.

4. 97 Cong. Rec. 10842 (August 30, 1951); Food and Agriculture Organization, *The State of Food and Agriculture 1948* (Washington, DC: Food and Agriculture Organization, 1948), 4–12.

5. Benn Steil, *The Marshall Plan* (Princeton, NJ: Princeton University Press, 2017).

6. Barry Eichengreen, *The European Economy since 1945: Coordinated Capitalism and Beyond* (Princeton, NJ: Princeton University Press, 2007), 6. Separate from the Marshall Plan, the United States exercised great influence over the economies of West Germany and Japan, which were ruled by military occupation authorities for several years after the war.

7. The quotation is from a speech by Robert Schuman on May 9, 1950. The agreement was codified as the Treaty Constituting the European Coal and Steel Community, April 18, 1951 (*American Journal of International Law* 46, no. S4 (1952): 107–48, doi:10.2307/2213971).

8. Eichengreen, *European Economy*, 82, 84. Productivity and income data are from the Groningen Growth and Development Centre and in the Conference Board Total Economy Database, both derived from the work of Angus Maddison. On Italy's exports, see Alfred Maizels, *Industrial Growth and World Trade* (Cambridge: Cambridge University Press, 1963), 479.

9. Maizels, *Industrial Growth*, 8, 133–34, 535, 539.

10. Maizels, 122–23, 243.

11. Quoted in Marc Levinson, *An Extraordinary Time* (New York: Basic Books, 2016), 36–46.

12. David M. G. Newbery and Joseph E. Stiglitz, *The Theory of Commodity Price Stabilization* (Oxford: Oxford University Press, 1981), 13; UNCTAD, Convention on a Code of Conduct for Liner Conferences, Geneva, April 6, 1974, UN *Treaty Series* 1334: 15 and 1365: 360, article 2.

13. UNCTAD, *Review of Maritime Transport 1968* (New York: UN, 1968), 4.

Chapter 5

1. Marc Levinson, *The Box: How the Shipping Container Made the World Smaller and the World Economy Bigger*, 2nd ed. (Princeton, NJ: Princeton University Press, 2016), 21–46.

2. Quoted in *Containers*, no. 12 (December 1954), 20. Author's translation.

3. Levinson, *Box*, 47–71.

4. US International Trade Commission (USITC), *Automotive Trade Statistics 1964–80*, Publication 1203, December 1981 (Washington, DC: USITC, 1981).

5. Joseph Grunwald and Kenneth Flam, *The Global Factory* (Washington, DC: Brookings, 1985).

Chapter 6

1. For a more technical discussion, see Robert Triffin, *Gold and the Dollar Crisis* (New Haven, CT: Yale University Press, 1960).

2. Duty-free allowances were lowered in Public Law 87–132. The tax on foreign securities issues, the Interest Equalization Tax, was enacted in 1964 as Public Law 88–563, but was retroactive to July 1963. On the collapse of the Bretton Woods system, see Paul Volcker and Toyoo Gyohten, *Changing Fortunes* (New York: Times Books, 1992), 18–136; Eichengreen, *Globalizing Capital*, ch. 4.

3. Eric Helleiner, *States and the Reemergence of Global Finance* (Ithaca, NY: Cornell University Press, 1994), 101–6 (quote 101).

4. Federal Deposit Insurance Corporation (FDIC), *History of the Eighties: Lessons for the Future*, vol. 1, *An Examination of the Banking Crises of the 1980s and Early 1990s* (Washington, DC: FDIC, 1997), 196–97; Harold James, "International Capital Movements and the Global Order," in Neal and Williamson, *Cambridge History of Capitalism*, 285.

5. William Seidman, an economic adviser to US president Gerald Ford in the mid-1970s, later wrote that "the entire Ford administration, including me, told the large banks that the process of recycling petrodollars to the less developed countries was beneficial, and perhaps a patriotic duty." See Seidman, *Full Faith and Credit* (New York: Crown, 1993), 38. The Wriston comment, which he repeated in many forms, first appeared in his article, "Banking against Disaster," *New York Times*, September 14, 1982, but was not original to Wriston.

6. Basel Committee on Bank Supervision, "Report to the Governors on the Supervision of Banks' Foreign Establishments," September 26, 1975.

7. Gerardo Della Paolera and Alan M. Taylor, "A Monetary and Financial Wreck: The Baring Crisis, 1890–91," in *Straining at the Anchor*, ed. Della Paolera and Taylor (Chicago: University of Chicago Press, 2001), 67–79; Kris James Mitchener and Marc D. Weidenmier, "The Baring Crisis and the Great Latin American Meltdown of the 1890s," *Journal of Economic History* 68 (2008): 462–500; Jon R. Moen and Ellis W. Tallman, "The Bank Panic of 1907: The Role of Trust Companies," *Journal of Economic History* 52 (1992): 611–30; Anna Grodecka, Seán Kenny, and Anders Ögren, "Predictors of Bank Distress: The 1907 Crisis in Sweden," Lund Papers in Economic History 180 (2018); Mary T. Rodgers and James E. Payne, "How the Bank of France changed U.S. Equity Expectations and Ended the Panic of 1907," *Journal of Economic History* 74 (2014): 420–48; Richard Roberts, *Saving the City: The Great Financial Crisis of 1914* (Oxford: Oxford University Press, 2013), 195–227.

8. The World Bank estimates the foreign-currency debts of low- and middle-income countries to have been $601 billion at the end of 1982, but this figure excludes foreign obligations of several major debtor countries, notably Argentina ($44 billion in 1982), South Korea ($37 billion), and Poland ($27 billion).

9. Susan M. Collins and Wong-Am Park, "External Debt and Macroeconomic Performance in South Korea," in *Developing Country Debt and the World Economy*, ed. Jeffrey Sachs (Chicago: University of Chicago Press, 1989), 121–40; Rüdiger Dornbusch, "Our LDC Debts," in *The United States in the World Economy*, ed. Martin S. Feldstein (Chicago: University of Chicago Press, 1988), 192.

10. Volcker and Gyohten, *Changing Fortunes*, 226.

11. International Monetary Fund (IMF), *Annual Report 1985* (Washington, DC: IMF, 1985), 21; Jerome I. Levinson, "A Perspective on the Debt Crisis," *American University International Law Review* 4 (1989): 504–8; Lois M. Plunkert, "The 1980's: A Decade of Job Growth and Industry Shifts," *Monthly Labor Review*, September 1990, 3–16.

Chapter 7

1. Vincent P. Carosso and Richard Sylla, "U.S. Banks in International Finance," in *International Banking 1870–1914*, ed. Rondo Cameron and V. I. Bovykin (New York: Oxford University Press, 1991), 68; Roberts, *Saving the City*, 169, 195.

2. Tommaso Padoa-Schioppa and Fabrizio Saccomanni, "Managing a Market-Led Global Financial System," in *Managing the World Economy: Fifty Years after Bretton Woods*, ed. Peter B. Kenen (Washington, DC: Institute for International Economics, 1994), 262.

3. Herbert Baum, "Possibilities and Limits of Regulation in Transport Policy," in *Possibilities and Limits of Regulation in Transport Policy*, by European Conference of Ministers of Transport (ECMT) (Paris: ECMT, 1983), 5–106.

4. Walter Y. Oi and Arthur P. Hurter, *Economics of Private Truck Transportation* (Dubuque, IA: W. C. Brown, 1965).

5. Bureau of Transport Economics, "Overview of Australian Road Freight Industry: Submission to National Inquiry, 1983" (Canberra: Australian Government Publishing Service, 1984); Michael Beesley, "UK Experience with Freight and Passenger Regulation," in *The Role of the State in a Deregulated Market*, by ECMT (Paris: ECMT, 1991), 45–76; Martha Derthick and Paul J. Quirk, *The Politics of Deregulation* (Washington, DC: Brookings Institution, 1985), 36.

6. The laws were the Railroad Revitalization and Regulatory Reform Act (1976), the Air Cargo Deregulation Act (1977), the Airline Deregulation Act (1978), the Motor Carrier Regulatory Reform and Modernization Act (1980), the Household Goods Transportation Act (1980), the Staggers Rail Act (1980), the Bus Regulatory Reform Act (1982), the Shipping Act (1984), and the Surface Freight Forwarder Deregulation Act (1986).

7. In the United States in 1978, one in forty orders for freight cars was not met; see US General Accounting Office, *Economic and Financial Impacts of the Staggers Rail Act of 1980* (Washington, DC: Government Printing Office, 1990), 55. Damage claims against railroads routinely exceeded 1.3% of their freight revenues; see Marc Levinson, "Two Cheers for Discrimination: Deregulation and Efficiency in the Reform of U.S. Freight Transportation, 1976–1988," *Enterprise and Society* 10 (2009): 178–215.

8. Aden C. Adams and Carl W. Hoeberling, "The Future of Contract Rates," *ICC Practitioners' Journal* 47 (1980): 661–64; US Federal Maritime Commission, *Section 18 Report on the Shipping Act of 1984* (Washington, DC: Federal Maritime Commission, 1989), 162, 178.

9. "Rates on Overseas Phone Calls Decline," *New York Times*, May 19, 1982; US Census Bureau, *Statistical Abstract of the United States 1992* (Washington, DC: Government Printing Office, 1990).

10. Guillermo Barnes, "Lessons from Bank Privatization in Mexico," World Bank policy research working paper WPS 1027 (1992).

11. Mary M. Shirley, "The What, Why, and How of Privatization: A World Bank Perspective," *Fordham Law Review* 60 (1992): S23–S36.

12. Brian Pinto and Sergei Ulatov, "Financial Globalization and the Russian Crisis of 1998," World Bank policy research working paper 5312 (2010); World Bank, *Economic Growth in the 1990s: Learning from a Decade of Reform* (Washington, DC: World Bank, 2005), 192 (quote); Saul Estrin and Adeline Pelletier, "Privatization in Developing Countries: What Are the Lessons of Recent Experience?" *World Bank Research Observer* 33 (2018): 65–102. For a defense of the benefits of privatization, see Alberto Chong and Florencio López-de-Silanes, eds., *Privatization in Latin America: Myths and Reality* (Washington, DC: World Bank, 2005).

13. Shane Greenstein, *How the Internet Became Commercial* (Princeton NJ: Princeton University Press, 2015).

Chapter 8

1. For estimates of trade to gross domestic product, see Findlay and O'Rourke, "Commodity Market Integration," 41. According to World Trade Organization (WTO) data, the merchandise exports of the six EC members rose a mean 384% between 1960 and 1973, while Denmark's merchandise exports increased 218%, Great Britain's 79%, and Ireland's 299%.

2. Thorn's address to the European Parliament on February 15, 1984, published in Commission of the European Communities, *Programme of the Commission for 1984* (Luxembourg: Office for Official Publications of the EC, 1984), 8, 10.

3. Productivity data are from the Conference Board's Total Economy Database; "Key Issues for Talks," *New York Times*, June 8, 1984; Herbert Giersch, "Eurosclerosis," Kiel Discussion Papers no. 112, Institut für Weltwirtschaft, Kiel (1985), 4.

4. Commission of the European Communities, *Completing the Internal Market*, COM 85 (310) (Brussels, June 14, 1985); Eichengreen, *European Economy*, 345.

5. The Single European Act was signed in 1986, but it did not take effect until ratified by Denmark and Ireland in 1987.

6. In 1979, 540 border factories, commonly known as "maquiladoras," were in operation. Their output could not be sold within Mexico. See Leslie Sklair, *Assembling for Development* (Boston: Unwin Hyman, 1989). López Portillo's statement was made in a meeting with US president Jimmy Carter in Mexico City on February 14, 1979; see "Memorandum of Conversation," in *Foreign Relations of the United States, Foreign Relations 1977–1980*, vol. 23, *Mexico, Cuba, and the Caribbean*, ed. Alexander O. Poster (Washington, DC: Government Publishing Office, 2016), 358.

7. President Ronald Reagan is sometimes credited for originating the idea of free trade in North America; see "Ronald Reagan's Announcement for Presidential Candidacy," Ronald Reagan Presidential Library, November 13, 1979, https://www.reaganlibrary.gov/11-13-79. However, this was not the first suggestion of tripartite talks; at a meeting with Carter and López Portillo in the White House on February 15, 1977, Mexican foreign minister Santiago Roel García said, "I think it would be helpful if there could be talks between Mexico, the U.S. and Canada—the three nations of North America and three democracies." See *Foreign Relations 1977–1980*, 23: 289. Nothing resulted from Roel García's comments. See Richard Lawrence, "Hopes for Closer U.S.-Mexican Ties Deflate," *Journal of Commerce*, May 13, 1982; comments of Deputy US Trade Representative Alan Wolff, "Summary of Conclusions of a Policy Review

Committee Meeting," January 19, 1979, *Foreign Relations 1977–1980*, 23: 344; and Robert J. Mc-Cartney, "Mexico to Lower Trade Barriers, Join GATT," *Washington Post*, November 26, 1979.

8. George W. Grayson, *The Mexico-U.S. Business Committee* (Rockville, MD: Montrose, 2017), 96–98.

9. General Agreement on Tariffs and Trade (GATT): Punta del Este Declaration (September 20, 1986), SICE Foreign Trade Information System, http://www.sice.oas.org/trade/punta_e.asp.

10. *Washington Post*, December 14, 1992. Perot's statement was made during the second presidential debate of the 1992 election campaign, October 15, 1992.

11. Ernest H. Preeg, *Traders in a Brave New World* (Chicago: University of Chicago Press, 1995), 165–73; quote from "The Uruguay Round," WTO, accessed February 2, 2019, https://www.wto.org/english/thewto_e/whatis_e/tif_e/fact5_e.htm.

12. IMF and World Bank, *Market Access for Developing Countries' Exports* (2001), 15–25.

13. Arvind Subramanian and Martin Kessler, "The Hyperglobalization of Trade and its Future," Peterson Institute for International Economics working paper 13-6 (2013), 24; WTO Regional Trade Agreements Information System, https://rtais.wto.org/UI/PublicMaintain RTAHome.aspx.

14. Christian Marx, "Reorganization of Multinational Companies in the Western European Chemical Industry," *Enterprise and Society* 21 (2020): 38–78.

Chapter 9

1. On Onassis, see Harlaftis, *Creating Global Shipping*, 193.

2. Steel production data are from the World Steel Association. Quote from Center for Naval Analysis, "A Brief History of Shipbuilding in Recent Times," CRM D0006988.A1/Final (September 2002); OECD, *Trade and Structural Adjustment: Embracing Globalization* (Paris: OECD, 2005), 244–51; OECD Working Party on Shipbuilding, "Imbalances in the Shipbuilding Industry and Assessment of Policy Responses," C/WP6(2016)6/final (April 2017). From 1956 to 1970, US shipbuilding subsidies exceeded $1 billion. US House of Representatives, Committee on Ways and Means, *Trade with Japan*, Serial 96–121 (Washington, DC: Government Printing Office, 1980), 123, citing Ira C. Magaziner and Thomas M. Hout, *Japanese Industrial Policy* (London: Policy Studies Institute, 1980).

3. Alice H. Amsden, *Asia's Next Giant: South Korea and Late Industrialization* (New York: Oxford University Press, 1989), 269–90.

4. Korean shipyards chartered six containerships to ship lines unable to complete planned purchases in 1984. Lars Bruno and Stig Tenold, "The Basis for South Korea's Ascent in the Shipbuilding Industry, 1970–1990," *Mariner's Mirror* 97 (2011): 201–17.

5. OECD Council Working Party on Shipbuilding, "Peer Review of Japanese Government Support Measures to the Shipbuilding Sector," C/WP6(2012)26 (2012), 7.

6. "Fünfte Kolonne," *Der Spiegel*, April 16, 1973.

7. Erik Lindner, *Die Herren der Container* (Hamburg: Hoffmann und Campe Verlag, 2008), 87–97, quote 91.

8. European Commission, "Community Guidelines on State Aid to Maritime Transport," 97/C 205 (July 5, 1997), 11; European Commission, "Community Guidelines on State Aid to Maritime Transport," 2004/C 13 (January 17, 2004), 6.

9. Ole Andersen, "The Rise and Fall of German Shipping," *Shippingwatch*, May 2014.

10. Ulrike Dauer, "Commerzbank Moves to Repay More State Aid," *Wall Street Journal*, March 13, 2013; Arno Schuetze and Jan Schwartz, "State Owners Sell Germany's HSH Nordbank to Buyout Groups," Reuters, February 28, 2018, https://uk.reuters.com/article/us-hsh-nordbank-sale/state-owners-sell-germanys-hsh-nordbank-to-buyout-groups-idUKKCN1GC1YJ; UNCTAD, *Review of Maritime Transport 2018* (New York: UN, 2018), 29.

11. Myrto Kalouptsidi, "Detection and Impact of Industrial Subsidies: The Case of Chinese Shipbuilding," *Review of Economic Studies* 85 (2018): 1111–58. A separate subsidy program, established in 2009 to encourage state-owned Chinese ship lines to scrap older ships and buy new, less polluting ones, had much the same effect. Maersk's cost comparisons were made in April 2007. "Container Market Crash on the Horizon?" *Fairplay*, September 22, 2005; "New Decade of Bursting Yards Predicted," *Fairplay*, October 13, 2005.

12. Margot Roosevelt, "Battles Erupt over Warehouse Jobs as the Legislature Moves to Curb Subsidies," *Los Angeles Times*, May 13, 2019; Office of Inspector General, United States Postal Service, "Terminal Dues in the Age of Ecommerce," RARC-WP-16-OU3 (December 14, 2015).

Chapter 10

1. On measurement and amounts of subsidies, see WTO, *World Trade Report 2006* (Geneva: WTO, 2006).

2. Steve Dryden, *Trade Warriors* (New York: Oxford University Press, 1995), 38.

3. James T. Walker, "Voluntary Export Restraints between Britain and Japan: The Case of the UK Car Market (1971–2001)," *Business History* 59 (2017): 35–55; Laurent Warlouzet, "Towards a European Industrial Policy?: The European Economic Community (EEC) Debates, 1957–1975," in *Industrial Policy in Europe after 1945*, ed. C. Grabas and A. Nützenadel (London: Palgrave Macmillan, 2014), 213–35; Christian Marx, "A European Structural Crisis Cartel as a Solution to a Sectoral Depression?" *Economic History Yearbook* 58 (2017): 163–97; Étienne Davignon, interview with Étienne Deschamps, Brussels, Centre virtuel de la connaissance sur l'Europe, January 14, 2008, www.cvce.eu; Stuart W. Leslie, "The Biggest 'Angel' of Them All: The Military and the Making of Silicon Valley," in *Understanding Silicon Valley*, ed. Martin Kenney (Stanford, CA: Stanford University Press, 2000), 48–67.

4. Arvind Panagariya, "Evaluating the Case for Export Subsidies," World Bank policy research working paper 2276 (2000).

5. I. M. Destler, Haruhiro Fukui, and Hideo Sato, *The Textile Wrangle: Conflict in Japanese-American Relations, 1969–1971* (Ithaca, NY: Cornell University Press, 1979), 66 (Nixon quote); "Agreement on Wool and Man-made Fibers" in US Department of State, *United States Treaties and Other International Acts*, vol. 23, part 3 (Washington, DC: Government Printing Office, 1972), 3167; Japan guidance quote from Japan Industrial Structure Council, *Japan in World Economy: Japan's Foreign Economic Policy for the 1970s* (Tokyo: Ministry of International Trade and Industry, 1972), 48–50.

6. Takafusa Nakamura, *The Postwar Japanese Economy: Its Development and Structure, 1937–1994* (Tokyo: University of Tokyo Press, 1981), 224; Konosuke Odaka, "Are We at the Verge of a Stagnant Society?" in "Recent Developments of Japanese Economy and Its Differences from Western Advanced Economies," ed. Hisao Kanamori, Center Paper 29, Japan Economic Re-

search Center (September 1976), 33; Yoshimitsu Imuta, "Transition to a Floating Exchange Rate," in *A History of Japanese Trade and Industry Policy*, ed. Mikiyo Sumiya (Oxford: Oxford University Press, 2000), 528; Sueo Sekiguchi, "Japan: A Plethora of Programs," in *Pacific Basin Industries in Distress*, ed. Hugh Patrick (New York: Columbia University Press, 1991), 437.

7. William Diebold Jr., *Industrial Policy as an International Issue* (New York: McGraw-Hill, 1980), 162; Japan Automobile Manufacturers Association, *Motor Vehicle Statistics of Japan 2014* (s.l., 2014) 16, 32.

8. Gary R. Saxonhouse, "Industrial Restructuring in Japan," *Journal of Japanese Studies* 5 (1979): 273–320; Steven Englander and Axel Mittelstädt, "Total Factor Productivity: Macroeconomic and Structural Aspects of the Slowdown," *OECD Economic Survey* 10 (1988): 36. The term "deindustrialization" was popularized by Barry Bluestone and Bennett Harrison, *The Deindustrialization of America* (New York: Basic Books, 1982).

9. As examples of the many warnings of diminishing US competitiveness and continuing Japanese advance, see Ezra F. Vogel, *Japan as Number One* (Cambridge, MA: Harvard University Press, 1979); Bruce R. Scott and George C. Lodge, eds., *U.S. Competitiveness in the World Economy* (Boston: Harvard Business School Press, 1985); and Clyde V. Prestowitz Jr., *Trading Places: How We Allowed Japan to Take the Lead* (New York: Basic Books, 1988), subsequently reissued with several other subtitles.

10. Jimmy Carter, "American Bolt, Nut, and Large Screw Industry Memorandum from the President," December 22, 1978, Pub. Papers (1978, bk 2), 2284; "Proclamation 4632—Temporary Duty Increase on the Importation into the United States of Certain Bolts, Nuts, and Screws of Iron or Steel," January 4, 1979, Pub. Papers (1979), 3; US Department of Commerce, International Trade Administration, "An Economic Assessment of the United States Industrial Fastener Industry (1979 to 1986)," March 1987; Gary Clyde Hufbauer and Howard Rosen, *Trade Policy for Troubled Industries* (Washington, DC: Institute for International Economics, 1986), 20.

11. Stephen D. Cohen, "The Route to Japan's Voluntary Export Restraints on Automobiles," working paper no. 20, National Security Archive (1997); USITC, *A Review of Recent Developments in the U.S. Automobile Industry Including an Assessment of the Japanese Voluntary Restraint Agreements* (Washington, DC: USITC, 1985), 4–11. The Reagan quote appeared in Richard J. Cattani, "Carter, Reagan Cast for Votes among Blacks, Auto Workers," *Christian Science Monitor*, September 3, 1980.

12. Dale W. Jorgenson and Masahiro Kuroda, "Productivity and International Competitiveness in Japan and the United States, 1960–1985," in *Productivity Growth in Japan and the United States*, ed. Charles R. Hulten, (Chicago: University of Chicago Press, 1991), 45; Philip Turner and Jean-Pierre Tuveri, "Some Effects of Export Restraints on Japanese Trading Behavior," *OECD Economic Studies* 2 (1984): 94–107.

13. Amsden, *Asia's Next Giant*, 69–80 (Park quote 69; Amsden quote 80); Somi Seong, "Competition and Cooperation among Asian Countries and the Future Prospect of Korean Industrial Policy," working paper, Korea Development Institute, January 1, 1996.

14. Hee-Yhon Song, "Economic Miracles in Korea," in *Economic Interaction in the Pacific Basin*, ed. Lawrence B. Krause and Sueo Sekiguchi (Washington, DC: Brookings Institution, 1980), 117–46. According to Kwang Suk Kim, "Lessons from Korea's Industrialization Experience," Korea Development Institute monograph no. 8105 (1981), the manufacturing sector grew at a compound annual rate of 17.1% between 1963 and 1980.

15. Chong-Hyun Nam, "Protectionist U.S. Trade Policy and Korean Exports," in *Trade and Protectionism*, ed. Takatoshi Ito and Anne O. Krueger (Chicago: University of Chicago Press, 1993), 183–222; USITC, *DRAMS of One Megabit and Above from the Republic of Korea*, Publication 2629 (Washington, DC: USITC, 1993), I-99.

16. Kim Gyu-Pan, "Korea's Economic Relations with Japan," *Korea's Economy* 31 (2017): 23–29. According to the OECD Trade in Value Added database, 21 percent of the value of Chinese electronic and optical products in 2015 originated in Korea; see "Trade in Value Added (TiVA): Origin of Value Added in Gross Imports," OECD.Stat, December 2018, https://stats .oecd.org.

Chapter 11

1. Carl E. Walter and Fraser J. T. Howie, *Red Capitalism* (Singapore: Wiley, 2011), 32, 153.

2. Joe Studwell, *How Asia Works* (London: Profile Books, 2013), 184; USITC, *China's Economic Development Strategies and Their Effects on U.S. Trade*, Publication 1645 (Washington, DC; USITC, 1985), 23–32.

3. Dennis Tao Yang, Vivian Weija Chen, and Ryan Monarch, "Rising Wages: Has China Lost Its Global Labor Advantage?" *Pacific Economic Review* 15 (2010): 482–504; Don Oberdorfer, "Trade Benefits for China Are Approved by Carter," *Washington Post*, October 24, 1979. The European Community reduced tariffs on Chinese goods in the late 1970s. Congress had blocked the Soviet Union from receiving similar tariff treatment owing to its human rights record, particularly restrictions on emigration of Jews.

4. China's market share of global manufactured exports in 1986 was less than 1%.

5. On the withdrawal from the GATT, see Monica Hsiao, "China and the GATT," *Pacific Basin Law Journal* 12 (1994): 433–34.

6. Donald C. Clarke, "GATT Membership for China?" *University of Puget Sound Law Review* 17 (1994): 517–31; Preeg, *Brave New World*, 106.

7. Dori Jones Yang and Maria Shao, "China's Push for Exports Is Turning into a Long March," *Business Week*, September 15, 1986, 66. The number of fatalities in the Tiananmen incident has been disputed. A diplomatic cable from Alan Ewan Donald, British ambassador to China, to London on June 5, 1989, referred to "atrocities committed by 27th Army," adding, "Minimum estimate of civilian dead 10,000." A US government report at the time concluded that "civilian deaths probably did not reach the figure of 3,000 used in some press accounts, but they surely far outnumbered official figures." The Chinese government gave figures in the low hundreds; Japan's Kyodo news service reported 7,000. Cable, US Embassy, Beijing, to Secretary of State, "What happened on the night of June 3/4?" June 19, 1989. For Deng quote, see Liang Zhang (compiler), *The Tiananmen Papers*, ed. Andrew J. Nathan and Perry Link (New York: Public Affairs, 2001).

8. Roderick MacFarquhar, "Deng's Last Campaign," *New York Review of Books*, December 17, 1992; "Full Text of Jiang Zemin's Report at 14th Party Congress," *Beijing Review*, accessed March 15, 2020, http://www.bjreview.com.cn/document/txt/2011-03/29/content_363504 .htm.

9. Takashi Kawakimi, "Uniqlo's China Factories Key to Success," *Nikkei Asian Review*, October 21, 2014, https://asia.nikkei.com/Business/Uniqlo-s-China-factories-key-to-success.

General Motors first opened a purchasing office in China in 1997; Norihiko Shirouzu, "Big Three's Outsourcing Plan: Make Parts Suppliers Do It," *Wall Street Journal*, June 20, 2004.

10. Nicholas R. Lardy, "China's WTO Membership," *Policy Brief* (Brookings Institution), April 1, 1999; Loren Brandt, Johannes Van Biesebroeck, Luhang Wang, and Yifan Zhang, "WTO Accession and Performance of Chinese Manufacturing Firms," *American Economic Review* 107 (2017): 2784–820, and the related correction at *American Economic Review* 109 (2019): 1616–21; Chang-Tai Hsieh and Zheng Song, "Grasp the Large, Let Go of the Small: The Transformation of the State Sector in China," *Brookings Papers on Economic Activity* (2015): 295–362.

11. Office of the US Trade Representative, "Background Information on China's Accession to the World Trade Organization," December 11, 2001, https://ustr.gov/archive/Document _Library/Fact_Sheets/2001/Background_Information_on_China%27s_Accession_to_the _World_Trade_Organization.html; Alan Matthews and K. Ingersent, "The WTO Negotiations in the Field of Agriculture and Food," European Parliament Directorate-General for Research, working paper AGRI 135 EN (2001), 58–59; Joseph Fewsmith, "The Political and Social Implications of China's Accession to the WTO," *China Quarterly* 167 (2001): 573–91.

12. WTO, "Special and Differential Treatment Provisions in WTO Agreements and Decisions," WT/COMTD/W/239 (October 12, 2018).

13. Peter T. Kilborn, "Wal-Mart's 'Buy American'" *New York Times*, April 10, 1985; Nelson Lichtenstein, *The Retail Revolution* (New York: Metropolitan Books, 2009), 159–78; David Barboza and Elizabeth Becker, "Free of Quotas, China Textiles Flood the U.S.," *New York Times*, March 20, 2005; Mei Fong, "Trade Disputes Cause Liz Claiborne to Change China Sourcing Levels," *Wall Street Journal*, September 29, 2005; "Trade in Value Added (TiVA): Origin of Value Added in Gross Imports: 5," OECD.Stat, December 2018, https://stats.oecd.org/.

14. James Kynge, *China Shakes the World* (Boston: Houghton Mifflin, 2006), 57–60.

15. Importers paid a weighted average tariff of 41% in 1992, falling to 16% in 1997, but some imports faced tariffs exceeding 100% as late as 2001. See Dani Rodrik, "What's So Special about China's Exports," NBER working paper 11947 (2006). Data on exports as share of output are from the World Bank.

16. Surafael Girma, Yundan Gong, Holger Görg, and Zhihong Yu, "Can Production Subsidies Explain China's Export Performance?: Evidence from Firm Level Data," *Scandinavian Journal of Economics* 111 (2009): 862–91; Zhi Wang and Shang-Jin Wei, "What Accounts for the Rising Sophistication of China's Exports," NBER working paper 13771 (2008). For the Chinese government's description of some of the subsidies available in the late 1990s, see WTO, "Accession of the People's Republic of China," Annex 5A, WT/L/432 (November 23, 2001).

17. USITC, *Certain Passenger and Light Truck Vehicle Tires from China*, Publication 4085 (Washington, DC: USITC, 2009), and *Certain Passenger and Light Truck Vehicle Tires from China*, Publication 4545 (Washington, DC: USITC, 2015).

18. OECD, "Measuring Distortions in International Markets: The Aluminum Value Chain," *OECD Trade Policy Papers* 218 (2019).

19. For other examples, see Usha C. V. Haley and George T. Haley, *Subsidies to Chinese Industry* (Oxford: Oxford University Press, 2013).

20. OECD, "Recent Developments in the Automobile Industry," *Economics Department Policy Notes* 7 (2011); Shang-Jin Wei, "Foreign Direct Investment in China: Sources and Conse-

quences," in *Financial Deregulation and Integration in East Asia*, ed. Takatoshi Ito and Anne O. Krueger (Chicago: University of Chicago Press, 1996), 77–105; Joshua B. Freeman, *Behemoth* (New York: Norton, 2017), 272–74.

Chapter 12

1. Andrea Andrenelli, Iza Lejàrraga, Sébastien Miroudot, and Letizia Montinari, "Micro-evidence on Corporate Relationships in Global Value Chains," OECD trade policy paper 227 (2019).

2. Samuel J. Palmisano, "The Globally Integrated Enterprise," *Foreign Affairs*, May–June 2006.

3. Alex Barker and Peter Campbell, "Honda Faces the Real Cost of Brexit in a Former Spitfire Plant," *Financial Times*, June 29, 2018; US National Highway Traffic Safety Administration (NHTSA), "Part 583 American Automobile Labeling Act Reports," NHTSA, June 4, 2019, https://www.nhtsa.gov/part-583-american-automobile-labeling-act-reports.

4. Andrew B. Bernard, J. Bradford Jensen, Stephen J. Redding, and Peter K. Schott, "Global Firms," *Journal of Economic Literature* 56 (2018): 565–619; John R. Baldwin and Beiling Yan, "Global Value Chain Participation and the Productivity of Canadian Manufacturing Firms," Institute for Research in Public Policy, March 17, 2016, https://on-irpp.org/2JDRQsR.

5. Marc J. Melitz and Daniel Trefler, "Gains from Trade when Firms Matter," *Journal of Economic Perspectives* 26 (2012): 91–118; Carolyn Freund and Martha Denisse Pierola, "The Origins and Dynamics of Export Superstars," Peterson Institute of International Economics working paper 16–11 (2016); Ricardo Monge-González, *Moving up the Global Value Chain: The Case of Intel Costa Rica* (Lima: International Labour Organization, 2017).

6. IHS Markit, "iPhone 3G S Carries $178.96 BOM and Manufacturing Cost, iSuppli Teardown Reveals," press release, Omdia, June 24, 2009, https://technology.ihs.com/389273/iphone-3g-s-carries-17896-bom-and-manufacturing-cost-isuppli-teardown-reveals.

7. Yuqing Xing and Neal Detert, "How the iPhone Widens the United States Trade Deficit with the People's Republic of China," Asian Development Bank Institute working paper 257 (2010).

8. No public information is available on Apple's net profit from selling iPhone 3Gs. The estimate of Apple's profit per phone applies its net margin during the four quarters of calendar year 2009, which was approximately 19%, to the average selling price per iPhone 3G. The net margin is calculated as net income divided by total revenue. iPhones of all models and related products accounted for 30% of Apple's sales during its fiscal year 2009 and 39% in its fiscal year 2010, and it is possible that the net margins on the iPhone 3G were higher or lower than those of the entire company.

9. Teresa C. Fort, "Technology and Production Fragmentation: Domestic versus Foreign Sourcing," *Review of Economic Studies* 84 (2017): 650–87; Richard Baldwin and Javier Lopez-Gonzalez, "Supply-Chain Trade: A Portrait of Global Patterns and Several Testable Hypotheses," *World Economy* 38 (2015): 1682–721.

10. This section draws on the OECD-WTO Trade in Value Added database.

11. WTO, *World Trade Statistical Review 2017*, table A54, https://www.wto.org/english/res_e/statis_e/wts2017_e/wts2017_e.pdf.

Chapter 13

1. Daniel Jessel, "Banking on the Dragon," *Fairplay*, January 6, 2005.

2. A. P. Møller-Maersk A/S, *Annual Report 2003*, 10–12.

3. The discussion in this section draws on documents from Maersk Archives, Department 131, Stubkjaers Secretariat, boxes 229488 and 229470 and various chronological notebooks.

4. Robert Wright, "World's Fastest Containerships Mothballed," *Financial Times*, February 22, 2010.

5. UNCTAD, *Review of Maritime Transport 2003* (New York: UN, 2003), 63; quotation from Knud Stubkjaer, then head of Maersk Line, i. "Maersk Deal Will Stir Up Liners," *Fairplay*, May 19, 2005.

6. The largest containership operating in 2005 reported capacity of 9,200 TEU; see *Containerisation International Yearbook 2005*, 7. *Emma Maersk*'s capacity was reported as 15,500 TEU in *Containerisation International Yearbook 2012*; one year earlier the yearbook had stated her capacity as 14,770 TEU. Reported capacity depends, in part, on assumptions about average weight per container. Gregory Richards, "Emma Maersk May Be as Big as a Container Ship Can Get," *Virginian-Pilot* (Norfolk, VA), August 23, 2006.

7. "Are Shipbuilders Hurtling Towards Overcapacity?" *Fairplay*, September 8, 2005.

8. Peter T. Leach, "Shakeup at Maersk," *Journal of Commerce*, July 1, 2007.

Chapter 14

1. Brent Hunsberger, "Worried about Lockout at West Coast Ports, Some Importers Cancel Orders," *Oregonian*, October 3, 2002; John Gallagher, "Shippers' Nightmare," *Traffic World*, October 14, 2002; David Teather, "Gap Warns of Knock-On as US Dock Strike Ends," *Guardian*, October 11, 2002; Daniel B. Wood, "Dock Backlog Likely to Hit Christmas Sales," *Christian Science Monitor*, October 10, 2002; Danielle Herubin, "Retailers Say They Think Port Delays Will Cause Toy Shortages for Christmas," *Orange County Register*, October 29, 2002.

2. Peter V. Hall, "'We'd Have to Sink the Ships': Impact Studies and the 2002 West Coast Port Lockout," *Economic Development Quarterly* 18 (2004): 354–67.

3. Freeman, *Behemoth*, 138–44.

4. Andrew Pollack, "Shortage of Memory Chips Has Industry Scrambling," *New York Times*, March 12, 1988; Jason Amaral, Corey A. Billington, and Andy A. Tsay, "Safeguarding the Promise of Production Outsourcing," *Interfaces* 36 (2006): 220–33.

5. Ila Manuj, "Risk Management in Global Sourcing: Comparing the Business World and the Academic World," *Transportation Journal* 52 (2013): 80–107 (quotes 92).

6. Stephan M. Wagner and Christoph Bode, "An Empirical Investigation into Supply Chain Vulnerability," *Journal of Purchasing and Supply Management* 12 (2006): 301–12; "BMW to Recall Faulty Diesel Cars," *BBC News*, February 1, 2005, news.bbc.co.uk/2/hi/business/4227159.stm.

7. Amy Chozick, "A Key Strategy of Japan's Car Makers Backfires," *Wall Street Journal*, July 20, 2007; April Wortham, "In Quake's Wake, Honda's U.S. Suppliers Lend a Hand," *Automotive News*, August 20, 2007.

8. Statement of Robert C. Bonner, Commissioner, US Customs, to the National Commission on Terrorist Attacks upon the United States, January 26, 2004, National Commission on

Terrorist Attacks upon the United States archived website, https://govinfo.library.unt.edu/911/hearings/hearing7/witness_bonner.htm.

9. See, for example, Genevieve LeBaron, *The Global Business of Forced Labor: Report of Findings* (Sheffield, UK: University of Sheffield Political Economy Research Institute, 2018).

10. "Statistics on Safeguard Measures," WTO, accessed April 20, 2019, https://www.wto.org/english/tratop_e/safeg_e/safeg_e.htm#statistics.

11. Vasco M. Carvalho, Makoto Nirei, Yukiko Saito, and Alireza Tahbaz-Salehi, "Supply Chain Disruptions: Evidence from the Great East Japan Earthquake," Columbia Business School research paper no. 17-5 (2016); Christoph E. Boehm, Aaron Flaaen, and Nitya Pandalai-Nayar, "The Role of Global Supply Chains in the Transmission of Shocks: Firm-Level Evidence from the 2011 Tōhoku Earthquake," *FEDS Notes*, Federal Reserve Board, May 2, 2016.

12. Sharon Silke Carty and Elaine Kurtenbach, "Tohoku Disaster May Bring Automakers to Their Knees," *Japan Times*, March 29, 2011.

13. Hans Greimel, "How Toyota Applied the Lessons of 2011 Quake," *Automotive News*, April 25, 2016; Thomas J. Holmes and Ethan Singer, "Indivisibilities in Distribution," NBER working paper 24525 (April 2018).

Chapter 15

1. World Bank, *Market Access for Developing-Country Exports* (Washington, DC: World Bank, 2001), 9; Wei, "Foreign Direct Investment"; Federico and Tena Junguito, "Tale of Two Globalizations," abstract. Direct investment statistics are from UNCTAD, bank lending statistics from Bank for International Settlements.

2. Kate Kelly and Serena Ng, "Bear Stearns Bails Out Fund With Big Loan," *Wall Street Journal*, June 23, 2007.

3. Meredith A. Crowley and Xi Luo, "Understanding the Great Trade Collapse of 2008–09 and the Subsequent Trade Recovery," *Economic Perspectives* 35, no. 2 (2011): 45; Richard Baldwin and Daria Taglioni, "The Great Trade Collapse and Trade Imbalances," in *The Great Trade Collapse: Causes, Consequences and prospects*, ed. Baldwin (London: Centre for European Policy Research, 2009), 47.

4. Kiyoyasu Tanaka, "Trade Collapse and International Supply Chains: Japanese Evidence," 201–8, and Ryuhei Wakasugi, "Why Was Japan's Trade Hit So Much Harder?" 209–22, both in Richard Baldwin, *Great Trade Collapse*.

5. Logan T. Lewis, Ryan Monarch, Michael Sposi, and Jing Zhang, "Structural Change and Global Trade," Federal Reserve International Finance Discussion Paper 1225 (2018); Przemyslaw Wozniak and Malgorzata Galar, "Understanding the Weakness in Global Trade," European Commission Economic Brief 033 (2018); US Bureau of Economic Analysis and US Census Bureau, US Imports of Goods by Customs Basis from Mexico, retrieved from FRED, Federal Reserve Bank of St. Louis, May 22, 2019, https://fred.stlouisfed.org/series/IMPMX; Eurostat, "Evolution of intra-EU trade in goods: 2002–2019," accessed March 15, 2020, https://ec.europa.eu/eurostat/statistics-explained/index.php?title=Intra-EU_trade_in_goods_-_main_features&oldid=452727#Evolution_of_intra-EU_trade_in_goods:_2002-2019.

6. Anna Ignatenko, Faezeh Raei, and Borislava Mircheva, "Global Value Chains: What Are the Benefits and Why Do Countries Participate?" IMF working paper 19/19 (2019).

7. Yuqing Xing, "How the iPhone Widens the U.S. Trade Deficit with China: The Case of the iPhone X," VoxEU, November 11, 2019, https://voxeu.org/article/how-iphone-widens-us-trade-deficit-china-0; Logan Lewis and Ryan Monarch, "Causes of the Global Trade Slowdown," Federal Reserve Board International Finance Discussion Paper note, 2016, https://www.federalreserve.gov/econresdata/notes/ifdp-notes/2016/files/causes-of-the-global-trade-slowdown-20161110.pdf; Jin Hongman, "China's Practice in Statistics of Goods for Processing," presentation, United Nations Regional Seminar on Trade Statistics, Beijing, October 24–26, 2011.

8. Scott Kennedy, *China's Risky Drive into New-Energy Vehicles* (Washington, DC: Center for Strategic and International Studies, 2018).

9. Tom Hancock and Yizhen Jia, "China Pays Record $22bn in Corporate Subsidies," *Financial Times*, May 27, 2018.

10. Bela Belassa, "Trade Liberalisation and 'Revealed' Comparative Advantage," *Manchester School* 33 (1965): 99–123; S. M. Ali Abbas and Alexander Klemm, "A Partial Race to the Bottom: Corporate Tax Developments in Emerging and Developing Economies," IMF working paper WP/12/28 (2012); United Nations, *Design and Assessment of Tax Incentives in Developing Countries* (New York: UN, 2018); Dorsati H. Madani and Natàlia Mas-Guix, "The Impact of Export Tax Incentives on Export Performance: Evidence from the Automotive Sector in South Africa," World Bank policy research working paper 5585 (2011).

11. Greg Leroy, *The Great American Jobs Scam* (San Francisco: Berrett-Koehler, 2005); Mike Pare and Dave Flessner, "Volkswagen Won Most Subsidies in Tennessee, but Were They All Necessary?" *Chattanooga Times Free Press*, September 16, 2017; Jason Spencer, "Spartanburg Takes a Look Back at Landing BMW," *State*, July 13, 2014; David Wren, "BMW's South Carolina Plant Remains Top Car Exporter Despite Higher Tariffs," *Post and Courier*, March 8, 2019; European Commission, "State Aid Scoreboard 2018," accessed March 15, 2020, http://ec.europa.eu/competition/state_aid/scoreboard/index_en.html; John Lester, "Business Subsidies in Canada," University of Calgary School of Public Policy Publications, *SPP Research Paper* 11, no. 1 (January 2018).

12. "Global Production Patterns from a European Perspective," *ECB Economic Bulletin* 6 (2016): 44; European Central Bank, "Understanding the Weakness in Global Trade," occasional paper 178 (2016), 30.

Chapter 16

1. Ragnhild Balsvik, Sissel Jensen, and Kjell G. Salvanes, "Made in China, Sold in Norway: Local Labor Market Effects of an Import Shock," IZA discussion paper no. 8324 (2014); Vicente Donoso, Víctor Martín, and Asier Minondo, "Do Differences in the Exposure to Chinese Imports Lead to Differences in Local Labour Market Outcomes?: An Analysis for Spanish Provinces," *Regional Studies* 49 (2015): 1746–64; David H. Autor, David Dorn, and Gordon H. Hanson, "The China Syndrome: Local Labor Market Effects of Import Competition in the United States," *American Economic Review* 103 (2013): 2121–68. For an early but still cogent critique of the costs of globalization, see Dani Rodrik, *Has Globalization Gone Too Far?* (Washington, DC: Institute for International Economics, 1997).

2. Facundo Alvaredo, Lucas Chancel, Thomas Piketty, Emanuel Saez, and Gabriel Zucman, coordinators, *World Inequality Report 2018* (World Inequality Lab, 2017), 64, 66.

3. IMF, *World Economic Outlook* (Washington, DC: IMF, April 2018), ch. 3.

4. Jeff Rubin, "Has Global Trade Liberalization Left Canadian Workers Behind?" Centre for International Governance Innovation Papers no. 163 (2018), 12.

5. Francisco Costa, Jason Garred, and João Pessoa, "Winners and Losers from China's 'Commodities-for-Manufactures' Trade Boom," VoxEU, September 24, 2017, https://voxeu.org /article/winners-and-losers-china-s-commodities-manufactures-trade-boom; Adrian Wood and Jörg Mayer, "Has China De-industrialised Other Developing Countries?" Oxford University Department of International Development working paper 175 (June 2010); Robert Neuwirth, *Stealth of Nations: The Global Rise of the Informal Economy* (New York: Pantheon, 2011).

6. Alvaredo et al., *World Inequality Report 2018*, 200; Bank of Japan, Research and Statistics Department, "Recent Developments of Japan's External Trade and Corporate Behavior," October 2007 (English translation of Japanese original released August 27, 2007), https://www.boj .or.jp/en/research/brp/ron_2007/data/ron0710a.pdf; Hitoshi Sasaki, "Import Competition and Manufacturing Employment in Japan," Bank of Japan working paper 07-E-25 (2007).

7. Gabriel Zucman, *The Hidden Wealth of Nations* (Chicago: University of Chicago Press, 2015); Annette Alstadsaeter, Niels Johannesen, and Gabriel Zucman, "Tax Evasion and Inequality," *American Economic Review* 109 (2019): 2073–2103.

8. "OECD Secretary-General Report to the G20 Leaders," Osaka, Japan, June 2019; Ernesto Crivelli, Ruud de Mooij, and Michael Keenan, "Base Erosion, Profit Shifting, and Developing Countries," IMF working paper WP/15/118 (2015); Jane Gravelle, "Tax Havens: International Tax Avoidance and Evasion," Congressional Research Service Report R40623 (2013); Thomas Wright and Gabriel Zucman, "The Exorbitant Tax Privilege," NBER working paper 24983 (2018).

9. See, for example, Micah White and Kalle Lasn, "The Call to Occupy Wall Street Resonates around the World," *Guardian*, September 19, 2011; Naomi Klein, "Occupy Wall Street: The Most Important Thing in the World Now," *Nation*, October 6, 2011, https://www.thenation.com /article/archive/occupy-wall-street-most-important-thing-world-now/.

10. Michael E. Waugh, "The Consumption Response to Trade Shocks," NBER working paper 26353 (2019).

11. Percy Ashley, *Modern Tariff History: Germany, United States, France* (London: John Murray, 1920), 297–306; Douglas A. Irwin, "From Smoot-Hawley to Reciprocal Trade Agreements," in *The Defining Moment: The Great Depression and American Trade Policy in the Twentieth Century*, ed. Michael Bordo et al. (Chicago: University of Chicago Press, 1998), 343; United States, *Reciprocal Trade Agreement between the United States of America and Cuba* (Washington, DC: Government Printing Office, 1934). Journalist Philip Stephens recalled how British prime minister Margaret Thatcher pushed for a European Union regulation on lawnmower noise to pre-empt more stringent German regulations that effectively barred British-made lawnmowers from Germany; see "After Brexit, Britain Will Be a Rule-Taker," *Financial Times*, March 7, 2019.

12. Sébastien Miroudot, Dorothée Touzet, and Francesca Spinelli, "Trade Policy Implications of Global Value Chains," OECD trade policy paper no. 161 (2013); Sébastien Miroudot and Charles Cadestin, "Services in Global Value Chains: From Inputs to Value-Creating Activities,"

OECD trade policy paper no. 197 (2017); Kommerskollegium (Swedish National Board of Trade), *Adding Value to the European Economy* (Stockholm: Kommerskollegium, 2007).

13. ComRes, "Independent/Sunday Mirror December 2016 Political Poll," ComRes Global, https://www.comresglobal.com/wp-content/uploads/2016/12/Sunday-Poll-December-2016 .pdf; GEG, "'Maintenant ce sont les patriotes contre les mondialistes': Traduction d'extraits d'un entretien de Marine Le Pen à Bjørn Bredal de Politiken, 19 mars 2017," Medium, April 2, 2017, https://medium.com/@LLDD/marine-le-pen-%C3%A0-politiken-principal-journal -danois-maintenant-ce-sont-les-patriotes-contre-les-41875ac8ef6d; Rory Horner, Daniel Haberly, Seth Schindler, and Yuko Aoyama, "How Anti-globalisation Shifted from a Left to a Right-Wing Issue—and Where It Will Go Next," Conversation, January 25, 2018, https:// theconversation.com/how-anti-globalisation-switched-from-a-left-to-a-right-wing-issue-and -where-it-will-go-next-90587 (May quote).

Chapter 17

1. US Army Corps of Engineers, New York District, *Bayonne Bridge Air Draft Analysis*, September 2009, 23.

2. Maersk Line reported a loss of $602 million in 2011 on volume of 8.1 million forty-foot containers. A. P. Møller-Maersk A/S, *Group Annual Report 2011*, 22.

3. Drewry Maritime Research, cited in *Containerisation International Yearbook 2012*, 5; comment by Gianluigi Aponte to Lloyd's List, cited in "Mediterranean Shipping Company (MSC)," Fitch Solutions, December 17, 2012, https://www.fitchsolutions.com/corporates/industrials -transportation/mediterranean-shipping-company-msc-17-12-2012; International Transport Forum, *The Impact of Mega-Ships* (Paris: OECD, 2015), 18, 29.

4. Michele Acciaro, "Naval Gigantism: Rationale and Limits," speech to Federagenti, Rome, Italy, December 16, 2015.

5. Olaf Merk, *The Impact of Mega-Ships* (Paris: International Transport Forum, 2015), 41; Adam Carey and Richard Willingham, "Port of Melbourne: Ships May Soon Be Too Big to Pass under West Gate Bridge," *Age*, September 15, 2015.

6. Bundesstelle für Seeunfalluntersuchung, "Investigation Report 34/16: Grounding of the CSCL Indian Ocean in the River Elbe on 3 February 2016," October 14, 2016; Port of Gothenburg, "The Impact of Megaships: The Case of Gothenburg," 2015, 2, 15, 26; International Transport Forum, *The Impact of Alliances in Container Shipping* (Paris: International Transport Forum, 2018), 61; Chabeli Herrera, "Despite Recent Dredge, Port Miami Still Can't Fit Some Large Ships. New Project in the Works," *Miami Herald*, July 8, 2018.

7. UNCTAD, *Review of Maritime Transport 1999* (New York: UN, 1999), 71; presentation of Robin Carruthers, World Bank consultant, to Transportation Research Board, Washington, DC, January 14, 2020.

8. OECD Working Party on Shipbuilding, "Peer Review of the Korean Shipbuilding Industry and Related Policies," C/WP26(2014)10 (January 13, 2015); Joyce Lee, "South Korea's Daewoo Shipbuilding Unlocks $2.6 Billion Bailout after Bondholder Approval," Reuters, April 18, 2017, https://uk.reuters.com/article/us-daewoo-restructuring/south-koreas-daewoo -shipbuilding-unlocks-2-6-billion-bailout-after-bondholder-approval-idUKKBN17K0KX; Xiaolin Zeng, "South Korean Shipbuilders' Fight for Life," *Fairplay*, April 6, 2017; Costas Paris,

"Korea Extends Aid Package to Hyundai Merchant Marine," *Wall Street Journal*, January 27, 2017; Costas Paris, "South Korea Sends Another $5 Billion to Hyundai Merchant Marine," *Wall Street Journal*, October 10, 2018.

9. Costas Paris, "Taiwan Approves $1.9 Billion Aid Package to Troubled Shipping Companies," *Wall Street Journal*, November 17, 2016; NYK president quoted in Leo Lewis and Robert Wright, "NYK, MOL and K Line to Combine Container Shipping Units," *Financial Times*, October 31, 2016.

10. Market share data from Alphaliner as of July 31, 2018.

11. Quote from Richard Milne, "Maersk Shares Slide as Chief Warns on US-China Trade War Risks," *Financial Times*, May 18, 2018; Costas Paris and Dominic Chopping, "Maersk Will Restrain Costs, Expand Logistics Services on Weak Shipping Outlook," *Wall Street Journal*, November 15, 2019.

Chapter 18

1. Global population was 5 billion in 1987, and of those, according to World Bank estimates, about 70%—3.5 billion—had electricity. By 2017, global population was 7.5 billion, of whom 87%—6.5 billion—had electricity. According to OECD figures, global beef consumption increased from 47 million metric tons in 1990 to nearly 70 million in 2017. By one estimate, the economic gains from international trade were 161 times the economic cost of environmental harm caused by greenhouse-gas emissions. See Joseph S. Shapiro, "Trade Costs, CO2, and the Environment," *American Economic Journal: Economic Policy* 8 (2016): 220–54.

2. Jean-Yves Huwart and Loïc Verdier, *Economic Globalisation: Origins and Consequences* (Paris: OECD, 2013): 114; Elizabeth Economy, *The River Runs Black* (Ithaca, NY: Cornell University Press, 2004); "China's War on Particulate Pollution Is Causing More Severe Ozone Pollution," *Science Daily*, January 2, 2019; Jintai Lin, Da Pan, Steven J. Davis, Qiang Zhang, Kebin He, Can Wang, David G. Streets, Donald J. Wuebbles, and Dabo Guan, "China's International Trade and Air Pollution in the United States," *Proceedings of the National Academy of Sciences of the USA* 111 (2014): 1736–41.

3. *International Union for the Protection of Nature* (Brussels: Imprimerie M. Hayez, 1948).

4. Rachel Carson, *Silent Spring* (Boston: Houghton Mifflin, 1962); Paul Ehrlich, *The Population Bomb* (New York: Ballantine Books, 1968); Donella H. Meadows, Dennis L. Meadows, Jørgen Randers, and William W. Behrens III, *The Limits to Growth* (New York: Universe Books, 1972), 23.

5. Mario J. Molina and F. S. Rowland, "Stratospheric Sink for Chlorofluoromethanes: Chlorine Atomic-Catalysed Destruction of Ozone," *Nature* 249 (1974): 810–12; "Life under the Ozone Hole," *Newsweek*, December 8, 1991; C. Ford Runge, *Freer Trade, Protected Environment* (New York: Council on Foreign Relations, 1994), 89–93.

6. Marc Levinson, "The Green Gangs," *Newsweek*, August 2, 1992; Frances Cairncross, "How Europe's Companies Reposition to Recycle," *Harvard Business Review*, March–April 1992, 34–45. A panel of GATT legal experts ruled in Mexico's favor, but the United States and Mexico agreed that the decision should not be adopted because of the ongoing trade negotiations; see "Mexico etc versus US: 'Tuna-Dolphin,'" WTO, accessed March 15, 2020, https://www.wto.org/english/tratop_e/envir_e/ediso4_e.htm.

7. Jordi Diéz, "The Rise and Fall of Mexico's Green Movement," *European Review of Latin American and Caribbean Studies* 85 (2008): 81–99.

8. Jaime de Melo and Nicole A. Mathys, "Trade and Climate Change: The Challenges Ahead," Fondation pour les études et recherches sur le développement international, working paper P14 (2010); Joseph S. Shapiro, "The Environmental Bias of Trade Policy" NBER working paper 26845 (2020).

9. Glen P. Peters, Jan Minx, Christopher Weber, and Ottmar Edenhofer, "Growth in Emission Transfers via International Trade from 1990 to 2008," *Proceedings of the National Academy of Sciences of the USA* 108 (2011): 8903–8.

10. Rahel Aichele and Gabriel Felbermayr, "Kyoto and the Carbon Content of Trade," VoxEU, February 4, 2010, https://voxeu.org/article/kyoto-and-carbon-content-trade.

11. Graham K. MacDonald, Kate A. Brauman, Shipeng Sun, Kimberly M. Carlson, Emily S. Cassidy, James S. Gerber, and Paul C. West, "Rethinking Agricultural Trade Relationships in an Era of Globalization," *BioScience* 65 (2015): 275–89; Jing Zang, "Chilean Fruit Exports to China Grow by 11% in 2018/19 Season," *Produce Report*, April 21, 2019, https://www.producereport .com/article/chilean-fruit-exports-china-grow-11-201819-season; Choy Leng Yeong, "NW Salmon Sent to China before Reaching U.S. Tables," *Seattle Times*, July 16, 2005; Yossi Sheffi, *Logistics Clusters: Delivering Value and Driving Growth* (Cambridge, MA: MIT Press, 2012).

12. Angela Paxton, *The Food Miles Report: The Dangers of Long-Distance Food Transport* (London: SAFE Alliance, 1994).

13. By one estimate, forcing consumers to pay the full environmental cost of their choices would reduce Dutch trade in agricultural products by 4.2%, because some domestic products would then become cheaper than imports. See Lóránt Tavasszy, Jorrit Harmsen, Olga Ivanova, and Tatyana Bulavskaya, "Effect of a Full Internalization of External Costs of Global Supply Chains on Production, Trade, and Transport," in *Towards Innovative Freight and Logistics*, ed. Corinne Blanquart, Uwe Clausen, and Bernard Jacob (Paris: Transport Research Arena, 2014), 337–51; Caroline Saunders and Andrew Barber, "Carbon Footprints, Life Cycle Analysis, Food Miles: Global Trade Trends and Market Issues," *Political Science* 60 (2008): 73–88; Alison Smith et al., *The Validity of Food Miles as an Indicator of Sustainable Development* (London: Department of the Environment, Food, and Rural Affairs, 2005). Anca Cristea, David Hummels, Laura Puzzello, and Misak Avetisyan, "Trade and the Greenhouse Gas Emissions from International Freight Transport," *Journal of Environmental Economics and Management* 65 (2013): 153–73, found that approximately one-fourth of international trade, mainly in minerals and foodstuffs, resulted in lower greenhouse-gas emissions than had the trade not occurred.

14. Alan C. McKinnon, "Options for Reducing Logistics-Related Emissions from Global Value Chains," European University Institute working paper RSCAS 2014/31 (2014).

15. David Hummels, "Transportation Costs and International Trade in the Second Era of Globalization," *Journal of Economic Perspectives* 21 (2007): 131–54; International Air Transport Association, "IATA Cargo Strategy" (2018); Ralph Sims, Roberto Schaeffer, Felix Creutzig, Xochitl Cruz-Núñez, Marcio D'Agosto, Delia Dimitriu, Maria Josefina Figueroa Meza, et al., "Transport," in *Climate Change 2014: Mitigation of Climate Change*, ed. O. Edenhofer et al. (Cambridge: Cambridge University Press, 2014), 646.

16. Alan McKinnon, "The Possible Influence of the Shipper on Carbon Emissions from Deep-Sea Container Supply Chains: An Empirical Analysis," *Maritime Economics and Logistics*

16 (2014): 1–19. While data from the International Maritime Organization and the International Energy Agency suggested that greenhouse-gas emissions from the shipping industry stabilized or declined after 2008, Naya Olmer, Bryan Comer, Biswajoy Roy, Xiaoli Mao, and Dan Rutherford, *Greenhouse Gas Emissions from Global Shipping, 2013–2015* (Washington, DC: International Council for Clean Transportation, 2017), found annual increases as late as 2015.

17. International Maritime Organization, "Initial IMO Strategy on Reduction of GHG Emissions from Ships," Resolution MEPC.304(72) (April 13, 2018). The maximum sulfur content in ship fuels was reduced from 4.5% to 0.5%.

18. Leslie Hook and John Reed, "Why the World's Recycling System Stopped Working," *Financial Times*, October 25, 2018.

Chapter 19

1. John N. Boucher, *History of Westmoreland County* (Chicago: Lewis, 1906); the origin of the name is explained on the municipal website, https://www.cityofmonessen.com/, accessed July 10, 2019. Bob Dvorchak, "Decaying Company Town Pinched Further by Steel Strike with Wheeling-Pittsburgh," Associated Press, July 24, 1985, https://apnews.com/7bba5b6b7c989cc fb1b31e46b66a2039.

2. Trump quoted in David Jackson, "Donald Trump Targets Globalization and Free Trade as Job-Killers," *USA Today*, June 28, 2016; Daniel Moore, "A Future Made of Coke?" *Pittsburgh Post-Gazette*, January 28, 2019.

3. The shoe manufacturer was Pou Chen Corporation; see Adidas Group, "Primary Suppliers and Subcontractors," January 1, 2019. The medical device manufacturer was Jabil Corp. The apparel maker was Sae-A Trading Company; Deborah Belgum, "Why Manufacturers Are Turning to Central America for Quick-Turn Apparel," *California Apparel News*, June 1, 2017.

4. Michael Laris and Ian Duncan, "Boeing Knew of Problems with Wing Parts but Told FAA Planes Were Safe, Agency Alleges," *Washington Post*, December 7, 2019.

5. US Department of Commerce, International Trade Administration, "The Current State of the U.S. Automotive Parts Market," April 2013.

6. Bown and Irwin, "GATT's Starting Point." Data on weighted average effective duties in the 2010s are taken from UNCTAD, "Import Tariff Rates on Non-agricultural and Non-fuel Products," accessed March 15, 2020 https://unctadstat.unctad.org/.

7. Wilders quoted in Ian Traynor, "Le Pen and Wilders Forge Plan to 'Wreck' EU from Within," *Guardian*, November 13, 2013; Salvini quoted in "Lega, Salvini contro euro: 'Crimine contro l'umanità,'" ANSA.it, December 15, 2013, http://www.ansa.it/web/notizie/rubriche /politica/2013/12/15/Lega-Salvini-contro-euro-Crimine-contro-umanita-_9781968.html.

8. Chiara Criscuolo and Jonathan Timmis, "The Changing Structure of Global Value Chains: Are Central Hubs Key for Productivity?" *OECD International Productivity Monitor*, Spring 2018, and "The Relationship between Global Value Chains and Productivity," *OECD International Productivity Monitor*, Spring 2017; Ang Jian Wei, Athreya Murugasu, and Chai Yi Wei, "Low-Skilled Foreign Workers' Distortions to the Economy," in *Annual Report 2017*, by Bank Negara Malaysia, 35–43 (quote 39); Xin Li, Bo Meng, and Zhi Wang, "Recent Patterns of Global Production and GVC Participation," and David Dollar, Bilal Khan, and Jiansuo Pei, "Should High Domestic Value Added in Exports Be an Objective of Policy?" both in *Global Value Chain*

Development Report 2019: Technological Innovation, Supply Chain Trade, and Workers in a Global-ized World, by World Bank and WTO (Washington, DC: World Bank Group, 2019), 9–44, and 141–54.

9. X. Li, Meng, and Wang, "Recent Patterns," 39; Shawn Donnan, "Trump's Top Trade Adviser Accuses Germany of Currency Exploitation," *Financial Times*, January 31, 2017.

10. X. Li, Meng, and Wang, "Recent Patterns," 27–34.

Chapter 20

1. Ward's Reports, Inc., *Ward's Automotive Yearbook* 1989 and 2017; Dharshini David, "The Real Price of Buying Cheap Clothes," *BBC News*, August 7, 2019, https://www.bbc.co.uk/news/business-49248921; US Department of Commerce, *2017 Characteristics of New Housing*, 345, https://www.census.gov/construction/chars/pdf/c25ann2017.pdf; "2015 RECS Survey Data," US Energy Information Administration, May 31, 2018, table HC3.3 (appliances by year of construction), https://www.eia.gov/consumption/residential/data/2015/.

2. United Nations World Tourism Organization, *Tourism Highlights 2000*, 2nd ed. (August 2000), https://www.e-unwto.org/doi/pdf/10.18111/9789284403745, and "International Tourism Growth Continues to Outpace the Global Economy," press release, January 20, 2020; Facebook, Inc., Form 10-K for the year ended December 31, 2018, https://www.sec.gov/Archives/edgar/data/1326801/000132680119000009/fb-12312018x10k.htm; UNCTAD, *World Investment Report 2019* (New York: UN, 2019), 20–21.

3. World Bank, "Manufacturing, Value Added (% of GDP)," accessed March 15, 2020, https://data.worldbank.org/indicator/NV.IND.MANF.ZS.

4. For the median age, see United Nations Division of Economic and Social Affairs, Population Division, *World Population Prospects 2019* (New York: UN, 2019). Households' spending, measured as a share of the world's total consumption, had crept up for decades, reaching 60% around the turn of the twenty-first century, but in the 2010s it retreated to 57%. By the World Bank's estimates, consumer outlays around the world grew at an average annual rate of 2.4% in the 2010s, down from 2.75% over each of the two prior decades; OECD, "Annual National Accounts Data," table 5, "Final Consumption Expenditure of Households," OECD.Stat, accessed March 15, 2020, https://stats.oecd.org/Index.aspx?DataSetCode=SNA_TABLE5; European Central Bank Statistical Data Warehouse, series SHI.A.V1.DWEL.A, accessed March 15, 2020, https://sdw.ecb.europa.eu/browse.do?node=70499.

5. David Barboza, "An iPhone's Journey, from the Factory Floor to the Retail Store," *New York Times*, December 29, 2016, https://www.nytimes.com/2016/12/29/technology/iphone-china-apple-stores.html; Kathrin Hille, "Foxconn: Why the World's Tech Factory Faces Its Biggest Test," *Financial Times*, June 10, 2019.

6. Ondrej Burkacky, Johannes Deichmann, Georg Doll, and Christian Knochenhauer, "Rethinking Car Software and Electronics Architecture," McKinsey & Company, February 2018, https://www.mckinsey.com/industries/automotive-and-assembly/our-insights/rethinking-car-software-and-electronics-architecture.

7. Marc Bain, "A New T-shirt Sewing Robot Can Make as Many Shirts per Hour as 17 Factory Workers," *Quartz*, August 30, 2017, https://qz.com/1064679/a-new-t-shirt-sewing-robot-can-make-as-many-shirts-per-hour-as-17-factory-workers/.

8. Canute James, "Caribbean Nations Savor Boom in Data Processing," *Journal of Commerce*, June 15, 1987; Proinnsias Breathnach, "Information Technology, Gender Segmentation and the Relocation of Back Office Employment: The Growth of the Teleservices Sector in Ireland," *Information Communication and Society* 3 (2002): 320–35.

9. Jay Solomon and Kathryn Kranhold, "In India's Outsourcing Boom, GE Played a Starring Role," *Wall Street Journal*, March 23, 2005; Rahul Sachitanand, "India's $150 Billion Outsourcing Industry Stares at an Uncertain Future," *Economic Times*, January 15, 2017; Calvin L. Scovel III, "Aviation Safety: FAA Oversight of Foreign Repair Stations," testimony before the US Senate Committee on Commerce Science and Transportation Subcommittee on Aviation Operations, Safety, and Security, June 20, 2007; Prakash Loungani, Saurabh Mishra, Chris Papageorgiou, and Ke Wang, "World Trade in Services: Evidence from a New Dataset," IMF working paper WP/17/77 (2017).

10. On advances in translation, see Richard Baldwin, *The Globotics Upheaval* (New York: Oxford University Press, 2019).

11. Michael O'Sullivan, *The Levelling* (New York: Public Affairs, 2019), ch. 6.

12. Dun & Bradstreet, "Business Impact of the Coronavirus," special briefing, 2020, p. 5, https://www.dnb.com/content/dam/english/economic-and-industry-insight/DNB_Business _Impact_of_the_Coronavirus_US.pdf.

13. Chad P. Bown and Douglas A. Irwin, "Trump's Assault on the Global Trading System," *Foreign Affairs* 98 (2019): 136 (quote); Jung Suk-yee, "S. Korea's Investment in China Almost Halved This Year," BusinessKorea, September 18, 2017, http://www.businesskorea.co.kr/news /articleView.html?idxno=19332.

INDEX

Acciaro, Michele, 188

acid rain, 200, 207

additive manufacturing, 223

aging of global population, 220

agricultural exports, 139, 162, 203–4

Airbus Industrie, 108, 170

aircraft manufacturers, subsidized, 108, 170

aircraft technology: developed with US defense budget, 108; software replacing hardware in, 222

airfreight: carrying materials and components, 210; financial crisis of 2008 and, 165, 186; flourishing in Third Globalization, 205–6; organization of value chains and, 133; pollution associated with, 205–6; spreading of supply chains and, 129; time sensitive or highly valuable, 2; used by retailers during port lockout, 153

airlines: COVID-19 and, 227; foreign repair stations for, 225

air pollution: by China, 197–98; transportation sources of, 205–7. *See also* greenhouse-gas emissions

aluminum, production of: Chinese subsidies for, 125–26; greenhouse-gas emissions and, 203

Amazon, 159

American Airlines, 224, 225

American Company, 14–15, 22

American Telephone and Telegraph Company, 79, 80

Amsden, Alice, 115

APL Panama, 196

A. P. Møller-Maersk, 145, 150, 194–95

APM Terminals, 193

Apple Inc.: chip shortage delaying color screen, 154, 156–57; iPhone 3G, 135–37, 167, 168, 249n8; iPhone X, 168

artificial intelligence, 225–26

asset-light companies, 154

austerity, imposed on indebted LDCs, 74

autarky: abruptly abandoned in Mexico, 92; in China before industrialization, 5, 117; of many large countries in Second Globalization, 5

auto industry: car-sharing services and, 221; China as major parts supplier for, 121, 126, 140; China as world's largest market for, 127; China's huge expansion of, 126–27; Chinese subsidies for, 125, 168–69, 214; Chinese tariffs on cars, 122; complicated value chains in, 209–10; computer programs in vehicles and, 222–23; containers of parts between Canada and Detroit, 161; electric vehicles in, 168–69, 223; incentives of US states to German companies, 170–71; in interwar period, 40–41; Japanese exports in, 109–10, 111, 112–13; Japanese reliance on China in, 127, 140; problems caused down the value chain, 156; regional trade patterns in, 140; of South Korea, 115, 140; Tohoku Earthquake and, 159

automation: driving down wages, 25; increasingly sophisticated, 223; job loss due to, 173, 174, 223; opportunities for workers in, 224; outsourced services related to, 131

A NOTE ON THE TYPE

This book has been composed in Arno, an Old-style serif typeface in the classic Venetian tradition, designed by Robert Slimbach at Adobe.

.

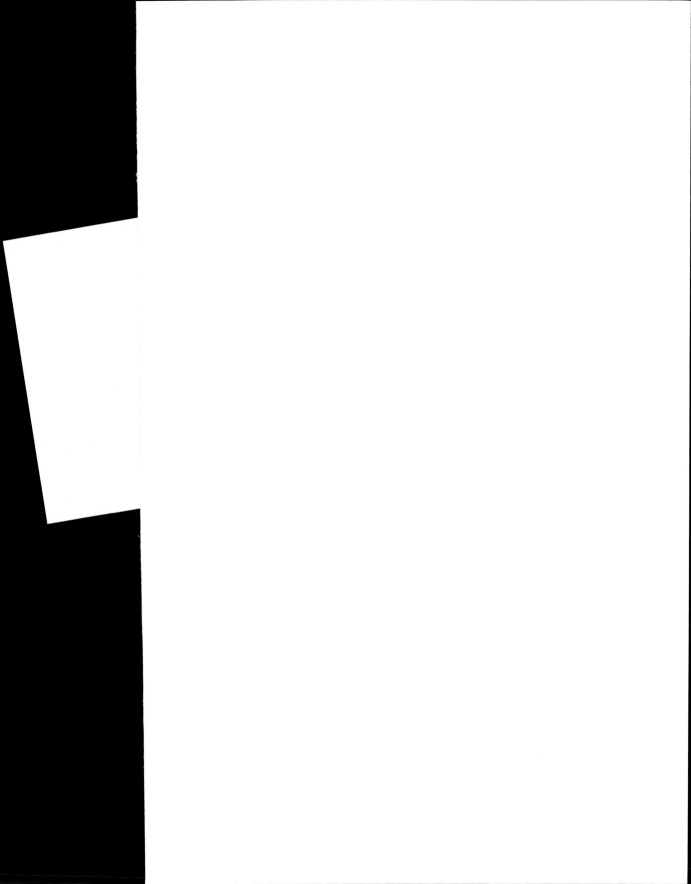

DATE DUE

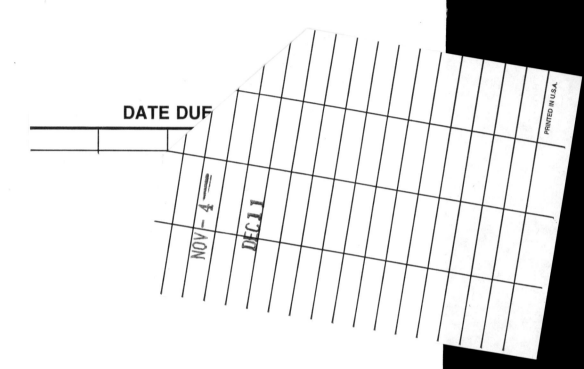

NOV – 4

DEC 11

PRINTED IN U.S.A.